The Politics of Common Sense

The Politics of Common Sense

How Social Movements Use Public Discourse to Change Politics and Win Acceptance

DEVA R. WOODLY

OXFORD
UNIVERSITY PRESS

OXFORD
UNIVERSITY PRESS

Oxford University Press is a department of the University of
Oxford. It furthers the University's objective of excellence in research,
scholarship, and education by publishing worldwide.

Oxford   New York

Auckland   Cape Town   Dar es Salaam   Hong Kong   Karachi
Kuala Lumpur   Madrid   Melbourne   Mexico City   Nairobi
New Delhi   Shanghai   Taipei   Toronto

With offices in

Argentina   Austria   Brazil   Chile   Czech Republic   France   Greece
Guatemala   Hungary   Italy   Japan   Poland   Portugal   Singapore
South Korea   Switzerland   Thailand   Turkey   Ukraine   Vietnam

Oxford is a registered trademark of Oxford University Press
in the UK and certain other countries.

Published in the United States of America by
Oxford University Press
198 Madison Avenue, New York, NY 10016

Library of Congress Cataloging-in-Publication Data
Deva R. Woodly
The politics of common sense : how social movements use public discourse to
change politics and win acceptance/Deva R. Woodly.
pages cm
ISBN 978–0–19–020398–6 (hardback) — ISBN 978–0–19–020399–3 (paperback)
1. Communication in politics—United States.   2. Communication in social action—United
States.   3. Social movements—Political aspects—United States.   4. Living wage movement—Political
aspects—United States.   5. Same-sex marriage—Political aspects—United States.   6. Politics,
Practical—United States.   I. Title.
JA85.2.U6W65 2015
322.4—dc23
2014038890

For Anthony, Vaughn, and Layla

CONTENTS

ILLUSTRATIONS

Figures

Charts

Tables

ACKNOWLEDGMENTS

It is difficult to begin to thank all the people who have helped to bring this book to fruition; however, I will make the sincerest attempt. First and foremost, I would like to thank my family, especially my husband, Anthony Davis, who has never ceased to cheer me on and give the emotional, material, intellectual, and co-parenting support I have needed throughout the writing process. I would also like to thank my parents, Ann and Donnell Woodly, who have always encouraged me to go, do, or be whatever sparks my passion, exercises my energy, and utilizes what talent I have. I have never doubted that when I turned around to see if anyone was watching out for me, they would both be there.

I would also like to thank a whole, irreplaceable slew of mentors, colleagues, and friends, including Daniel Reid, who has been my boon buddy and prose editor since college, always standing at the ready with a big heart and a red pen, which is an invaluable combination; Shawn and Dave Campbell, who were very good friends to me at a time that would otherwise have been very lonely; Danielle Allen, who has always believed in me and is an example of the kind of heterodox, big thinker I aspire to be; Neve Gordon, who offered his bold insights, valuable time, and incredible personal kindness in the reading (and rereading) of early drafts with a dauntless enthusiasm and a humbling commitment to mentorship; Catherine Rottenberg, whose kindness and intellectual generosity helped me commit to my own voice; and Patchen Markell, a longtime mentor and friend who has never hesitated to lend a helping hand. I also want to thank all of the following for comments, expertise, and inspiration: John Brehm, Moon-Kie Jung, Sara Farris, David Eng, Didier Fassin, Joan Scott, Jennifer London, David Plotke, and Cathy J. Cohen. I must also shout out Paul Richardson for diligent and critical IT support!

I would also like to acknowledge the Institute for Advanced Study, particularly the Friends of the Institute, who sponsored my fellowship year, 2012–2013, which allowed me needed time to revise this manuscript.

To anyone I have omitted: my apologies. Know that I am full of gratitude, and even if my brain has failed to recall you in this moment, my heart never will. My cup overflows. Selah.

Introduction

The Talk of Movements

The way movements communicate matters because changing public discourse changes power relations, and altered power relations change politics—the principles and policy that are at stake in the struggle over who shall govern and how. Changing politics requires not merely a series of victories in discrete policy battles but an ongoing struggle that shapes political meanings in the public sphere. Indeed, for political challengers who set out to transform policy, shifting the mainstream public discourse is the best—and in most cases the only—way to achieve lasting change. Without this crucial ingredient, other movement successes—recruiting and empowering members in an expanding social organization; raising public awareness; and even convincing power holders to change policy in a desired direction—may prove ephemeral. By contrast, a movement that effectively alters the terms of discourse can overcome considerable opposition and structural disadvantages to achieve sustained, meaningful change.

In this book, I offer a theory of *political acceptance* to explain the role of discourse in the relative success of challenger political movements. Using a theoretical and empirical investigation of two contemporary movements—the push for marriage equality and the fight to attain a living wage—I argue that a critical battleground for movements is mainstream political discourse, the general public sphere in which political issues take on popular meaning and affect the *common-sense understandings* of members of the polity. This project takes seriously the power of movement discourse to not only advance particular interests, but to actually *change politics itself*, rewriting the common understandings present in the discursive field upon which political possibilities are considered and wherein binding decisions are made. By illuminating the way that popular political meanings matter for the general public's political understandings, I reveal mainstream political discourse as an underrated, yet indispensable resource for political challengers, and establish a new framework for analyzing the progress of individual social movements toward lasting political change.

A Tale of Two Movements: Two Kinds of "Success"

The marriage equality and living wage campaigns both appeared as self-declared movements in the early 1990s. Each movement was shaped by similar indigenous "political processes" (McAdam 1982), but embodied different organizational structures, distinct organizational cultures and inter-organizational environments, and divergent choices of political venues and tactics. As a result, by the mid-2000s, a startling and counterintuitive phenomenon had emerged. Although the living wage movement had scored much higher on many of the indicators of traditional politics—especially shaping and passing favorable policies—it was marriage equality that had the most impact on the national political landscape by influencing national campaigns, shaping the contours of national discourse, and impacting public understandings and opinion.

Between 1994 and 2004, the living wage movement enabled the passage of over 120 local ordinances, guaranteeing municipal employees and contractors wage raises of varying amounts and, in most cases, improved access to affordable health benefits. However, this policy success was marred by a number of ambiguous outcomes. For example, though local living wage movements are often highly energized and successfully lean on municipal politicians to support their legislation, most states keep few or no records about the effects of living wage ordinances on localities. Further, many ordinances remain un- or under-enforced, with no apparatus for sanction or oversight to see that the laws on the books are followed. Perhaps most important for the movement, neither the general public in the locations where ordinances are passed nor national audiences seem to be familiar with or politicized around the issue beyond the tenure of the local campaign (Luce 2004). Fundamentally, despite hotly contested and skillfully executed local legislative campaigns that have often led to policy victories, the public's ideas about the relationship between government, capital, and citizens has remain unchanged. That means that while movement leaders have won many policy battles, they have generated little public interest, created very little lasting public awareness, and garnered only slight political capital to deploy on related issues of labor and fairness.

By contrast, the movement for marriage equality suffered numerous judicial and legislative defeats in the 1990s and early 2000s and incited an extremely hostile and well-organized countermovement: forty-one states passed some form of legislation legally limiting the definition of marriage to a union that can only exist between one man and one woman. However, despite these policy losses, the idea of "gay marriage" became an issue of national attention, causing officials at all levels of government to take stands on the merits of marriage equality—forcing them to articulate arguments for or against what had previously been unthinkable inclusion. While marriage equality advocates were losing the vast majority of judicial and legislative battles at both local and national levels, their deliberate and disciplined attempt to *persuade* Americans through popular public discourse on the merits of marriage equality was succeeding. The social imagination of Americans expanded to include gay people and indicators of public support for a variety of gay rights, such as nondiscrimination in employment and hate crimes legislation, rose quickly and steadily over the decade.

My research on the two movements shows that advocates for marriage equality deliberately sought to make a compelling and consistent case to a wide American audience that marriage is fundamental to the individual pursuit of happiness as well as a civil right, infusing the issue with a gravitas that merited continual revisiting in the national political conversation. It was a framing that ultimately outdid alternative frames, both the dominant conservative arguments that attempted to cast same-sex marriage variously as an absurdity; evidence of the moral downfall of the nation; a threat to the "natural" definition of marriage; and otherwise fundamentally detrimental, particularly to the institution of the "traditional family." It also outdid more radical arguments that pointed out the deficiencies of the institution of marriage as a vehicle for social justice.

This discursive outdoing was actually an undoing—not the triumph of a battle for news-cycle domination between competitive frames, but instead a dogged and consistent effort to alter the *political meaning* and *public understanding* of the social significance and political possibilities at stake regarding the issue of marriage equality. So, while the marriage equality movement enjoyed few judicial and legislative victories during the decade after its emergence as a social movement, and indeed, suffered many crushing defeats, advocates nevertheless successfully persuaded the American polity of the merits of their case and the viability of their solution to benefit previously invisible gay families.

This strategy has continued to succeed in the years since 2004. In 2012, American majorities came to consistently favor marriage equality; the sitting president of the United States, Barack Obama, announced his personal support for marriage equality; three states (Maine, Maryland, and Washington) voted to legalize same-sex marriage by referendum, and one (Minnesota) rejected a constitutional amendment to ban the practice. In 2013, the Supreme Court heard two cases bearing on the legality of same-sex marriage, *United States v. Windsor* and *Hollingsworth v. Perry*; both were decided in favor of proponents of marriage equality. Since the Supreme Court decisions, five states (Delaware, Rhode Island, Minnesota, Hawaii, and Illinois) have legalized same-sex marriages through their legislatures. In an additional ten states, judges have issued rulings overturning same-sex marriage bans (Indiana, Pennsylvania, Arkansas,

Idaho, Michigan, Oklahoma, Texas, Utah, Virginia, and Wisconsin) and in three others judges have issued rulings deigning to immediately overturn bans, but indicating their doubt that the bans can survive scrutiny by higher courts (Kentucky, Ohio, and Tennessee). Further, as of 2014, gay people can legally marry in 35 states. In addition, there is no state in which same-sex marriage bans are not under challenge in state or federal court. Such favorable policy outcomes were inconceivable just twenty years ago. The rapid change in the attention accorded the issue by political elites and the American public alike is the result of a movement-initiated change in the common understanding of what the issue means for individuals, society, and the nation.

The living wage movement, on the other hand, despite stunning policy success and expertly executed pressure politics, has suffered the disbanding of ACORN (Association of Community Organizations for Reform Now), the movement's lead organization, due in large part to a smear campaign spearheaded by conservative media provocateurs and congressional Republicans. While the movement continues to win new living wage policies, those wins are as subject to nonenforcement as they were a decade ago, and the work is still largely outside the majority of the public's awareness. It is important to keep in mind that this lack of awareness is not only regarding a dearth of knowledge about new policies that are passed, but more importantly, the lack of a politically accepted common-sense framework that gives meaning and context, explaining the significance and implications of such policy wins for American workers.

The success of the negative campaign against ACORN and the relative obscurity of the living wage movement in popular discourse are two symptoms of the same problem. That problem is neither organizational weakness nor lack of political savvy, nor is it merely the inherent difficulty of making political claims on behalf of an economically disadvantaged group. Instead, it is the neglect of the most powerful resource that political challengers have at their disposal: public speech. While the living wage movement contains several established organizations that have "built power" by recruiting members, sustaining action organizations, and garnering influence among sympathetic legislators and political officials, the movement has had little presence in the awareness of the general public and therefore struggles to keep local governments accountable for the laws that they have passed under pressure bought to bear by movement actors. This has been less a conspiracy of media silence than the lack of a movement-wide campaign to engage in a broad public conversation about the issue. Put differently, living wage advocates have been slow to articulate a consistent and broad political meaning for their cause, and that lack has put the movement at a severe disadvantage—as it would any political challenger.[1]

The differential developments in the marriage equality and living wage movements illustrate a sea change in the momentum of one movement and evidence of a crippling inertia in the life of the other. Looked at in comparison, the lessons that these two movements have to teach students of American politics, democratic theory, political communications, and social movements are manifold. The first and most important one is this: there is more to being a successful social movement than winning immediate or direct favorable outcomes in either the legislative or judicial arenas. Social movements have their most lasting and permanent effect not through particular policy victories but instead by changing politics, redefining what is at stake and what can and ought to be done about a politicized problem.

How can political challengers, the authors of social movements, accomplish such a feat? I argue that this kind of change generally, and the outcomes of these two contemporary struggles in particular, are rooted in the discursive power available in mainstream democratic discourse—specifically in a phenomenon that I call *political acceptance*, whereby an issue takes on national importance so that it is routinely covered by the media, attended to by the public, and addressed by elected officials. In this book, I explain how and why marriage equality achieved political acceptance in the decade after its emergence as an issue, between 1994 and 2004, while the living wage did not. Political acceptance focuses on the ways that mass-mediated public discourse functions as an important site of influence and authority for political challengers who seek to alter the status quo distributions of power and privilege.

Though political challengers are at a disadvantage vis-à-vis the regular arrangements of political influence, not only including access to financial resources but also to discursive resources such as media, the attention of decision-making elites, and a politically effective voice within organized political parties,[2] my research demonstrates that social movement actors *can* influence mainstream political discourse over time in such a way that they are able to gain credibility and contest, not only particular public officials and the policies they sponsor, but more importantly standing conceptions of what is politically possible, desirable, and just. In this way, challengers obtain both a hearing for their views and the opportunity to "change the structure of political conflict," so that all political participants, including their traditionally more powerful opponents, must begin talking about their issue, taking into account the way challengers have framed the debate (Baumgartner, De Boef, and Boydstun 2008, 10).

Indeed, while there are a number of ways to influence public policy, political actors without a ready-made apparatus of Washington-based interest organizations or routine access to elected officials *must* go through the public sphere. It is here that such groups are able not only to publicize their organizations or to get the word out about their current campaigns, but also to communicate the definition of the problem they see and the contours of the "common-sense" logic that leads them to their preferred solutions. I argue that for social movements, the difference between long-term success and stultifying inertia can come down to their ability to win such a hearing in the mainstream public sphere repeatedly over time and thus to create new opportunities to negotiate policy, persuade powerful potential allies, accumulate monetary and other kinds of resources, and eventually prevail in policy disputes. In other words, when political challengers deliberately seek to make new political issues into common touchstones and change mainstream political meanings, they greatly increase their chances to effect lasting and, occasionally, even transformational political change.

Power and Political Speech

We know that public speech has power, but what does that power consist in? In political theory, there are two dominant strains of thought that might answer this question. One is the school of communicative ethics (or communicative action) established by Jürgen Habermas. The other is discourse theory in the genealogical tradition exemplified by Michel Foucault. In neither tradition is the common public speech of political debate the chief article of inquiry. In the first case, mainstream discourse is not as important as the normative ethical model represented by the "ideal communication community," which demonstrates a form of intersubjective interaction that aims toward understanding and cooperation rather than conflict and advantage. In the second case, public speech is important only insofar as it reveals the history, or genealogy, of how subjects come to be conditioned in taken-for-granted ways that are misremembered or misrecognized as natural and/or necessary.

To the extent that we can piece together the underlying significance of public discourse in each school of thought, it seems that its chief characteristic for communicative ethicists is as the conduit of reason, the vehicle that people can use to talk among themselves and coordinate cooperative political action. For genealogists, common public speech is a text, of more or less equal importance with any other kind of text, such as medical journals, religious tomes, or popular novels. In this tradition, the main use for all texts, including mainstream public discourse, is to decipher logics of governance as they develop across time and manifest in psychological, social, and state practices as exercises of power.

Power, it should be noted, is differently conceived in each tradition of thought. Foucault's work has complicated the simple designation of power as subject A having power over subject B to the extent that they can get B to do something that B would not otherwise do (Dahl 1957) in most contemporary conceptions. Still, it is fair to say that those who take the ethics of discourse to be of central concern tend to view power's significance as primarily rooted in the ability of the more powerful to use it to dominate the less powerful (Lukes

2005). For example, Steven Lukes writes that "power as domination is the ability to constrain the choices of others, coercing them or securing their compliance, by impeding them from living as their own nature and judgment dictate" (Lukes 2005, 85).[3] Foucauldians, on the other hand, reject the notion that people's natures and judgments are ever uncontaminated by power. They take power to be constitutive of all relations (psychological, interpersonal, social, and political) and find power's primary significance not in domination but in what the knowledge of how power has come to be exercised, obscures or reveals. In the first instance, the danger presented by power is its misuse by the few to dominate the many, which can be prevented by developing a well-conceived and regulated political community. In the second, we have a conception of power in which the dangers it presents are not (only) those of domination, but (primarily) those of normalization. In this conception, to "solve" the problem of power, insofar as this is possible, every subject is tasked with resistance, defined as the empirical and historical interrogation of the given or normal. That is, one must engage in critique at every level—personal, social, and political—if one hopes to be free.[4]

As we shall see in the next chapter, the movement actors in the living wage and marriage equality movements seem to interpret political power in distinctly different terms, along lines that roughly mirror Luke's notion in the first case and Foucault's in the second. These two different conceptions of power have significant ramifications for the ways the movements developed and maintain themselves organizationally as well as the ways that each has chosen to engage politically, leading to very different kinds of movement success.

In my view, both of these schools of thought have illuminating (and complimentary) things to say on the questions of the ethics of communication and the revelatory potential of discursively based genealogy, but neither takes seriously the unique power of common public speech *in its own right* as a major site where the momentum of the "multiplicity of force relations," of which power consists, can be disrupted, redirected, organized, and changed. The question of domination *is* important, and the paradigm of the ideal communication community highlights the egalitarian potential embedded in ethical conceptions that take interpersonal participation and engagement as their theoretical basis. But it is also essential to remember that domination is only one of many possible power relations, and an exclusive focus on it may obscure more than it illuminates in terms of both how power works and the ways that those positioned lower in hierarchies of advantage can and do exercise power. This is because such a focus often ignores the ways that power constrains and influences *all actors* in significant ways, including those who are traditionally more advantaged. The reality is, even those who engage in politics from advantageous positions exercise power in the context of common public understandings about what is and is not possible, significant, or permissible and what can and should be done.

It is my contention that, as Hannah Arendt knew, public speech is important because public speech acts *create*. What they create is common political understandings of what is at stake in a political issue as well as what the polity can do to answer those stakes. This power of public speech to create political understandings is critical because what we think of as political is both *contingent* and *constrained* by common-sense notions that develop out of the interactions among our background conceptions of the way the world is—what Aristotle called *endoxa*—with new ideas, practices, and laws. These interactions play out through public discursive processes that shape individuals' interpretation of new political problems and solutions.

For example, the notion that marriage is the culmination of a search for the unique person one can love for all time—familiar from popular culture in all its forms—is, genealogically speaking, an invention of the eighteenth-century novel (Swidler 2001). Ann Swidler argues that during the rise of bourgeois individualism at the beginning of the Industrial Revolution, the common understanding of love underwent a major change. While the notion of romantic love had been present in Western cultural traditions since the troubadours sang their stories of the ennobling passion of courtly love in the late eleventh century, those stories were most often tragedies that ended in the deaths of the lovers when their passion defied social obligation. The modern love story, on the other hand, "ends with a marriage in which the autonomous individual finds his or her proper place in the social world. 'Bourgeois love' thus alters the tension between individual morality and social demands, reconciling the two through a love that tests and rewards a person's true merits" (Swidler 2001, 113). This not only recasts marital love as essentially romantic, but makes this romantic love the basis of legitimate adult social relations. This view of love is still predominant today, and this myth, now embedded in *endoxa*, has been an essential trope for making the new idea of same-sex marriage intelligible.[5] However, the relation between the new notion of same-sex marriage and the doxic understanding of love is not inherent and did not become a part of the contemporary American common understanding through an automatic or inevitable process. Instead, marriage equality advocates deliberately and consistently made room for their new notion within an old paradigm and, in so doing, have changed the common understanding of who marriage might and ought to include.[6]

Take, as another example, the neoliberal idea that American individualism ought to equate to capitalist entrepreneurialism in all aspects of life (Brown 2003). This logic, which Wendy Brown argues is a normative rather than ontological project, has become a part of the baseline and background beliefs embedded in American *endoxa*. In this way, neoliberal thinking has become naturalized, a part of common doxa, and it leads to a political understanding of business interests as synonymous with the economic interests of the whole society as well as the privileging of the importance of employers and capitalists (idealized as "self-made makers") over the employed, who must work for a wage (casts as "entitled takers"). This *doxic* truism certainly has a normative valence, but it is particularly powerful because it has become a part of common-sense public understanding, a "neoliberal commonsense" (Woodly 2014), often deployed discursively as though it were a fact even by those who are uncomfortable with current distributions among capital and labor.[7]

This neoliberal commonsense holds that business interests are more important than those of workers because businesses are "job creators," making them both more virtuous than workers ("makers") and casting their fates as significant to more people. This status is accorded companies despite the empirical reality that businesses exist not to create jobs, but to make profits, a goal that, in practice, leads to eliminating jobs almost as often as creating them. Nevertheless, such belief leads to a logic that takes the desire and well-being of business owners to be paramount, superseding that of workers, communities, cities, or states. This neoliberal logic, though empirically dubious, is still the starting point for economic commentary across the political spectrum, even by political actors who wish to challenge its accuracy, veracity, and morality. This means that the idea that what's good for business is good for the economy overall is now embedded in American *endoxa*. However, the notion is much newer than that of courtly love. Indeed, as recently as 1937, the president of the United States proclaimed in his second inaugural address:

> Today we reconsecrate our country to long-cherished ideals in a suddenly changed civilization. In every land there are always at work forces that drive men apart and forces that draw men together. In our personal ambitions we are individualists. But in our seeking for economic and political progress as a nation, we all go up, or else we all go down, as one people.... The test of our progress is not whether we add more to the abundance of those who have much; it is whether we provide enough for those who have too little. (Roosevelt 1937)

Franklin D. Roosevelt's interpretation of American individualism accommodated prioritizing the well-being of "those who have too little" in the assessment of "economic and political progress," leading to policies that took the maximization of decent employment, rather than the maximization of business profits, to be of paramount importance to the health of the economy overall. The political meanings and public understandings that made Roosevelt's interpretation of American individualism possible also shaped the boundaries of the policy options that Congress and the president were able to consider in the 1930s and 1940s. By contrast, the reinterpretation of the doxic notion of American individualism, persuasively articulated by a different American president in a different political time, yielded a very different range of policy options. President Ronald Reagan declared in 1980:

> If we look to the answer as to why, for so many years, we achieved so much, prospered as no other people on Earth, it was because here, in this land, we unleashed the energy and individual genius of man to a greater extent than has ever been done before. Freedom and the dignity of the individual have been more available and assured here than in any other place on Earth. The price for this freedom at times has been high, but we have never been unwilling to pay that price.

The point is not to decide which interpretation of the American individualism is right or true. Instead, it is to observe the ways that old ideas, present in the *endoxa*, can be put to use for new purposes, which are present in the politics of a particular age. Public articulations of "the way things are" that are repeated in terms that ordinarily competent members of the polity find both intelligible and resonant can and do provide very different logics for social and political problem-solving. This is the fundamental reason why public speech has power, because it can bring new understandings into being, and new understandings precipitate new possibilities for political action.

Framing: How Public Meanings Change

Ultimately, success for social movements hinges on persuading others, which is the unique purview of common public discourse. Whereas most of the literature on attitude change takes the psychological individual as the unit of measure, I assert that political persuasion is primarily a *public* process, and my theory of political acceptance highlights the crucial relationship between the public meaning of common discourse, political persuasion, and political impact. The colloquial form of persuasion occurs when an individual experiences an avowed change of heart and/or mind, but other important forms of persuasion are possible. Public opinion research on priming and framing has shown that even though people do not easily change their personal attitudes, differences in the topics and frames discussed as a part of the regular public debate do change people's perceptions of issue salience as well as what is at stake in political debates. This general assessment of what is important and what kinds of options are sayable and doable in public changes over time. That means that individual attitudes need not be the first element to shift in the process of political persuasion; public discourse can and often does change first. As a frame is frequently repeated in the media (a process referred to in the literature as "priming"), it may have a "framing effect" that causes people to change not their values and principles but rather the way they associate those predispositions with particular issues. This can result in changes to individuals' policy preferences without necessarily altering their underlying political attitudes (Zaller 1992) (Chong and Druckman 2007, Baumgartner, De Boef, and Boydstun 2008).

The classic example of this kind of framing effect is an experiment in which respondents are asked whether the Ku Klux Klan should be allowed to march down a local street. It has been shown that if the argument is framed in terms that emphasize the constitutional right of free speech, more people are likely to tolerate a march than if the question is framed in terms of public order (Nelson, Clawson, and Oxley 1997). In the case of discourse on marriage equality, we witness a dramatic shift away from the emphasis on the presumed sexual deviance of "homosexual acts" and reliance on the explanatory power of an exclusive and static "definition" of marriage in the public discourse that prevailed in the early 1990s, and toward an emphasis on the fundamental similarity of individuals who form romantic and familial bonds according to their own "orientation" and their attendant civil rights that became widespread by the mid-2000s.

There has been much less mainstream public discourse on the living wage, but in the discourse that emerged during the period of study, the terms of debate have evinced no change. Moreover, the discourse of support for the living wage has remained variable and inconsistent, while the terms of opposition to the living wage have been coherent and consistent. Most news coverage is focused on competing claims. In such a context, when claims differ in consistency, the interpretation will favor the consistent claims, particularly when they are undergirded by doxic understandings of "the way things are."

The most frequent pro-living wage frame that appears in news coverage is the basic affirmative definition of the term, which is simply that those who work full time should make enough to sustain themselves. However, living wage opponents use a "rhetoric of reaction" against that powerful basic claim, by emphasizing the presumed jeopardy that mandatory wage increases would cause for local business, the perverse effects that might manifest in the loss of low-skilled jobs, and the futility of marginal wage increases to bring the poor out of poverty (Hirschman 1991).

Frames are made up of arguments that co-occur together repeatedly. The most frequent and resonant frame containing arguments against the living wage focused on the potential perverse effects of implementing and/or raising a wage floor. This type of argument allowed living wage opponents to sidestep the moral imperative of the living wage argument by emphasizing a technical (and inaccurate) (see Card and Krueger 1995, Doucouliagos and Stanley 2009) economic orthodoxy, which dictates that wage floors must cause job losses and other negative economic outcomes, so living wage laws cannot achieve the desirable end they are designed to bring about, but instead would actually cause harm to low-skilled workers. Albert Hirschman writes that, in the face of lofty objectives that seem morally compelling, "reactionaries are not likely to launch an all-out attack on that objective. Rather, they will endorse it, sincerely or otherwise, but then attempt to demonstrate that the action proposed or undertaken is ill conceived; indeed, they will most typically urge that this action will produce, via a chain of unintended consequences, the *exact* contrary of the objective being proclaimed and pursued" (Hirschman 1991, 11). As he notes, these kinds of arguments create anxiety about changing things, even when change is desired. During the decade from the mid-1990s to the mid-2000s, researchers were able to produce quite a bit of evidence that living wages do not produce job losses in the locales where they have been implemented; however, the orthodoxy cautioning against perverse effects has been slow to change among economists, political elites, and the public at large.

Beyond the fundamental premise of the living wage, advocates presented a host of different frames in support of the policy, including highlighting the problem of poverty in general, as well as the usually bad conditions of low-wage work, and directly rebutting economic orthodoxy with empirical evidence. However, principal component analysis of the arguments reveals that the various arguments did not cohere well into recognizable and resonant frames (meaning that these arguments were not mentioned together in predictable and patterned ways). The rhetoric of reaction deployed by opponents, on the other hand, cohered very well. These two rhetorical problems, the inability to effectively combat common economic understandings despite the availability of evidence, as well as inconsistent use of resonant rhetoric, produced an unfavorable situation for living wage advocates. The many different arguments of living wage supporters who were challenging the status quo against the consistent arguments put forward by living wage opponents, arguments undergirded by orthodox economic beliefs, made for a public understanding of the issue that favored the status quo, even though the policy desires of the public were (and continue to be) aligned with the movement. In addition, popular public discourse on the topic was infrequent in mainstream media, limiting general public awareness and discussion of the issue.

However, as the marriage equality movement makes clear, it is possible for political challengers to shift the terms of debate to more favorable terrain if they employ resonant arguments and sustain their efforts to make these arguments salient in popular political discourse. We can observe changes in public discourse by analyzing mainstream news media as texts that help us to apprehend the evolution of common understandings of the issue under investigation; particularly the questions of what is at stake and what can be done. As the same range of frames and their framing effects persist over time, the issue becomes commonly regarded as *inherently* connected to the prevailing frame, and therefore *necessarily* connected to the principle(s) invoked by the most usual framing. Marches or protests by the Ku Klux Klan and, more contemporarily, the Westboro Baptist Church (a group that protests at the funerals of fallen soldiers because of their conviction that "God hates gays") are seen as inherently evocative of the right to free speech, rather than, for example, a threat to public order. Similarly, marriage equality, in a dramatic shift, becomes inseparable from our ideas about the basic value of romantic and familial love as well as the inseparability of that concept from the pursuit of happiness and individual civil rights. Such a change in the common perception of an issue is not automatic or inevitable but is instead a result of public contention over political ideas and social policy in common, popular discourse. Interestingly, political scientists have rarely studied the effects of public meaning in this capacity. As Katherine Kramer Walsh argues, "Political scientists have given the act of *understanding politics*, also referred to . . . as the act of interpreting or making sense of politics, far less attention than the act of . . . *making political choices*" (2004, 2). However, understanding politics and the public meanings encoded therein is the only way to fully account for lasting political change, especially change from the bottom up.

The Political Character of Persuasion

Ample literature in political science has shown that people's political opinions may be influenced by opinion leaders, political advertisements, or everyday talk around the kitchen table (Mainsbridge 1999, Popkin 1994, Iyengar 1995). However, individuals have also been shown to reject, modify, reinterpret, or ignore all of these sources of influence under various conditions (Druckman and Chong 2010, Druckman and Nelson 2003). In their book *The Decline of the Death Penalty and the Discovery of Innocence*, Frank Baumgartner, Suzanna De Boef, and Amber Boydstun observe that American public opinion approving the use of the death penalty for capital offenses has been stable for decades. Though there have always been moral and religious arguments for and against the death penalty, the "morality frame"—the idea that the state should simply never kill—which was the most prevalent anti-death penalty argument for most of the life of the nation, did not succeed in persuading more than a third of the populace. However, since the mid-1990s, there has been a rise in the acceptance of a new frame that shapes the way that Americans view the death penalty, which Baumgartner and his coauthors call the "innocence frame." The argument underlying the innocence frame is that, no matter how one feels morally about the justice (or injustice) of the death penalty, evidence, particularly DNA evidence that became available in the last decade of the twentieth century, shows that hundreds of erroneous convictions have occurred in capital cases and that innocent people may sometimes be executed for crimes that they did not commit. The power of this new frame is that it reshapes the contour of the death penalty debate, shifting the attention of both regular citizens and decision-making officials from the morality of the death penalty, toward the vexing problem of the state-sanctioned killing of innocents resulting from error. Baumgartner and his coauthors show that "this shift in the nature of public discourse has driven changes in public opinion and in policy outcomes" and points to the ways that "framing and attention-shifting in American politics more generally ... affect not only public opinion, but the direction of public policy as well" (Baumgartner, De Boef, and Boydstun 2008, 9–10).

This finding indicates that the traditional notion of persuasion as idiosyncratic, psychological changes in the preferences of individuals, what we might call personal persuasion, is relatively rare. Instead, it seems that John Zaller's supposition that "political attitudes" are instead the result of the gradual change in the mix of information and the balance of considerations at play in people's assessments of political issues, or what we might think of as public persuasion, is more common (Zaller 1992). This aspect of persuasion is characterized by a dynamic social process that is circumscribed, though not determined, by the already present understandings, interpretations, values, and principles that publics claim and ascribe to themselves. For example, the American *endoxa* are populated with ideas of Americans as innovative, optimistic, individualist, capitalist, conservative, private, free, equal, favored by God, and so on. These notions need not be true, in the sense of empirically observable or provable, in order for them to be a part of the affective understanding that helps Americans *make sense of themselves* in the world. The empirical (in)correctness of these self-ascriptions is less important to prevailing political understandings than the political fact that Americans publically avow these characteristics, repeating them to each other in formal and informal settings so often that they become background truisms in any story that America tells about itself. Notably, even those that aim to critique, challenge, or change elements of the American tale based on the actual experiences of individuals and groups experiencing systematic disadvantage and injustice must incorporate elements of these *endoxa* in some way—not in order to tell a true story, but instead, in order tell an intelligible one.

While Baumgartner, De Boef, and Boydstun show how the shift from the "morality frame" to the "innocence frame" has had quantifiable effects on both public opinion and policy around the death penalty, they do not attempt to answer the question of *why some arguments resonate* with officials and the public while others do not. One of the aims of my project is to offer a theory that addresses this question. In addition, I develop a statistical method, adapted from the evolutionary frame analysis designed by Baumgartner, De Boef, and Boydstun, to measure the resonance of arguments presented in mainstream public discourse.

In order to analyze the data set of mainstream discourse on marriage equality and the living wage that I built, I use principal component analysis to empirically identify two rhetorical phenomena. First, I statistically identify frames that are present in the news discourse over the ten-year period between 1994 and 2004. Second, I measure how well multiple frames cohere to form resonant arguments. This allows me to observe the common understandings present in the discourses on the living wage and marriage equality during the period of study.

The combined theoretical and statistical examination of the two shows that arguments become persuasive in the public sense when they make consistent connections between their issue and existing cultural and political logics. The establishment of the connection between the new issue and existing *endoxa* creates a rhetorical resonance that allows advocates a chance to win political acceptance for themselves, for their organizations, and most importantly, for the terms that they use to wage the public debate. Political acceptance is evidenced by an issue's persistent salience in mainstream media discourse, an increase in public awareness of the issue, and official responses to the issue in the form of position-taking and policy accommodation. Note that, as I discuss in the next section, political acceptance does not refer to the acceptance of a *position* by a portion of the public but rather the acceptance of an *issue* into the set of topics that are recognized as compelling subjects in mainstream political discourse.

Resonance and Fit: How Political Acceptance Happens

For political challengers with limited access to monetary resources, official authority, or elite networks, political acceptance in mainstream discourse is the only way to acquire the kind of public authority and credibility they need to make their case to the general public. As E. E. Schattschneider observed in his pragmatic analysis of American politics, *The Semisovereign People*, if political disputes were always limited to occurring among contesting groups in private, then the power ratio between groups at the outset would directly determine the winner. He explains, "Private conflicts are taken into the public arena precisely because someone wants to make certain that the power ratio among the private interests most immediately involved shall not prevail" (Schattschneider 1975, 37). When challengers are able to alter status quo arrangements of power and push through policies they prefer, it is because they have been able to establish enough public authority to compete with the preexisting arrangements of prestige, prerogative, and authorization. They are able to do this most effectively when they make arguments in new, yet resonant terms that can shift the structure of political conflict in their favor (Schattschneider 1975, Swidler 1995, Gamson 2006, Baumgartner, De Boef, and Boydstun 2008).

In order to get a chance to shift attention to a new issue, political challengers must first win what Robert Dahl calls an "effective hearing." An effective hearing is distinct from merely "making a noise." It requires that "one or more officials are not only ready to listen to the noise, but expect to suffer in some significant way if they do not placate the group, its leaders, or its most vociferous members" (Dahl 1961, 145). Winning an effective hearing requires at least two observable moments: *emergence* and *political acceptance*. The moment in which concern *emerges* from a marginal community into the mainstream occurs when the press, officials, and other elites take notice of a new or newly problematized set of political circumstances. However, the emergence of a new topic into the mainstream does not necessarily make a lasting impression on either decision-making officials or the mass public. Indeed, the general public is usually still unaware of new political issues at the moment of emergence. In such situations media gatekeepers and public officials may choose to dismiss or ignore, or merely fail to prioritize, challengers' claims, and the assertions of grass-roots communities may fall back into the category of "noise." In order to ensure an effective hearing, new ideas must appear in the public sphere with regularity and persist over time, taking a place in the regular subject matter of mainstream political discourse. The regular and frequent appearance of an issue in the news, the corresponding awareness and attention of the public, and the public position-taking and policy accommodation of decision-makers is what I refer to as *political acceptance*. Without political acceptance it is impossible for challenger groups to gain an effective hearing, because their new issue will not have a chance of penetrating mainstream public awareness, which in turn makes it impossible to generate public concern, influence the terms of debate, and earn enough public authority to effectively challenge those who already have power.

After a historiographical recounting of the political emergence of each issue in the following two chapters, the bulk of my attention will be devoted to developing the criteria for the political acceptance of an issue that has already emerged, with particular attention to the role that resonance plays in the process. It is crucial to understand that *political acceptance* is not the same as *political agreement*. Political acceptance is the chance that challengers get to make their case in the generally accessible public sphere, which is manifest in and through mainstream political discourse, and evidenced in mass-mediated communication like national daily newspapers. The acceptance I refer to is not of a *policy position* but of the relevance of challenger *issues* in the limited lexicon of regular political subjects that the mainstream media covers, the public acknowledges as significant, and officials are compelled to address.

This uptake of challenger issues in mainstream discourse is not random. Instead, political acceptance depends on the resonance of the issue. Successful political acceptance can be demonstrated empirically by the measurable, persistent appearance of challenger issues in mainstream discourse combined with an increase in public awareness and widespread, observable position-taking by elites who develop or endorse policy accommodations to political challengers. This dynamic process must persist over time, for at least one year, and often will continue for many more.

Outline of the Book

I carry out my examination of political acceptance in two ways: one primarily theoretical and the other empirical. The theoretical examination integrates the insights of several disparate political philosophers to posit thinking about democratic discussion and political discourse in a way that emphasizes the process that enables members of the polity in mass-mediated democracies to develop common understandings about new political issues. For this reason, this project focuses on the mainstream news discourse present in actually existing American polity rather than emphasizing the principled or theoretical ground for a well-ordered or just democratic society. The empirical investigation consists of a historically and institutionally grounded accounting of the development of the marriage equality and living wage movements as well as unstructured interviews with key activists who have been at the heart of these movements since their inception. In addition, I use existing survey data to analyze public awareness, opinion, and general issue salience throughout the decade of study, for each case. I also perform a textual analysis on ten years of articles referencing the two movements between 1994 and 2004. My textual analysis has two levels. The first is a close reading of the news discourse using a rhetorical technique called rhetorical criticism; the second is content analysis, which yields information about discourse that can be interpreted quantitatively. My quantitative content analysis includes an examination of the principal components of the news discourse on each topic, which allows me to statistically determine what frames exist in the debate and whether and to what degree those frames appear to be resonant.

This book proceeds broadly from the theoretical and general to the empirical and particular. In chapter 1, I make the case for discourse as an essential location of study for the understanding of politics generally and for political change in particular. In chapters 2 and 3, I embark on a detailed political history of the emergence of the two social movements onto the American political landscape.

In chapter 4, I describe what I take to be the architecture of resonance as the theoretical underpinning of my theory of political acceptance. I seek not only to explain the conceptual context that undergirds the empirical phenomenon that I examine, but also to make an original contribution to theoretical knowledge about the relationship between communicative action and the genealogy of public discourses. In chapter 5, I explain the relationship between political acceptance and the process of political change. I also detail my contribution to the literature on social movements, with special emphasis on my finding that the degree to which a movement is able to win policy battles in the short term may say little about its ability to win a favorable political understanding of its issue, and with it enduring success, in the long term. In chapter 6 I turn my attention to direct quantitative analysis of the content of the mainstream discourses surrounding the living wage and marriage equality as they appear in the *New York Times* and *USA Today* between 1994 and 2004. I also examine the ways that public opinion on the topics shifts over time. In my analysis, I focus on determining whether the differences in the discourses characterizing the two movements can help to explain why marriage equality has become a staple on the national political agenda, while the living wage has not. Finally, in the conclusion, I address the general applicability of the theory of political acceptance and the potential for its use in both reform and radical movements.

The combined use of historical accounting, theoretical examination, both qualitative and quantitative discourse analysis, interviews with activists, and public opinion data shows that the discursive characteristics of political debates make a significant difference in whether an issue achieves mainstream political acceptance or is consigned to continued peripheral struggle. It is important to note that, regardless, political challengers will struggle, and acceptance of an issue does not entail agreement with a position. However, on balance, political challengers achieve more durable and lasting success when the struggle they undertake is in full public view and actively invites the polity to come to new understandings about what is at stake, influencing the interpretation of what range of policy outcomes is possible, probable, and desirable. My aim in this book is to show that movement-driven changes in popular public discourse can create new possibilities for political change by altering commonplace understandings about what counts as a pressing national concern and how it can be resolved.

1

Mainstream Discourse, Public Meaning, and the Political Character of Persuasion

What is it about discourse, specifically mainstream public discourse, that makes it a better tool for explaining how political change happens from the bottom up than institutional pressure group politics, structural hierarchies, resource mobilization, or a myriad of other potential explanations that scholars have used to analyze the differential political success of groups and movements? The answer is simply this: the way that we talk about issues in public both reflects and determines what solutions are considered desirable or plausible in the commonplace logics that shape the politics of a particular moment. Close attention to public discourse not only allows us to keep up with politics as it happens, but also reveals important truths about the meaning, linkages, and effects of the non-discursive activities we traditionally consider political, such as voting, interest group activities, and movement campaigns.

Public discourse is also a key site for the creation and contestation of political meaning. The prevailing view, implicit or explicit in most contemporary political analysis, that the meanings of political phenomena are either self-evident—autonomously and spontaneously generated by individuals engaged in self-contained, rational analysis—or simply irrelevant, causes scholars to miss the mechanisms of action and interaction that are actually at play in politics generally, and the process of political change, in particular.

In this chapter, I lay out my understanding of the relationship between popular political discourse, public meaning, and the specifically political character of persuasion. I argue that scholars of politics must be concerned with questions of meaning to more accurately conceptualize, observe, and describe politics as it actually happens. This account explores the importance of meaning to understanding—and changing—politics and reveals the critical role of political acceptance to the process of political change.

.ie Political Importance of Semiotic Contexts

.ι science tends to conceive the study of politics as a study of institutions
.ciples, procedures, organizations) on the one hand and individuals (atti-
.des, interests, choices) on the other. Where these two subjects intersect—the
neglected site where political meaning is made—is in the ways that people
articulate and understand politics in the context of their political time and place
and the ways that they understand those contexts as meaningful. The context
I am referring to, including the experience of and participation in politics, is culture. As Lisa Wedeen argues, *culture*, in this sense, is not meant to connote what
Sherry Ortner describes as "a deeply sedimented essence attaching to, or inher-
ing in, particular groups" (Ortner 1997, 8–9) but instead consists of "practices
of meaning-making" that render our world, including what we consider to be
material or political interests, intelligible (Wedeen 2002).

Culture conceived in this way consists of "semiotic practices"; it "refers to
what language and symbols *do*—how they are inscribed in concrete actions and
how they operate to produce observable political effects" (Wedeen 2002, 714).
These semiotic practices, which I refer to in this book as *discourses*, allow us to
study the ways that people both produce and receive meanings, not through
individual psychological processes, but instead as part of a public organization
of practices (including work, social mores, routines, gender norms, etc.) and systems of signification (the ways we make sense of words and other symbols, see
Swidler 1995, Wedeen 2002). Culture, then, is not something inside people's
heads, the essence of which they come to embody, or even a set of deeply held,
more or less stable values and beliefs. Instead, it is a set of *public practices* that
organize patterns of understanding and (inter)action among self-acknowledged
collectivities such as families, associations, regions, and nations. Culture is not
static and fixed, but dynamic and flexible. It is not about inchoate values, but
about the tools (skills, habits, and repertoires of action) with which people
design the "strategies of action" (Bourdieu 1977) that they use to navigate the
world they share with others (Arendt 1958). This means that culture is in no
way ephemeral, amorphous, or invisible. "Culture in action" can be *observed* in
discourses (Swidler 1995).

At present, political theory does not give us much guidance for evaluating
discourse as it happens outside what Habermas calls the "formal realm" of deliberative interaction. Though Habermas is arguably the most influential theorist
of communication in contemporary democratic theory and has developed a
detailed theory of communicative action (also called communicative reason)
over the last four decades, his schema is not very helpful when trying to pinpoint
the dynamics and effects of actual, mediated public discourse. Habermas takes as
his model the interpersonal communication between two equal subjects whose

communication is by its nature rational and aims at understanding (Habermas 1996). While he acknowledges that mass-mediated communication is an important factor in how modern political communication actually works (Habermas 1996), his account of communicative action does not consider the implications of mediated communication as it extends across an entire polity.

Since people in industrialized democracies mostly encounter political speech in mediated forums like newspaper, television, the Internet, and mobile devices—not through the explanatory interpersonal exchanges that we might call deliberations—facts, arguments, and frames distributed to large audiences by mass media are a fundamental part of the experience of contemporary democratic politics. Indeed, mass-mediated communication is the principal kind of communication that actually influences politics. Despite the deficiencies of mass media that have been noted by scholars and laymen alike, it serves a necessary function in the transmission and interpretation of political information. Without it, our experience of democratic politics would be barely recognizable.

Habermas explicitly focuses his theory on an idealized version of interpersonal communication, setting aside the messier world he calls the "general public sphere," of which he writes:

> Opinion formation uncoupled from decisions is effected in an open and inclusive network of overlapping, subcultural publics having fluid temporal, social, and substantive boundaries. Within a framework guaranteed by constitutional rights, the structures of such a pluralistic public sphere develop more or less spontaneously. The currents of public communication are channeled by mass media and flow through different publics that develop informally inside associations. Taken together they form a wild complex that resists organization as a whole. (1996, 307)

Habermas concedes the importance of the informal discourses that people engage in casually and constantly, writing that "democratically constituted opinion- and will-formation depends on the supply of informal public opinions that ideally develop in structures of an unsubverted public sphere." But what he views as the anarchy of the lifeworld—in contrast to the ordered and rules-governed political public sphere—prevents him from engaging it analytically (Habermas 1996, 308).

This artificial separation prevents analysis of how discourses move from the fecund general public sphere into the political public sphere, where binding policy decisions are made. This is a serious limitation of Habermas's framework, restricting both its explanatory power and normative purchase. How can we understand bottom-up discursive and political change if we have no analytic to

such communicative activity is possible, let alone whether it fol-
᠁natic patterns that can be explored and explained?
᠁d of beginning our analysis of communication with the formal and
᠁at ideal, it might be useful to begin with the most basic definition of dis-
᠁rse: the expression of thoughts through the exchange of speech or writing.
Because discourse—unlike, for example, reflection—is rooted in the notion
of exchange between two or more persons, it is necessarily intersubjective and
therefore implies a context of common symbols and other knowledge that is
accessible to the parties involved in conversation. When we talk about political
discourse we are speaking of the conduit of public meaning and the site where
political understandings develop. It is the space in which what Pierre Bourdieu
calls "commonplaces" are produced and maintained. It is also the place in which
these commonplaces can be challenged, interrupted, and revised.

Discourses are the way that we make sense of what actions mean in a political context. The action of lowering a flag to half-mast, for example, is a powerful communicative act only for those who understand what it is meant to
commemorate. Even seemingly straightforward political actions like voting for
a particular candidate may mean different things depending on a combination
of contingent factors that range from the personal (which candidate do I trust?)
to the institutional (which candidate does my union support?) to the symbolic
(which candidate represents something I believe in?) to the strategic (which is
the candidate who can win?).

The study of discourse is different from other empirical endeavors in that it
is not primarily concerned with determining the material facts of situations or
the cause of epiphenomenal events. Instead, it is concerned with the semantic
tools and social processes that help people interpret and evaluate political life.
I examine news discourses, as representative of commonly accessible political
discourse, in order to discover how facts and narratives come to be regarded by
majorities as worth considering—or not. This inductive examination of public
discourse sheds light on the question of why and how certain political topics and
political framings are taken up, becoming regular features of public discourse,
while others are not.

We cannot discover the answer to this question by focusing exclusively on
the formal realm of political action, as theories of communicative rationality
following Habermas might, but neither can we rely on a conception of politics
concerned only with "material interests and the relative success or failure of the
individuals articulating them," which has been the most frequent approach in
empirically based political science (Wedeen 2002, 714). A purely rational and/
or decision-focused approach to understanding political choices and change is
inadequate because most political actors do not make decisions about what is
important, including how their material interests are constituted and how to

the articulate the necessity of those interests to the wider polity, wholly on the basis of fact-based, cost-benefit analyses. To truly understand how people make choices about what is politically important, we have to take much greater notice of the elements that *shape the interpretation* of facts, symbols, events, and problems and their solutions. This in turn requires us to undertake two things at once. The first is to examine meanings as they have been made in political time, and the second is to consider how this meaning-making functions both in politics and as a politics. I have designed this study with the intention of accomplishing both of these goals.

Public Meaning

Examining discourses allows us to recognize how ideas and the logics associated with them become commonplace. When I speak of generally intelligible meaning, shared understanding, or common political culture, I do not refer to universal ideas or deep cultural knowledge that we all possess *inside* us; rather, I refer to the meanings that observably exist *between* us. This is important for the study of politics because it causes us to rethink some of the assumptions inherent in methodological individualism. Examining public discourses can reveal the ways that people's choices and actions, which are important and may be motivated by more or less self-contained psychological processes, are nevertheless *always* enabled and constrained by what they *understand* those choices to *signify* to others in the polity. This signification is what *public meaning* consists of, and this public meaning is decided in and through contestation in what I variously call mainstream, popular, or common public discourse. All these designations are synonymous and meant to describe the common currency of ideas, logics, and practices that are intelligible to most people most of the time—even to those who do not agree with them or believe to be inaccurate descriptions of the world. The elements of common public discourse are broadly recognizable even when their truth or implications are disputed.

In sum, the way that we receive and produce meaning in politics is based on popular public discourse. In this way, persistent shifts in political discourse can change politics because they entail changes in public meanings and political understandings, thereby altering what we take to be political, what issues are generally considered problematic and in need of solution, who we think is responsible, and what we think it is feasible and/or desirable to do in response. Put another way, "the boundaries of political community, the legitimacy of political institutions, the acknowledgement of social structures and the nature of justice" all exist in practice as publicly discussed ideas with contingent and contested meanings, rather than as immutable and knowable facts (Ball, Farr, and Hanson 1989, 3). Our political and social worlds are "constructed from a 'moral language that maps political possibilities and impossibilities; it enables us to do certain things even as it discourages or disables us from doing others'" (Rochon 1998, 14). It is for this reason that "altering cultural codings is one of the most powerful ways that social movements actually bring about change" (Swidler 1995, 33).

Ann Swidler argues in "Cultural Power and Social Movements" (1995) that we need to understand the relationship between culture and action—that is, between the ways that semiotic codes organize our interactions at both the interpersonal and structural levels of analysis—as a relationship not primarily about the way that deeply felt or internalized values impact personal motivation and choice, but instead as "global, impersonal, institutional and discursive" (31). Discourses have explanatory power because they reveal how political understandings can develop independent of people's deeply held values, and how externally based, commonplace interpretations of reality—or, to use Emile Durkheim's term, "social facts"—facilitate and constrain our interpretations of the way things are, the way they ought to be, and what we can do about them within a particular polity at a particular time.

Making an effort to understand how the meanings that affect political life are generated, maintained, challenged, overcome, and occasionally transformed ensures that political scientists do not become mere social accountants—measuring a close-fitting line to the discrete occurrences that we are able to gather together. This is not to say that accounting, in this fashion, is not important work. It is, especially because such analysis lets us know what fact(or)s might characterize and help to explain particular phenomena. However, without considering how social and political meanings affect both the choices we make about what problems to address as well as the way we imagine and interpret possible solutions, the explanatory potential of accounting is quite limited.

As John Dewey observed, "Many persons seem to suppose that facts carry their meaning along with themselves on their face. Accumulate enough of them and the meaning stares at you. . . . But the power of physical facts to coerce belief does not reside in the bare phenomenon" (1954, 3). Or as Hannah Pitkin puts it, "That thing may be what it is [whatever we call it] but as soon as we try to say what it is we invoke a conceptual system, which governs what we can say about reality [and] certainly also affects what we perceive" (52). In practice, facts alone, no matter how accurately measured and worthy of consideration, do not make a case, let alone a persuasive one likely to affect the understandings and practices of individuals or the polity as a whole.

This point is underscored by research on the configuration of political attitudes that shows that people's opinions vary by context, and the weight that individuals give to one value or another in deciding a political conflict can and does change depending on a variety of factors, including differential emphasis on the contested meanings in a given political situation (Druckman 2001, Druckman and Nelson 2003, Peffley and Hurwitz 2007, Scheufele and Tewksbury 2007). Therefore, attention to meaning as it is presented in the content of mainstream discourse over time in combination with trends in public opinion offers an opportunity to better understand politics in general and the process of political change, in particular, especially when change is initiated by those who do not have an established place in the normal routines of voice, money, and policy influence. Shifts in popular public meaning are particularly relevant because they give us clues about the range of political possibilities that mainstream audiences find credible from one era to the next and the way those understandings shape political activity.

For example, Frank Baumgartner, Suzanne De Boef, and Amber Boydstun (2008) have found in their groundbreaking *The Decline of the Death Penalty and the Discovery of Innocence* that there has been a precipitous decline in the use of the death penalty since the mid-1990s and that the explanation lies *not* in the change in the fundamental beliefs of Americans regarding whether the death penalty is moral, but rather in the rise of a new "innocence" frame in the death penalty debate. The authors observe that though there has been a gradual decline in the percentage of Americans who support the death penalty, large majorities of Americans continue to support the punishment in principle. Still, the average number of annual death sentences since 2000 has been half what it was in the 1990s. The authors attribute this dramatic shift in public practices to "the innocence movement," a movement that gained influence through the introduction of "a new argument in an old debate," which has shifted attention from what the authors call the "morality frame," chiefly concerned with the question of whether it is moral for a state to kill, to a new "innocence frame," which is primarily focused on the propensity of the state to kill the wrongly convicted (5). Baumgartner and his coauthors write:

> The "morality frame" has long been dominant in this debate, but the ascendance, since the mid to late 1990s of the innocence frame *has changed the political questions and thus policy options associated with this debate.* 'No matter what one thinks about the death penalty in the abstract,' this new argument goes, "evidence suggests that hundreds of errors have occurred in spite of safeguards designed to guarantee that no innocent people are executed." (9; emphasis added)

This new frame, the authors contend, has resulted in a process of "collective attention-shifting." Using statistical factor analysis of the content of public discourse on the topic, they find that "as legal scholars, judges, journalists, and others have focused new attention on this old problem of innocence, the debate has been transformed.... Although Americans remain supportive of capital punishment *in theory*, they are increasingly concerned that the system might not work as intended *in practice*" (5). They conclude that "public opinion is shifting because of the rise of a new frame" and the way public policy is practiced, "measured by the number of death penalties imposed, has already been transformed" (10). While public opinion is slowly changing on the death penalty, the public understanding of what is at stake in the death penalty debate and the practices informed by that understanding are changing much faster.

This kind of study, which takes seriously the ways that "shift[s] in the nature of public discourse [can drive] changes in public opinion and in policy outcomes" (8), may help political scientists answer the long-bedeviling question of issue uptake, or why some events and not others seem to enable significant changes in policy, practice, and opinion, creating what social movement scholars call "political opportunities," while others do not (Tarrow 1998, Meyer and Minkoff 2004, Tilly 1978, McAdam and Snow 2009).

The Role of Agenda-Setting, Priming, and Framing in Shifting Public Attention

Scholars of public opinion have found that mass media influence what information is easily available for public consumption as well as how individuals who have taken in the information may make decisions after viewing, hearing, or reading the content (Bennett 2011, Iyengar 1987, W. Gamson 1992, Entman 2004). Beginning with Walter Lippmann in 1922, some of these scholars have posited that changes in public opinion may be caused by changes in the media agenda, and that changes in the issues, frequency, or depth of media coverage have a direct effect on citizens' attitudes toward issues. However, such a direct relationship has been highly disputed within the public opinion literature, and most recent scholarship posits an *indirect* relationship between media coverage and public opinion. The first empirical study of this phenomenon made the observation that while there is little evidence to support the claim that mass media are able to tell people *what to think*, it seems to be the case that the media influence what citizens *think about* (McCombs and Shaw 1972). While some have disputed even this finding (Patterson and McClure 1976), and others have found that the degree of influence that news has on citizens depends on their level of political awareness and sophistication (Gilens 2011), most agree that, generally speaking, there are "long-term effects on audiences, based on the ubiquitous and consonant stream of messages [news media] present to audiences" (Scheufele and Tewksbury 2007, 10).

Using a quasi-experimental research design and pushing a particular policy agenda in a local newspaper in order to "move community opinion and bring about policy change" over the course of a year, Mutz and Soss (1997) found that while news coverage has little effect on people's personal issue positions, coverage does change people's perceptions about whether an issue is salient as well as their perception of the dominance of certain opinions in their community as a whole. "In this manner," Mutz and Soss note, "increased media coverage of a political issue may help to construct citizens' perceptions of [the] issue as an important social problem" (1997, 434).

Since the 1990s such findings have been commonplace, but so too are the "negation models" of media influence on public opinion (McQuail 2005). In this paradigm, while scholars acknowledge that the news media can create "opinion environments" of the kind identified in the work of Mutz and Soss, they emphasize that such influence is mediated to varying degrees by individual predispositions, schemas, and the demographic characteristics of the audience (Scheufele and Tewksbury 2007, 11). Different individuals and groups process the idiomatic cues that they are given in different ways. However, it is possible to separate out the agenda-setting effects of media, which play out differently with different audiences, from the priming and framing effects, which seem to be more consistent. In terms of the effect that media has on influencing what people are likely to think about as political or politically important, it seems that the media's priming and framing power remains important (B. Cohen 1973, McCombs et al. 2011).

According to Iyengar and Kinder (2010), priming effects are a subset of agenda-setting in which the initial effects of influence deepen and become more specific over time. Priming effects are evidenced by "changes in the standards people use to make political evaluations" (Iyengar and Kinder 2010, 63). Priming effects differ from framing effects in that priming is a function of frequency, influencing the accessibility of information, while framing effects are a function of content, influencing the perceived applicability or relevance of different aspects of an issue (Scheufele and Tewksbury 2007).[1]

Framing, the phenomenon that has effects on public opinion based on the content of the discourse, is the most widely researched across public opinion, political communication, and social movement literatures. It refers to both a macro- and a micro-level construct. At the macro level, frames are the "modes of presentation that journalists and other communicators use to present information in a way that resonates with existing underlying schemas among their audience" (Shoemaker and Reese 1996). At the micro level, framing is the individual cognitive process that people use to form impressions regarding a particular issue. Thomas Nelson and his coauthors put it this way: "Frames affect opinions ... by making certain considerations seem more important than others; these considerations, in turn, carry greater weight for the final attitude" (Nelson, Clawson, and Oxley 1997, 569). In this way, "Frames are more than simply positions or arguments about an issue. Frames are *constructions* of the issue: they spell out the essence of the problem, suggest how it should be thought about, and may go so far as to recommend what (if anything) should be done" (Nelson and Oxley, 1999, 1057). Framing, at both levels, is about emphasizing what aspects of a particular issue are important, thereby shaping the kinds of connection people make between issues. Frames work by making it possible for people to distill complex arguments into a few takeaway points that, in turn, resonate with their already-existing heuristics and cognitive schemas (Druckman and Nelson 2003, Johnson-Cartee 2005, Scheufele and Tewksbury 2007, Klar, Robison, and Druckman 2013).

Frames are dynamic. In the real world of politics, frames are compared and evaluated with one another, meaning that "frames themselves are contestable" (Sniderman and Theriault 2004, 141). Since "the strategic use of framing to mobilize public opinion on a contested issue is a tactic available to all sides," then "the key to being an effective frame ... lies in the frame's strength," or the ability of the frame to stand out in people's minds given the context of competing frames (Druckman 2010, 101–102). Issue frames can impact people in different ways depending on the level of frame competition in political discourse as well as the level of engagement people have with politics (Chong and Druckman 2010, 2013). Researchers have also found that different groups can react to different frames in different ways. For example, Peffley and Hurwitz found that black and white respondents reported very different reactions to the same kinds of framing. In their most striking result, the authors found that while African American respondents to an experiment embedded in the 2000–2001 National Race and Crime Survey readily agreed with a racial discrimination frame when offering an opinion on the death penalty, whites resisted the same frame and in fact were more likely to support the death penalty once they learned that it discriminates against blacks (Peffley and Hurwitz 2007).

While the effects of agenda-setting, priming, and framing are well explored, if still hotly disputed, a fourth phenomenon, *persuasion*, is more rarely investigated in the literature. Persuasive discourse is characterized by the consistency and resonance of frames deployed in public debate. It is the only way that democratic decision-making can function without coercion, and it is a tool political challengers can use to effect change. While persuasion is not an inherently egalitarian art, it can be used to level the playing field between people or groups that begin a contest with asymmetrical resources. The potential for persuasion in discourse offers a way to amass authority and credibility through presentation and argument, rather than simply leveraging resources that accrue based upon preexisting advantages of wealth, official position, education, and the like.

One misconception is worth addressing at the outset of this discussion. Persuasive discourse is often dismissed as an attempt to distort reality in speech or writing in order to deceive political decision-makers about their interests and dupe them into supporting policies that will harm them and benefit the speaker. This common attitude is reductive to the point of misrepresentation, and it has obstructed our understanding of political change in democratic politics. If we are to take the description of reality as the guiding principle of social scientific research, then it is most productive to define persuasion practically, as the process by which people are compelled to consider, and sometimes alter, their perceptions, assumptions, preferences, and criteria for decision-making, or their decisions themselves. On these terms, to persuade is to urge successfully to think or believe something by speaking from, for, out of, or to a belief or set of beliefs.[2] Druckman elaborates that "persuasion . . . takes place when a communicator effectively revises the content of one's beliefs about the attitude object, replacing or supplementing favorable thoughts with unfavorable ones or vice versa" (Druckman 2001, 1044). But does *political* persuasion require the revision of personal attitudes? If culture is a distinctly public characteristic, might we think of persuasion as a public affect?

The Political Character of Persuasion

Let us consider that political persuasion might rely less on the revision of the content of individual principles and predispositions than on shifts in the public meaning of widely circulated semiotic codes, what I am calling mainstream public discourse. Some public opinion scholars, most notably John Zaller, have offered similar assessments. In his influential book *The Nature and Origin of Mass Opinion* (1992), Zaller argues that people change their opinions on political issues (as measured by survey responses) based on their exposure to and comprehension of elite cues, whether the arguments put forth by elites comport with their predispositions, and whether they can recall relevant considerations from their memory to help them make decisions about their positions on political issues (Zaller 1992).

Zaller's model, which he calls Receive-Accept-Sample (RAS), paves the way for thinking about persuasion as a public and political rather than a purely personal phenomenon. He argues that changes in public opinion do not necessarily indicate moral conversions or alterations of basic principles, but rather, differences in the salient considerations that rise to "the top of the head." In a related vein, Thomas Nelson and Donald Kinder point out that "public opinion . . .

depends importantly on the political *context*; the political environment helps determine the balance of forces that make up popular thinking about public issues" (Nelson and Kinder 1996, 1055). In contemporary democracies, where the main communicative medium is mass media, news is the most direct record of political discourse. As Mutz and Soss have observed, "Mass media . . . may provide mass publics with accessible, though fallible, means of monitoring their political environment, and it may aid elites in interpreting and anticipating public reactions" (1997, 432).

The lesson that Mutz and Soss take from this finding is that political elites, especially elected officials, may use news coverage as a proxy to help them anticipate public opinion and therefore act on "anticipations or perceptions of media influence on other political actors" regardless of whether their own or other citizens' issue positions have actually changed (Mutz and Soss 1997, 447). As a result, "Mass media's influence on citizens' perceptions of popular sentiment may have important implications for the strategies available to elites advocating opposing policy courses. By influencing the perceptual environment in which policy debates transpire, media coverage may have important effects on the balance of power among contending policy factions" (Mutz and Soss 1997, 447, Klar, Robison, and Druckman 2013).

I take this argument a step further and contend that elites are not the only group who may find influencing the perceptual environment fruitful for making their claims. In fact, political challengers must rely even more heavily on how the public perceives their claims than elites who may not need public support to press their preferred policy outcomes. I am especially interested in how challenger groups, who do not have routine access to official power or to mass news media, are nevertheless sometimes able to influence political discussion in such a way that they can alter the public perception of which issues and policies are important and how they ought to be discussed. Moreover, the changes in perception that Mutz and Soss observe, with sustained coverage over a period of years, might lead citizens to acknowledge arguments and take positions on issues that they previously did not know or care about, not primarily because they are personally convinced by the veracity of particular claims about those issues or because they have had personal changes of heart, but instead because they perceive the issue to be an important topic of discussion for the polity in general. I submit that this is how many issues *become* salient.

Salience is not always rooted in an aggregation of personal reflections, but instead is often constructed in a process of signification in which individuals weigh in on new issues simply because they perceive that many others are doing so (Druckman 2001, Klar, Robison, and Druckman 2013). An understanding of this discursively based impetus for members of the public to take positions on new issues will offer insight into one of the mechanisms that causes the political environment to change, creating opportunities for new interpretations of social problems and for new policy options to be offered up as solutions.

With this understanding, we can leave behind unhelpful notions that a concern with meaning and meaning-making necessitates a preoccupation with idiosyncratic individual predilections or with a cynical fascination with "spin." What is important for people interested in politics is that meanings that are generally intelligible draw on a common perception of certain contexts, background knowledge, and symbolic elements. I do not mean to suggest, of course, that the existence of shared public meanings implies that distinctions in their interpretation or lived experience are unimportant, or that universality is somehow the real truth of human experience. Instead, I have a rather thin and specific conception of shared, public meaning—that is, the collection of common concepts, symbols, historical interpretations, frames, and practices that can reasonably be considered apprehensible to any ordinarily competent member of the polity because the ideas circulate regularly and in public. Apprehension in this sense does not necessarily mean understanding in any deep sense—neither insight, nor realization, nor mastery is implied. However, there are certain elements of meaning that are widely represented in public discourse and that most citizens can interpret—more often than not, in similar ways (Paige and Shapiro 1992). Therefore, when I speak of meaning in this study, I am always referring to practical meanings and never intend to imply that the highlighted interpretations are "real" or "true," but only that some interpretations are usual, customary, and regular—commonsensical and prevalent rather than absolute and comprehensive (Boudieu 1977, Wedeen 2002).

It is for this reason that mainstream public discourse is the best place to look for evidence of changes in political understanding—changes that may affect the environment in which certain ideas or idioms develop and in which political decisions are made by both private individuals and the officials commissioned to represent, serve, or lead them. In this way, public discourse is the site of shared political meaning. As people share information and evaluate problems, they also share the stories, symbols, and logic that allow their interpretations to make sense. The kinds of attitudes and explanations that are commonly considered plausible, desirable, reasonable, effective, or in line with particular ends is a trove of valuable information for students of politics.

Of course, my acknowledgment of meaning and persuasion as key components of politics is not new. John Dewey argued, "If one wishes to realize the distance which may lie between facts and the meaning of facts, let one go to the field of social discussion" (Dewey 1954, 3). However, this observation and the questions it gives rise to—such as how certain facts come to be seen as legitimate (neither spurious nor unjustified) and move people to action and others do not—have been less prevalent in the literature since the mid-twentieth century. Social and political analysts like John Dewey, Robert Dahl, and E. E. Schattschneider were intensely interested in the political function of social meanings, but interest in such studies has receded in the face of the dominance of methodological individualism and the statistics-based analysis of individual's political decisions as well as traditional political events, such as campaigns and elections. While individual decision-making and political events are important ways of understanding the political, they do not capture the entirety of politics, particularly ignoring the part that is reflected in ongoing processes rather than singular events or individual decisions.

As Lisa Wedeen has argued, "thinking of meaning construction in terms that emphasize intelligibility, as opposed to deep-seated psychological orientations," which she terms a "practice-oriented approach," points the analyst's attention toward the aspects of meaning that affect people sharing the same public space (Wedeen 2002, 713). In other words, it is important to analyze the ways that things are generally understood (within a particular place at a particular his- torical moment) in order to examine how that widespread understanding may affect the choices and actions of members of the polity. Media helps shape this general understanding by framing issues, especially newly emergent issues, in what William Gamson and Andre Modigliani call "interpretive packages" that "typically impl[y] a range of positions, rather than any single one, allowing for a degree of controversy" (Gamson and Modigliani 1989, 3). This range of contro- versy does not capture the entire debate, but does represent the range of plau- sible alternatives referenced in mainstream political discussion, which we may consider generally intelligible and accessible to most people.

Political attitudes are not a given, nor are they so tied to individual socializa- tion as to be fruitless to investigate. People apply their values to problems in a variety of ways (Mutz 1994, Mutz and Soss 1997, Druckman 2001, Druckman and Nelson 2003, Klar, Robison, and Druckman 2013). This is why perspective matters at all, because the same facts (e.g., statistics about the effects of cohabi- tation versus marriage) and similar values (e.g., the well-being and security of individuals, families, and children in the polity) can result in very different con- clusions depending on how public rhetoric is deployed and received.

For example, in the early days of the mainstream debate over whether gay marriage ought to be legalized or banned, opponents and advocates both deployed arguments that made use of the common idea that marriage encour- ages monogamy, social cohesion, and personal stability, thereby improving the well-being of those involved. Both used similar statistics and anecdotal evidence to back up this claim. However, while opponents deployed these facts to prove that "traditional" heterosexual marriage is sacred, socially productive, and frag- ile, advocates used the empirical data about the benefits of "traditional" marriage as evidence that it ought to be expanded to anyone who wished to enter into this more socially productive relation, which seems to increase several indicators of well-being.[3] In a 1994 letter to the editor published in the *New York Times*, the writer inquires, "And how does gay marriage make for bad public policy? A committed relationship that is blessed by marriage, gay or straight, promotes stability and security in our society." In contrast, Robert Knight of the Family Research Council, an anti-gay marriage group in Washington, DC, argued in an article published on March 15, 1995, "Marriage is the basis of family life and families are central to civilization.... The law does not discriminate against homosexuals.... It merely states that each sex must be represented in marriage. Same sex couples do not qualify. It may be called a partnership, but if it's called marriage it's a counterfeit version. And counterfeit versions drive out the real thing."

In this way, the same basic belief is interpreted and framed in completely different terms, implying opposite conceptions of the central social problem to be solved and the appropriate policy options that might be used to solve it. However, this only tells part of the story. What I explore in chapter 4 is how framing can create shifts in the political *doxa*, with one set of associations becoming commonsensical and the other left open to (re)definition and contestation.

All social movements, especially those in democracies, depend upon the public and the authority and leverage that they may grant, not only as members and active allies of a movement, but as a sympathetic (or indifferent, or antagonistic) audience of judges. Without the willingness of the mass public to hear the cause of the movement and the subsequent impetus for elites to react to its claims, movements can have little influence. However, the implicit public power upon which all challenger movements not reliant on military might are built is often forgotten by practitioners and academics alike.

Conclusion

Background understandings of who "we" are as a polity or nation and how things are as material and social facts in the world set the stage for what constitutes public meaning. However, politics is a process filled with subjects who act. National political agendas do not merely develop; they are made by and through the speech and action of officials, elite opinion leaders, news media, interpersonal interactions, and the organized efforts of grass-roots political challengers. Those who seek to put new issues on the national agenda, increase the salience of existing issues, or change the way that those issues are perceived and acted upon have their most significant opportunity to *change the politics* that attend their issue by changing the structure of political conflict through influencing mainstream public discourse—reshaping the public meanings that attend the key symbols, reference points, facts, and perspectives that are routinely included in public discussion. This is especially true for advocates of communities that are, on balance, marginal from the point of view of the American idiomatic "mainstream," such as GLBTQ people, racial and ethnic minorities, or poor people.

Unless we consider the changing and polysemous reality of meaning, social scientists run the risk of treating values and attitudes as antecedent, given, and fixed. This is certainly not the case. On the individual level the evolution of opinions may be hard to trace, but as previous research in public opinion has hinted, the shifting concerns and preferences of mass publics may be available through much simpler means (Paige and Shapiro 1992). Observing changes in mainstream public discourse offers a direct and efficacious opportunity to gain access to these concerns. One cannot observe or prove that individuals in a particular mass public have had changes of heart that fundamentally alter their predispositions, but this is not necessary to analyze political change. As Campbell, Converse, Miller, and Stokes observed in the middle of the last century, Americans do not seem to make political decisions based on cohesive and coherent ideology, but instead consider information in light of values, attitudes, and predispositions that they may variously and contradictorily apply depending both on the political information they have and on the kinds of decisions they are asked to make (Zaller and Feldman 1992, Alvarez and Brehm 1995, 1997, Baumgartner, De Boef, and Boydstun 2008). A key rubric for these differential applications may be written right into the public record.

In the following two chapters, I examine the history of the struggles for a living wage and the fight for marriage equality. For each movement, I explore the origins, structure, organizational culture, and interorganizational environment of the two movement sectors. I explain how these characteristics are related to each movement's venue choice, or the predominant institutional pathways where these political challengers chose to press their claims, as well as the tactical preferences of each movement. This historiography helps to illuminate the differing understandings of political power that motivated each movement's regard for and approach to engaging mainstream public discourse. This engagement ultimately resulted in the dogged, but obscure, political subsistence of the one and the political acceptance of the other.

A Tale of Two Movements

Living Wage

The following two chapters contain an account of the emergence of two movements: the fight for a living wage and the struggle to win marriage equality. A timeline of activity in each movement is provided in figure 2.1. Though they both came into existence in the early 1990s, the two movements took different tracks to challenge existing political arrangements of resources, recognition, power, and privilege. Their differences cannot be explained only by the fact that the two movements advocated for different kinds of issues. Instead, their dissimilarity was manifold, beginning with two distinct conceptions of power that led to observably different *organizational structures, organizational cultures*, and *interorganizational environments* within the broader movements. These differences led the movements to make different choices regarding the institutional *venues* chosen for action as well as the preferred *tactics* that each employed. I will argue in subsequent chapters that these divergent features are critical to explaining the different outcomes of the two movements; here, I want to explore the ideology, structure, and trajectory of each movement in greater detail.

Power, Action, and Identity

At the outset, I want to call attention to an ideological contrast between notions of what constitutes power and action for each movement and how those notions shape their approaches to challenging status quo political arrangements. For the living wage movement, the way to seek political change is to "build power" through taking action. Power, from the perspective of both the intellectual history of the movement and the individual movement leaders I interviewed, consists of something like Steven Luke's notion of the first face of power: directly influencing the behavior of decision-makers in the desired direction on immediately relevant policy issues. Action, then, is conceived as whatever public

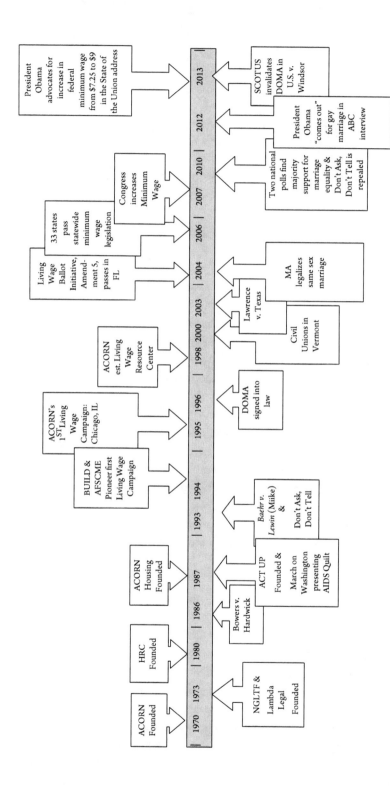

Figure 2.1 Living Wage and Marriage Equality Timeline.

force facilitates this influence. The marriage equality movement has a more Foucauldian notion of power and pursues political change by taking on "identity work," a kind of political action that involves the creation, articulation, negotiation, maintenance, and policing of intelligible and credible identities (Stryker, Owen, and White 2000, Snow and McAdam 2000). For the marriage equality movement, identity work is practiced as one of the most important components of political action; for the living wage movement, as we will see, identity work has not been considered an important component of political activism.

In addition the organizational culture that characterized the gay rights movement undertook identity work as a necessary, even habitual, practice, both internally in organizations and externally with the broad public. Leaders of the living wage movement, coming out of a more general labor-left framework, believed that the reasons people should support their cause and organize in favor of policy change were *objective* and *self-evident*, requiring little intentional identity work or broad public discussion to communicate the urgency, necessity, and efficacy of their cause. In addition, since most people in America fit into the socioeconomic category "low-to-moderate income," the living wage movement, especially from the point of view of the movement's lead organization, ACORN, was a majority movement waiting to be organized, rather than a minority movement in which identity ought to be cultivated, explained, and defended. In this way, the ACORN strategy was not a minority strategy. Its participants were not very concerned about winning understanding and sympathy from a broad public; instead, they were most concerned about "building power" to win the next, concretely identifiable political contest. The marriage equality movement, by contrast, always understood itself as a minority movement that needed to get people, including potential members and allies, the general public, and government officials, to care about its cause. In addition, the AIDS crisis created a personal, social, and political environment in which cooperation and coordination, even amid intense ideological and tactical disagreement, was paramount, a necessity made glaringly clear by the shocking mortality brought on by the modern-day plague.

Comparing the Living Wage and Marriage Equality Movements: An Overview

The living wage and marriage equality movements are alike in that they both became self-articulated movements at the same time and by similar processes. Both movements also began as outbursts within their broader movement sectors propelled by a surprise local victory. The emergence of the living wage was the result of an innovative campaign authored by church leaders and union officials working together to serve their local constituents in Baltimore. The marriage equality movement started in the courts, not as a self-conscious strategy of gay rights advocates, but due to the political promise of a surprising ruling handed down in Hawaii. Each movement began as existing organizations took advantage of surprise victories in legislative and legal venues, respectively. The living wage movement pursued discrete local fights, in part, because leaders believed that was where what social movement scholars call their "political opportunities" lay (Tilly 1978, McAdam 1999, Tarrow 1994, Meyer and Minkoff 2004). Political opportunity is the structural relationship between movements and the wider political environment including the "specific configurations of resources, institutional arrangement and historical precedents for social mobilization" (Kitschelt 1986, 58). Likewise, the marriage equality movement took advantage of the courts, because leaders believed, based on the twentieth-century history of the black civil rights movement, that this would be the best path to victory for a maligned minority group.

However, the political opportunity story is only a partial explanation for the differential success of these movements. It is also the case that the living wage "social movement sector" (McAdam, McCarthy, and Zald 1996) had an organizational structure that made national action difficult, even when there were potential elite allies at the national level, as well as an organizational culture that valued conceptions of power and action that were not easily compatible with either interest group politics or broad-based communication aimed at the general public. The marriage equality movement, on the other hand, had an organizational structure that privileged centralized, professionalized national organizations, as well as some space for more loosely networked, shorter-lived innovative groups.

In each case, these unexpected wins constituted opportunities to pursue significant and successful campaigns that activists and organizers in the well-developed movement sectors of labor justice and gay rights were prepared to take advantage of. However, each movement sector had its own historical, organizational, political, cultural, and resource predicaments that shaped the ways that the movements chose to nationalize their fights.

The living wage movement became the efficacious signature campaign of a loose network of community-based organizations (CBOs) that trace their philosophical origins to legendary Chicago organizer Saul Alinsky. By contrast, the marriage equality movement emerged out of a diverse and vibrant social movement sector forged into functional unity by the crucible of the AIDS crisis. In terms of *organizational structure*, the living wage movement is highly localized, even when conducted under the auspices of national organizations like ACORN, which built a large and powerful organization between 1970 and 2010. The *organizational culture* of secular CBOs tends to be task-centered, action-oriented, and confrontation-welcoming, rather than self-reflective, self-consciously philosophical, or interested in identity work (Swarts 2008, Rathke 2009). The *interorganizational environment* among CBOs tends to be rife with conflict over turf, with "little coordination or strategizing among them and no mechanism for discussion of how to best utilize their substantial resources in the most effective way" (Dreier 2009, 7). In terms of *venue choice*, CBOs target specific, local decision-makers who can deliver on some specific good. This often means local corporations, municipal bureaucrats, and local legislatures. *Tactically*, CBOs prize *action*. Action has a very particular meaning for those in the Alinsky school: it means creative, fun, combative demonstrations of power with the goal of achieving a concrete, immediate deliverable such as a specific change in corporate policy or practice, or a legislative vote on a particular policy.

The marriage equality movement, on the other hand, emerged within the broader gay rights movement sector, in which movement entrepreneurs and organizations had been forced to focus nationally and (reluctantly) cooperate among themselves, often by devising a functional division of labor, because of the literal threat to survival that the AIDS crisis created. This meant that the *organizational structure* of most gay advocacy organizations became centralized and professionalized in the 1990s and the *interorganizational environment* became movement-oriented, was relatively cooperative,[1] and was nationally focused from the beginning of the period of study. For gay rights movement sector, action necessarily entailed the identity work of creating publicly intelligible selves both for activists inside the movement and for the education of the general public.

For this reason, the gay rights movement sector had an *organizational culture* that was identity-centric in at least two senses. First, beginning in the mid-twentieth century, same-sex loving people began to create a self-conscious identity to name who they were and begin to articulate political demands. This was in response to federal and state policies allowing employers, landlords, and business owners to fire, evict, or exclude people on suspicion of "moral indecency." Second, organizations advocating for gay rights brought this identity focus into their engagement with the public sphere. Marriage equality activists exemplified this focus and had a broad conception of what kinds of activities are useful and count as movement work. They tended to create public campaigns making claims about the existence and worth of people with gay identities in addition to making political demands on behalf of the group. In terms of *venue choice* and *tactical preferences*, the gay rights movement had no single, uniform set of strategies that characterized the movement sector. Instead, there developed a division of labor, with different organizations specializing in different venues and tactics.

While each movement pursued local strategies with the intention of eventual national impact, living wage advocates usually chose to pursue those ends through a combination of interest group politics and direct action aimed at legislatures at the municipal and, more rarely, the state level, while marriage equality advocates predominantly pursued their claims in the courts. These predominant venue choices were never exclusive; however, each movement demonstrated a general tendency in regard to venue choice. These general differences in venue are partly a matter of preference and partly a matter of "political opportunity." This is because public opinion was not on the side of marriage equality, and it is hard to instigate political change through the legislature without the support of public sentiment as well as significant mobilization of people who are both local constituents and movement participants. For political challengers, the choice of what institutional venue is most likely to be most conducive to their claims is much influenced by whether or not public sentiment is with or against their cause. Challenger groups that have public opinion on their side, like the living wage movement, can press claims through legislatures that will yield policy wins. For those movement groups who are pressing claims not in line with public sentiment, like the marriage movement, the courts are the most logical venue to pursue claims.

The Political Emergence of the Living Wage

In 1994, the American Federation of State, County and Municipal Employees (AFSME) and Baltimoreans United in Leadership Development (BUILD), a group of local churches, led a campaign based on a novel idea. Instead of striving for a statewide or federal increase in the minimum wage, which seemed unattainable at the time, they targeted city service contractors and demanded that those who worked for them should receive an increase in pay that would allow them to live above the poverty line. They called the campaign the *living wage*, to communicate that the current wage paid by the targeted employer was not enough to allow a family to survive. In the end, the labor and faith coalition successfully pressured the city council to pass an ordinance that required city service contractors to raise the pay of their workers from $5.15 per hour to $7.70 per hour by 1999—and the living wage struggle became the signature issue of contemporary labor activists.

These activists are descended from the progressive labor movements that first made the regulation of working conditions a political priority in the nineteenth century. Specifically, the idea of the living wage borrows quite a bit from the older and more familiar rallying cry of the minimum wage, a policy with a long history and moderate but sustained political cachet. The difference between the minimum wage and a living wage is that minimum wages generally apply to all workers at either the state or federal level. Living wages, on the other hand, seek to affect employees of firms receiving public money:

> Our limited public dollars should not be subsidizing poverty-wage work. When subsidized employers are allowed to pay their workers less than a living wage, tax payers end up footing a double bill: the initial subsidy and then the food stamps, emergency medical, housing and other social services low wage workers may require to support themselves and their families even minimally. Public dollars should be leveraged for the public good—reserved for those private sector employers who demonstrate a commitment to providing decent, family-supporting jobs in our local communities. (ACORN 2007)

The success of the Baltimore living wage campaign quickly caught the attention of the nation's oldest and largest grass-roots organization of low-and-moderate income people, the Association of Community Organizations for Reform Now (ACORN). Jen Kern, the former director of the Living Wage Resource Center at ACORN, reports that the group was surprised and intrigued by the success of the Baltimore coalition. Though, as Stephanie Luce writes, "no one national organization has run the movement, and no one model of campaign has dominated," it is also true that ACORN "stands out as instrumental to the success of many of the campaigns" (Luce 2009, 131). In an interview I conducted with Kern she recounted, "The Baltimore campaign had nothing to do with [ACORN]—it happened totally organically"[2]—but the local approach was a natural fit for ACORN, a national institution that was, from its founding in 1970, based on a community-organizing model. At the time, Kern was a recent graduate of Grinnell College, a new staffer sent to discover what ACORN might learn from the local campaign. In nearby Washington, DC, "At the Library of Congress, she poured over regulations, court decisions, and state constitutions from around the country to find out if ACORN could mount campaigns in other cities" where it organized (Atlas 2010, 105). Her research showed that it was, indeed, possible, and over the next decade and a half, ACORN would become the most important national organization involved in both starting living wage campaigns and training unaffiliated organizers to run them on their own. Between 1994 and 2010, when ACORN disbanded, 120 living wage campaigns successfully advocated for municipal ordinances. Of these, ACORN was the initiator of fourteen, and a significant coalition partner in another twenty-one; for most of the remaining campaigns, ACORN played the role of trainer and expert, providing access to academics working on the issue like Robert Pollin, Mark Brenner, and Stephanie Luce, as well as to legal counsel from labor-friendly lawyers like Paul Sonn at the National Employment Law Project (Luce 2009).

After the 1994 win in Baltimore, ACORN stepped in to offer structure and support for what they viewed as a model of action that could be successfully exported to other cities, and sometimes pushed at the state level. "We very deliberately thought through what we could do to raise wages in cities. We knew the federal government could not be relied upon to raise wages to an appropriate level, and at the beginning we weren't strong enough to push the issue on the federal level."[3] This rationale is also elaborated by sociologist Stephanie Luce, who writes, "Unable to win a higher federal minimum wage due to political resistance, and lacking power in municipal wage bargaining due to threats of privatization, activists turned to their local governments to pass living wage ordinances" (Luce 2004, 27). Madeline Janis, the lead organizer of Chicago ACORN, put the matter this way: "[Movements must b]uild momentum and model success. You start where you can actually win. It makes no sense to start on the national level when you have no chance of getting anything adopted. We found we could win in cities." Plainly speaking, it is easier to win on the municipal level, so labor activists decided in the mid-1990s to try their hand at fighting some fights that they were confident could be won in order to alleviate negative conditions for some working people and to galvanize the labor movement in general (Pollin and Luce 1998).

By 1998, ACORN had set up the Living Wage Resource Center (LWRC), which sought to "track the living wage movement and provide materials and strategies to living wage organizers all over the country."[4] In addition, the LWRC held periodic National Living Wage Training Conferences, which drew organizers from across the country to "learn from each other about elements of a living wage campaign such as building local coalitions, doing research, working with city council, developing message and responding to the opposition, preparing for living wage implementation fights, and using living wage campaigns to build community and labor membership and power."[5] The organizers who saw the potential in the targeted living wage approach were proved correct. Within four years of the first ordinance, ACORN, often in partnership with local unions or church-based community organizations, had helped pass some kind of living wage ordinance in seventeen different cities, including New York, Los Angeles, Chicago, Jersey City, and Portland. However, along the way, movement leaders realized that there were some limitations to the living wage approach. Wage laws that cover municipalities have limited reach, and as ACORN attempted to spread the living wage model it learned some blistering lessons about the unmitigated vociferousness of business opponents. Kern remembers, "We tried to do [a living wage] in Houston, Texas, and one in Denver, Colorado, and we got our asses handed to us by the restaurant business. We were still new to things that we now know are important, like messaging."[6] Still, ACORN saw great potential in the living wage approach and began presenting it as one of a host of campaigns that it offered to help local groups put together and carry out.

Structure and Strategy: Organizational Structure, Organizational Culture, Interorganizational Environment, Venue Choice, and Tactics

In order to understand what kind of movement the living wage is and the logic that shaped its priorities, it is important to note that the organizational culture at ACORN—and thus for much of the living wage movement—shared a great deal with the larger twentieth-century labor movement. Labor had rejected (and been rejected by) the postmaterialist sectors of the New Left. Indeed, the work by ACORN founder Wade Rathke seemed a reaction against the New Left movements that were influenced by the thought of European scholars like Herbert Marcuse and Ronald Inglehart and eventually came to be analyzed by social movement scholars under the rubric of New Social Movements. These movements are said to diverge from those of the nineteenth and early twentieth centuries in that they abjure the classical Marxist paradigm in which "most significant social actors will be defined by class relationships rooted in the process of production and . . . all other social identities are secondary at best in constituting collective actors." Instead, the New Social Movements embrace the view that there are "other logics of action based in politics, ideology, and culture," which are "the root of much collective action" (Bucheler 1995, 442). Functionally, this means that those who analyze New Social Movements look to identities other than class, such as race, ethnicity, gender, and sexuality, as sites where collective identity is defined and collective action is motivated.

This account elides several important questions. For example, the newness of New Social Movements is somewhat dubious (Plotke 1990, Pichardo 1997), and a paradigmatic distinction between "class politics" and "identity politics" is deeply problematic, given the historical observation, made most incisively by Ira Katznelson, that class politics in the American case has generally been organized based upon ethnicity (Katznelson 1981). Likewise, feminist scholars, scholars of color, and queer scholars have written extensively about the class dimensions and class conflict that occur in movements organized on the basis of other kinds of identities and their intersections (Higginbotham 1993, Crenshaw 1991, Phillips 1987, Andersen and Collins 2006, Anthias and Yuval-Davis 1983, Bailey 1999, Cohen 1999). Still, it is certainly true that movement actors may conceive of themselves and their political project differently depending on whether they see their struggle as primarily aligned with the "old" labor Left or the "new" identity politics. And these differences can be important in terms of the development of organizational culture, venue choices, and tactical preferences.

ACORN was uniquely equipped by its *organizational structure* to spread the living wage as a winning legislative issue. Unlike other community-based organizations (CBOs), ACORN was a *"federated organization* with local bases but with a national infrastructure and the capacity to wage campaigns simultaneously at the local, state, and national levels" (Dreier 2009, 13). Rathke founded ACORN in Arkansas in 1970, after learning the basics of community organizing as a staffer for a group called the National Welfare Rights Organization (NWRO), which he had become involved with as a college student in Boston. Despite the designation "national" in the group's title, the NWRO, like most associations of CBOs, was only loosely affiliated, each local organization having almost complete autonomy in raising funds and deciding on goals, campaigns, staffing, tactics, and messaging.

CBOs constitute a wide field of civic and political activism in the contemporary United States. However, the organizations that make up this sector are often invisible to the general public (Swarts 2008). This inconspicuousness is not accidental: CBOs often remain locally focused with decentralized decision-making apparatuses on purpose. Even long-established CBOs with dozens of small affiliates in cities and towns all over America, many with impressive accomplishments under their belts, such as the Industrial Areas Foundation, PICO National Network, and Gamaliel Foundation, do not go out of their way to publicize themselves and have no explicit agendas outside their local communities. Saul Alinksy, whose book on community organizing, *Rules for Radicals*, became the organizational inspiration for many CBOs, held that in order to be effective, political organizing had to have an unrelentingly local focus: addressing concerns, cultivating leaders, and "building power" block by block (Alinsky [1971] 1989).

Along with this localism, Alinsky promulgated a deep suspicion of the usefulness of ideology to achieve concrete objectives, refusing to define his goals in abstract, normative terms. This aversion to ideology as a basis for organizing often translates, in Alinsky-inspired groups, to an *organizational culture* characterized by distaste for the abstract notion of social movement and the expressive protest tactics that sometimes accompany them. Michael Gecan, a longtime organizer for the Industrial Areas Foundation and author of *Going Public*, a contemporary take on the old rules for radicals, describes an antiglobalization protest he witnessed in 2001 this way:

> Five people stood at the corner of Broadway and Rector Street. Two
> had splashed black paint on their clothing and smeared black paint on

their faces. They writhed on the sidewalk while a graying demonstrator pounded a drum and a young woman harangued the passing crowd. Twenty-five cops eyed the scene, casually leaning against the building and stairs, their nightsticks in their belts, their riot helmets perched on their nightsticks.... [W]hat was their cause? The demonstrators held a hastily painted sign: "Save the U'Wa Tribe. . ." There was a reference to Fidelity Capital. The woman with the megaphone couldn't be easily understood.... For all their choreographed movement, the demonstrators seemed remarkably static. Still life: *Activists on a Manhattan Street.*... What crystalized for me that day in Manhattan was this: what I was observing was not an action at all, but a reenactment. (Gecan 2002, 50–51)

From the perspective of most CBOs, ideologically based movements are generally in the business of staging "non-strategic, expressive, symbolic demonstrations not designed to gain achievable results," while locally anchored community organizers focus on creating "actions" that take place in "strategic, instrumental, disciplined venues" where community leaders "make specific, negotiable demands and . . . win results" (Swarts 2008, 8).

Though ACORN also traced its organizational lineage to Alinsky, Rathke infused the organization with his own philosophy, based on the conviction that fundamentally improving the lives of poor people would require an organization that could mobilize members in the economic position shared by the majority of Americans. ACORN was multi-issue and multiracial, did not underestimate the power of electoral politics, and embraced tactical flexibility (Rathke 2009). The result was a federated organization anchored in communities with dues-paying members that was nevertheless more centralized than most CBOs, thanks to a professional national staff that helped to shape policy initiatives and develop useful strategies and replicable *tactics*. ACORN was therefore uniquely ready to coordinate activities at the municipal, state, and national levels (Dreier 2009). Heidi Swarts writes that unlike most CBOs, ACORN "unhesitatingly [sought] to form a *movement* that will change the status quo" (2008, 7). However, ACORN did share with many CBOs a suspicion of ideology. In her ethnographic study of CBOs, *Organizing Urban America*, Swarts writes that ACORN had an "instrumental and utilitarian organizational culture in which transcendent values and beliefs are seldom articulated. Organizers point to the conditions of poor people as *self-evident* motivation for organizing, and the organization does not have an elaborated ideology that it teaches members" (Swarts 2008, 44; emphasis added), although "long-term ACORN organizers . . . tend to see the organization as a solitary vanguard of principled leftists" (Swarts 2008, 29).

ACORN as an organization felt no responsibility for serving, articulating, or imagining a broader sociopolitical vision for either its staff and members, or for the political Left. "Organizers' ideals are less often articulated and more often inferred from their commitment to daunting work at low pay" (Swarts 2008, 34). The organization itself made only one statement about its philosophical underpinnings and political priorities, a document called *The People's Platform*, "a veritable laundry list of progressive positions challenging corporate power and championing 'the people'" (Swarts 2008, 33) conceived in 1978 "as a tool to consolidate new affiliates" (Delgado 2009, 272) and updated once in 1990, as a part of the organizations twentieth-anniversary celebration.

ACORN, like other CBOs in the Alinsky lineage, saw itself as an "action organization" that practiced a "down-to-earth, nonsectarian populism" (Swarts 2008, 33). The notion that the motivation for organizing is obvious and self-evident, requiring no lofty elaboration, is critical to understanding the orientation of ACORN and other CBOs toward delivering immediate policy results to their members, neighborhoods, and constituents, rather than spending limited resources attempting to win over the general public. For these kinds of organizations, values and vision are most convincing when demonstrated through commitment and action, not when articulated in persuasive speech. This view often led to a disregard for developing messaging strategies that were not campaign specific or a public face that engaged with the general public in general terms. In short, ACORN eschewed what David Snow and Doug McAdam (2000) have termed "identity work," the deliberate cultivation of a coherent "we-ness" among movement participants across campaigns. Rather, there was a conviction that there was an organic movement "out there," among "the people" that did not need to be constructed, only harnessed by enduring and powerful organizations.

That is why, though ACORN staffers spent little time cultivating a philosophical or political vision, Rathke and his colleagues nurtured an *organizational culture* focused on supporting, strengthening, and expanding the organization itself. In a reflection on the genesis of ACORN in 2009, Rathke wrote: "Few questions surprise me more than when outsiders, reporters or other well-meaning inquisitors ask me to state ACORN's biggest accomplishment or most important victory. After all is said and done, the organization itself is our largest achievement" (Rathke 2009, 40). When all was, suddenly, said and done in March 2010, ACORN had ample reason to be proud of the size and strength of the organization. ACORN had not only endured but grown and thrived for forty years. It raised and spent $100 million dollars annually on campaigns across the country and claimed over 500,000 individual dues-paying members in 1,200 chapters (Rathke 2009).

However, in the wake of a perfect storm of challenges including institutional reorganization, an embezzlement scandal involving the founder's brother, and a smear campaign orchestrated by right-wing media provocateur James O'Keefe and joined by Fox News and congressional Republicans, ACORN abruptly shut its doors. While it would have been tough for any organization to overcome these challenges, it is also true that ACORN had no reputation with the general public at the time. As large as it was, as many people as it had helped, as close as its ties were with some elected officials—notably Democratic senators Richard Durbin of Illinois and Charles Schumer of New York, as well as Bernie Sanders of Vermont, an independent, who appreciated ACORN Housing's important work and supported living wage campaigns in their states—stories of ACORN's "corruption" were the first occasion on which most people had ever heard of the group (Atlas 2010).

The living wage movement always transcended ACORN the organization, but ACORN had a hand in influencing many campaigns and provided a tactical model for many more. While the *interorganizational environment* among CBOs is diffuse and plagued by turf battles, ACORN was able to develop intensive training that other organizations found useful and replicated in their own communities. At the LWRC training conferences organizers learned basic guidelines for running successful living wage campaigns. Relying on her extensive experience, Kern argued that "the best campaigns . . . utilize both an 'inside track' and an 'outside track'" (Luce 2009, 135). The inside track referred to the relationship that the organizers developed with local legislators. The instructions on how to develop these relationships were detailed.

> The campaign should build a delegation to meet one-on-one with each city councilor. Each visit with a council member has two purposes. First, the delegation should gather information, assessing where the councilor stands on the ordinance and how strong his or her opposition is. Second, visits are meant to *pressure* and *persuade* the councilor to vote for the ordinance and to urge fellow councilors to do the same. In order to persuade, the delegations should demonstrate to the city council member the depth of the coalition. Delegations must involve prominent leaders from the community, especially those from the councilor's district or ward. The delegation should also make sure the councilor knows the full list of groups and individuals supporting the campaign. Hopefully, that list of supporters grows with each visit. Councilors must see that their constituents want the living wage passed, and they must understand that there will be political repercussions for failing to support the ordinance. (Luce 2009, 135–136)

In this strategy, persuasion is seen not as the successful transmission of ideas but the achievement of a specific outcome through the brute force of electoral power.

Persuasion is thus only a function of power, and power is conceived solely in terms of what Steven Lukes has called its "first face" (Lukes [1974] 2005). This means that power, for those involved in the organizations of the living wage movement, could only be equated with "success in decision-making. To be powerful is to win: to prevail over others in conflict situations" (Lukes [1974] 2005, 70). Michael Gecan elaborates on the theory of power and action for CBOs in the Alinsky tradition:

> When you say that you seek power, want power, you are headed into terra incognita. You are no longer a do-gooder holding hands and singing "Kumbaya.". . . Without power there's no real recognition, there's no reciprocity, there's not even a "you" to respond to . . . there's no relationship of respect. Without power, you can only be a supplicant, a serf, a victim, or a wishful thinker who soon begins to whine. Power in the new millennium is the same as power when Thucydides was writing about the Melians and the Athenians. It is still the ability to act. And it still comes in two basic forms—organized people and organized money. (Gecan 2002, 8, 36)

This view of power and persuasion, while partly correct, is also rather anemic. Those who enter political challenges with fewer resources, weaker institutions, and no official sanction can and should build power, in this sense, but this alone will ultimately be insufficient. As Steven Lukes writes in his famous meditation on the subject, power has at least three faces: direct influence, agenda-setting, and latent influence ([1974] 2005). If political challengers cultivate only one of these, they limit the tools at their disposal.

The "outside track" that ACORN-trained living wage campaigns were encouraged to follow entailed "the work done in the community" (Luce 2009, 136). This work consists of building coalitions, doing public education, and "demonstrating power." Luce reports:

> Kern works with campaigns to develop a strategic plan, involving escalating tactics. Early in the campaign, the coalition might focus on educational activities and non-confrontational tactics, like sending postcards to elected officials. A next step might be door knocking with a cell phone in hand, asking residents to support the campaign and call their councilors right there. From there, a coalition may hold rallies outside council members homes' or public actions, and even participate in civil disobedience. (2009, 136)

The inside track consists of one-on-one meetings used to demonstrate power and elicit cooperation by using the threat of electoral harm; the outside track consists of educating the public about the living wage and, again, mobilizing public pressure on legislators to elicit cooperation under the threat of electoral harm. This "outside track" is not very far outside direct contact with the legislator. Although public education is mentioned, there is little detail about how that ought to be conducted and very little guidance concerning whether or how an organizer should frame the issue with potential members, allies, or, through media, with the general public. When I asked Jen Kern what the strongest public arguments for the living wage were, her answer was indicative of the way that ACORN and its allies regarded communication strategies, especially those aimed toward the general public rather than toward potential members:

> I'm not a big messaging person. Some people say that the moral argument always trumps the economic argument, but I really think it's about power. For me, I can't make the pitch unless I know who I'm talking with.... In the end it's about whether you can bring more pain on the elected official than your opponents. It's all about how you come out in their calculation about who it's safer to piss off. It matters whether the people are behind it and whether that can be demonstrated.[7]

For Kern, who started her career as an organizer in ACORN and led the LWRC to many policy victories, there is only one way to "demonstrate power," and that is to win the argument by bringing the most pain. From this viewpoint, creating a portable verbal picture of the living wage that is generally intelligible in many contexts would not yield victory in the immediate context of a particular action—and those things that would not yield victory or directly build the organization were not worth spending scarce money, skills, and time on. During our interview, Kern admitted that the living wage movement had not "refined a central message" but she didn't feel this was a problem, arguing:

> There are some PR people who would say that's a problem. It's just sloppier than that in real life. But that sloppiness can be useful because you're talking to different people with different concerns. The idea that we could win if we just framed the message correctly is ... well, it's more complicated than that.... The most important takeaway is the importance of grass-roots organizing. [The living wage movement] has allowed the strengthening of the organizations that represent working people.

Indeed, ACORN's firm belief that ideology does not need to be clearly articulated because "objective" class conditions and the necessity of their immediate remedy are self-evident, influenced the way many who undertook living wage campaigns understood how to present their issue in the public sphere. The privileging of "action" over articulating what former ACORN organizer Gary Delgado calls "vision and values" may have caused the movement to be more narrowly focused on taking down powerful, discrete opponents and less concerned with developing public awareness, understanding, and concern about the issue itself (Delgado 1986).

There were people involved in the living wage movement who were aware that the tendency to privilege action over argument might be detrimental to the movement. Kristina Wilfore, former executive director of the Ballot Initiative Strategy Center (BISC), a consulting company that served progressive organizations pushing ballot initiatives, including some undertaking living wage campaigns, understood the power of creating a more general public discourse on issues, even when the ballot initiatives lost.

> I come from these issues at the state level. There has been an overemphasis of just federal policy. But the right wing has long understood the power of the states as a testing ground. You can do that even in losses. Look at the power of antichoice measures on the ballot. And the win rate against those is 90 percent, but what you have happen in the process is a public discussion that would otherwise not be in our discourse. Legitimized even in defeat simply by being on the ballot. U.S. term limits, extreme tax policies—these are issues that have done that as well.

Wilfore goes on to say that, in her experience, issues involving wages or the poor are the hardest to communicate about:

> Most issues that have to do with wages [are hard to communicate about] because we have to appeal to the middle class while still advocating for the poor. But their issues are slightly different.... It's tough to create *empathy that moves policy* rather than just empathy. That's been a challenge, to put it into that framework.

However, it is not only the complicated nature of the general public's understanding of wage issues that BISC struggled to overcome, but also living wage and labor organizers' skepticism about the efficacy of messaging.

> The Center for American Progress has raised a bunch of money—mostly federally on the issue of how we communicate about these issues—raise alternative ways of thinking and talking about this issue. So we've gotten better, but it has been hard to get people to understand [communicating with the public] it's not just a policy report. [It] often requires a more public conversation. You have to find out what they already believe.

You can't talk at them. That's why I love the [ballot] initiatives world, because it takes these issues from behind closed doors and moves them into the public debate. But most organizers are not hardwired around messaging. That's not limited to living wage, it's pretty much any economic policy. They know, "Okay we need that," but they're not most concerned about the communications aspect of the fight.[8]

When movement leaders are unconcerned about or uncomfortable with broadening the "scope of conflict" to include the general public, it can be disadvantageous because, as E. E. Schattschneider observed in his pragmatic analysis of American politics, *The Semisovereign People*, if political disputes occur only among contesting groups in private, the power ratio between groups at the outset will determine who succeeds. He goes on to say, "Private conflicts are taken into the public arena precisely because someone wants to make certain that the power ratio among the private interests most immediately involved shall not prevail" (Schattscneider 1975, 37). While the living wage movement became expert in how to leverage power in local contexts, it is also true that in terms of overall political impact, "the whole is smaller than the sum of its parts" (Dreier 2009, 12). Even when ACORN engaged the public through its "outside track," it did not engage the *general* public in a general way, which may have limited its ability to win broad-based and lasting gains.

In addition, though ACORN, unlike most other CBOs, declared its desire to participate in the building of a wider social movement and worked collaboratively with many diverse local organizations in neighborhoods and at colleges and universities all over the country, its first priority was always its organization rather than any abstract idea of social movement. Rathke writes that when he founded ACORN at twenty, in the waning years of the tumultuous and exciting civil rights and antiwar movements, he "wanted to build something that lasted longer than the sound of the shout and holler" (Rathke 2009, 41). For him, that meant building an institution that would endure regardless of the fortunes of various issues or, indeed, of the rising and falling political tides of any social movement. He puts the matter this way:

A membership organization is not a public-interest group with an amorphous, squishy, self-described constituency, but a real-life flesh eating machine that must be fed constantly on activity and victory. Neither does membership activity necessarily translate into a social movement.... Turning the wheels of the organization is not a matter of mobilizing disparate parts of the low-and-moderate income base we identify as our support but precisely and exactingly motivating and activating our membership base. (Rathke 2009, 49–50)

Though ACORN worked with partners in all the localities where it had branches and in many localities where it did not, Rathke characterizes these working partnerships this way:

> These relationships . . . while providing support, services and strength are situational and symbiotic rather than sustaining. Unions, churches or corporate partners will all be with ACORN as long as it serves their own interests, but they keep their distance when the fur is flying. These relationships are political, even when permanent, because they are driven by institutional interests that are autonomous and directed by self-determined instincts around survival and growth. We understand these interests because we share them. . . . The raison d'etre of permanent, mass-based organization has to be within its own base and never external. (Rathke 2009, 59)

As Heidi Swarts astutely observes, "If [Frances Fox] Piven and [Richard] Cloward wrote an unjustified brief against organizations, the community organizing sector traditionally committed the opposite sin by fetishizing them" (Swarts 2008, 185).

The laser-like focus on building power in the member base, developing concrete deliverables that could be clearly demanded of specific power holders, and prioritizing the survival and growth of the organization above all else facilitated the rapid and widespread success of the tactical models used to win living wage ordinances across the country, but it also tended to isolate ACORN and other CBOs from the awareness of the broader public. This kind of remoteness inhibits what Schattschneider calls the "socialization of conflict" and can prevent the phenomenon I call political acceptance, a process that gives challengers a chance to make their case in the public sphere, in terms that are more favorable to them in the long run.

Outcomes

Since 1994, over 120 living wage ordinances have been passed in twenty-six states.[9] There have been living wage laws passed in every region of the country, though the bulk of successful campaigns have been concentrated on the coasts. Since living wages are tailored to localities, these laws encompass different groupings of workers and the wage rates are set in different ways. A breakdown of these differences is provided in table 2.1. In 110 of the 125 living wage ordinances passed between 1994 and 2004, living wages cover those firms who have been granted public contracts by the city. In 47 cities, those businesses that have been given economic development grants also

Table 2.1 **Local Living Wage Laws, 1994–2010**

Municipality	Date Adopted	Rate	Covered
Baltimore, MD	1994 (2005)	($10.59)	Public contracts
Santa Clara, CA	1995	$10	Public contracts
Milwaukee, WI*	1995 (2005)	$8.80 ($10.59)	Public contracts/(citywide repealed 2005)
Portland, OR	1996 (1998)	$9.50 ($11.26)	Public contracts
Jersey City, NJ	1996	$10.50 ($13.60)	Public contracts
New York, NY	1996	**	Public contracts/local government employees
St. Paul, MN*	1997	$11.66 ($13.78)	Public contracts/local government employees/ economic development grants
Minneapolis, MN*	1997	$11.66 ($13.78)	Public contracts/economic development grants
Los Angeles, CA*	1997 (1999) (2003) (2005)	$10.30 ($11.55)	Public contracts/local government employees/ economic development grants
New Haven, CT*	1997 (2011)	$14.67	Public contracts
Milwaukee County, WI*	1997	$7.88	Public contracts/local government employees
Duluth, MN	1997	$8.64 ($9.63)	Public contracts
Boston, MA*	1997 (1998) (2001)	($13.02)	Public contracts
West Hollywood, CA	1997	$9.38 ($10.74)	Public contracts/economic development grants
Durham, NC*	1998	($11.40)	Local government employees/ Public contracts
Oakland, CA*	1998	$11.15 ($12.82)	Public contracts/economic development grants
San Antonio, TX	1998	($10.60)	economic development grants
Chicago, IL*	1998	($10.33)	Public contracts
Cook County, IL	1998	$10.57 ($13.21)	Public contracts
Pasadena, CA*	1998 (2008)	$10.14 ($11.88)	Local government employees/ Public contracts

(continued)

Table 2.1 **Continued**

Municipality	Date Adopted	Rate	Covered
Multnomah County, OR*	1998	$11.72	Public contracts
Detroit, MI*	1998	$11.03 ($13.78)	Public contracts/economic development grants
San Jose, CA	1998	$12.94 ($14.19)	Public contracts/economic development grants
Hudson County, NJ*	1999 (2005)	$8.25	Public contracts
Dane County, WI*	1999	($10.61)	Local government employees/ public contracts/economic development grants
Madison, WI*	1999	$11.66	Local government employees/ public contracts/economic development grants
Hayward, CA*	1999	$10.41 ($12.01)	Local government employees/ public contracts
Cambridge, MA*	1999	($13.69)	Local government employees/ public contracts/economic development grants
Miami-Dade County, FL	1999 (2009)	$11.60 ($13.29)	Local government employees/ public contracts
Somerville, MA*	1999	($11.22)	Local government employees/ public contracts
Ypsilanti Township, MI	1999	$8.50 ($10.00)	Public contracts/economic development grants
Ypsilanti, MI	1999 (2009)	$10.48 ($12.28)	Public contracts/economic development grants
Los Angeles County, CA	1999	$9.64 ($11.84)	Public contracts
Buffalo, NY	1999	$10.57 ($11.87)	Public contracts
Tucson. AZ*	1999	$9.17 ($10.32)	Public contracts
Hartford, CT*	1999	$11.66 ($17.78)	Public contracts/economic development grants
Corvallis, OR*	1999	($11.55)	Public contracts
Warren, MI*	2000	$11.25 (13.78)	Public contracts/economic development grants

(*continued*)

Table 2.1 **Continued**

Municipality	Date Adopted	Rate	Covered
Denver, CO*	2000	($10.60)	Public contracts
San Fernando, CA*	2000	$7.25 ($8.50)	Public contracts/economic development grants
Omaha, NE*	2000 (2001)	***	Local government employees/ public contracts/economic development grants
Toledo, OH*	2000	$11.67 ($13.79)	Public contracts/economic development grants
Alexandria, VA	2000 (2009)	($13.13)	Public contracts
Cleveland, OH	2000	($10.00)	Public contracts/economic development grants
Berkeley, CA	2000	$12.42 ($14.47)	Local government employees/ public contracts/economic development grants
St. Louis, MO*	2000	$11.33 ($14.47)	Local government employees/ public contracts/economic development grants
San Fransisco, CA*	2000 (2001) (2003) (2009)	$11.69	Public contracts
Eau Claire County, WI	2000 (repealed by state 2005)		
Santa Cruz, CA	2000	$13.60 ($14.83)	Local government employees/ public contracts
Meriden, CT*	2000	$10.64	Public contracts
Rochester, NY*	2001	$10.59 ($11.83)	Public contracts/economic development grants
Ferdale, MI	2001	$9.59 (11.00)	Public contracts
Ann Arbor, MI*	2001	$11.71 ($13.06)	Public contracts/economic development grants
Missoula, MT*	2001	$10.11 ($11.62)	economic development grants
Eastpointe, MI*	2001	$11.03 ($13.78)	Public contracts/economic development grants
Pittsfeild Township, MI*	2001	$10.97 ($12.86)	Public contracts/economic development grants
Miami Beach, FL*	2001 (2010)	$10.16 ($11.41)	Local government employees/ public contracts

(*continued*)

Table 2.1 **Continued**

Municipality	Date Adopted	Rate	Covered
Ventura County, CA	2001	$9.50 ($11.50)	Public contracts
Santa Monica, CA	2001 (repealed 2002)		
Pittsburg, PA	2001 (repealed 2002)		
Suffolk County, NY	2001	$10.83 ($12.33)	Public contracts/economic development grants
Gloucester County, NJ*	2001	($10.27)	Public contracts
Oyster Bay, NY	2001	$9.00 ($10.25)	Public contracts
Ashland, OR*	2001	($13.40)	Local government employees/ public contracts/economic development grants
Monroe County, MI	2001 (repealed 2003)		
Hempstead, NY	2001 (repealed 2001)		
Washtenaw County, MI	2001	$10.88 ($12.75)	Public contracts
Richmond, CA*	2001	$15.19 ($16.69)	Public contracts/economic development grants
Charlottesville, VA	2001 (2012)	$13.00	Public contracts
Burlington, VT	2001	$14.21 ($15.35)	Local government employees/ public contracts/economic development grants
Camden, NJ	2001 (repealed 2003)		
Cumberland County, NJ	2001	8.50 ($11.30)	Public contracts
New Britain, CT*	2001	($10.97)	Public contracts/economic development grants
Santa Cruz County, CA*	2001 (2002)	$13.60 ($14.83)	Public contracts
Bozeman, MT*	2001	$9.93 ($11.09)	Local government employees/ economic development grants

(*continued*)

Table 2.1 **Continued**

Municipality	Date Adopted	Rate	Covered
Marin County, CA	2002	$10.05 ($11.55)	Local government employees/public contracts
Hazel Park, MI	2002 (repealed 2002)		
New Orleans, LA	2002 (repealed 2002)		
Port of Oakland, CA	2002	$10.09 ($11.58)	Public contracts
Montgomery County, MD	2002	($13.00)	Public contracts
Oxnard, CA	2002	($13.25)	Public contracts
Southfield, MI*	2002	$11.03 ($13.78)	Public contracts/economic development grants
Fairfax, CA*	2002	$13.00 ($14.75)	Local government employees/public contracts/economic development grants
Watsonville, CA*	2002	$13.08 ($14.27)	Public contracts
Broward County, FL	2002	$11.13 ($12.57)	Local government employees/public contracts
Taylor, MI*	2002	$10.60 ($13.25)	Public contracts
Westchester County, NY	2002	$11.50 ($13.00)	Public contracts/economic development grants
Bellingham, WA*	2002	$11.97 ($13.18)	Public contracts
Cincinnati, OH*	2002	$10.60 ($12.10)	Local government employees/public contracts
Santa Fe, NM*	2003 (2007)	($9.85)	Citywide
Palm Beach County, FL	2003	($11.40)	Public contracts
Gainesville, FL	2003	$10.60 ($11.85)	Public contracts
Prince George's County, MD*	2003	($12.65)	Public contracts
Ingham County, MI*	2003	$10.00 ($12.50)	Local government employees/public contracts

(continued)

Table 2.1 **Continued**

Municipality	Date Adopted	Rate	Covered
Arlington, VA	2003	($11.20)	Public contracts
Dayton, OH*	2003	$10.60 ($12.72)	Public contracts
Lakewood, OH*	2003	$11.99 ($13.28)	Local government employees/ public contracts/economic development grants
Orlando, FL	2003	$8.50 ($10.20)	Local government employees/ public contracts
Lansing, MI*	2003	$13.79	Public contracts/economic development grants
Bloomington, IN*	2005	$8.50 ($11.25)	Public contracts/economic development grants
Santa Monica, CA	2005 (2008)	($13.27)	Public contracts
Lacrosse, WI	2005 (repealed 2005)		
Philadelphia. PA*	2005	($7.73)	Local government employees/ public contracts
Syracuse, NY*	2005	$11.60 ($13.70)	Public contracts
Brookline, MA	2005	($12.24)	Public contracts
Albany, NY*	2005	$10.25 ($11.91)	Public contracts/economic development grants
Macomb County, MI*	2005	$11.03 ($13.78)	Public contracts
Emeryville, CA	2005	$12.81	Local government employees/ public contracts/economic development grants
Nassau County, NY	2005	$12.50 ($14.16)	Public contracts
Washington, DC	2006	($12.50)	Public contracts/economic development grants
Santa Barbara, CA	2006	$13.24 ($15.45)	Public contracts
Sandia Pueblo, NM	2006	($8.18)	Citywide
Albuquerque, NM	2006	($7.50)	Citywide

(continued)

Table 2.1 **Continued**

Municipality	Date Adopted	Rate	Covered
Miami, FL	2006	$10.58 ($11.83)	Local government employees/ public contracts
Manchester, CT	2006	$12.19 ($15.54)	Public contracts/economic development grants
Ventura, CA	2006	$10.73 ($13.75)	Local government employees/ public contracts
Pine Bluff, AR*	2006	$9.30 ($10.55)	Local government employees/ public contracts/economic development grants
Memphis, TN	2006	$10.27 ($12.32)	Public contracts
Petaluma, CA	2006	$12.46 ($13.99)	Local government employees/ public contracts/economic development grants
Norwalk, CT*	2007	$12.19 ($15.19)	Local government employees/ public contracts/economic development grants
Revere, MA	2007	$10.78 ($12.16)	Local government employees/ public contracts
Irvine, CA	2007	$10.82 (13.16)	Public contracts
Shelby County, TN	2007	$10.02 ($12.01)	Local government employees/ public contracts
Ashville, NC*	2007 (2011)	$9.85 ($11.35)	Local government employees/ public contracts
San Leandro, CA*	2007	$11.67 ($13.17)	Local government employees/ public contracts/economic development grants
Pittsburg, PA	2010	**	Public contracts/economic development grants

*Indexed to inflation.

**Prevailing wage law, which means there is no set rate.

Note: Wage rates current as of December 2010, except Charlottesville, VA (March 2012).

Source: National Employment Law Project, retrieved on March 5, 2013, from http://nelp.3cdn. net/0ddf028c738728d7fb_alm6iv582.pdf.

come under the aegis of living wage laws. In nine cities, the living wage covers all local government employees. Fifty of the 125 cities covered combine these classes of covered workers in some way, with 27 providing living wages to both local government employees and public contractors, 10 providing coverage to those workers under public contracts or employed by firms giving economic development grants, and 13 covering all three types of workers. In 63 cities, the living wage is indexed to rise with inflation. In addition, most living wage ordinances demand allowances for healthcare coverage of full-time workers. Firms may either provide affordable healthcare options for their employees or provide a higher base wage so that employees have some chance of purchasing healthcare for themselves.

The outcomes of living wage ordinances beyond their passage are hard to measure, but the kinds of results that movement participants and observers usually consider in their accounts include number of people affected, the incremental amount of wages (and benefits), organization-building, coalition-building, greater public awareness, changed public debate, and winning favorable policy. The exact number of people affected by living wage ordinances is hard to estimate because few cities keep records of the number of workers covered (Luce 2009, 146). However, the average wage gains that accrue to those who are covered can be substantial (Pollin and Luce 1998, Howes 2005, Brenner 2005, Pollin, Brenner, and Luce 2008). In Los Angeles, the living wage ordinance passed in 1997 had increased pay for about 10,000 jobs by 2005. Luce found that for the initial 8,000 workers affected, the average pay raise was about $2,600 per year, or 20 percent. The remaining 2,000 workers saw a pay increase of about $1,300 per year (Luce 2009). In Boston, the living wage ordinance passed in 1998 resulted in an average $2.10 per hour raise, an increase of 23 percent, for those who had earned less than the living wage at the time of passage. Since firms often attempt to stabilize their costs by shifting part-time workers into full-time work, the average annual pay of workers in Boston actually increased by about $10,000 per year, from an average of about $16,990 to $26,990 due to longer hours worked (Pollin, Brenner, and Luce 2008). In addition, studies of job loss in municipalities that implement living wages do not find any disemployment effects (Brenner 2005, Dube, Lester, and Reich 2011).

This is because unlike the simple equation in neoclassical economics 101, labor market variables are best represented as flows with dynamic effects over a certain interval of time, rather than stocks with fixed effects observed at one instant. Labor economist Arindrajit Dube puts it this way:

> There are lots of things about the labor market that don't really fit well with the simplest competitive models of the labor market. In reality, there are good jobs and bad jobs, and workers try to get to a better job

whenever they can. So there's a lot of turnover and churning in the low-end of the labor market. To the extent that the minimum wage makes the lowest paid jobs better, it tends to reduce turnover and reduce vacancies. So an increase in the minimum wage may not kill jobs but kill vacancies in a low-end labor market.... So, minimum wage laws might make jobs more stable while raising wages. (Konczal 2013)

In other words, vacancies in the low-wage labor market often do not indicate that extra jobs are available to new workers. Instead, vacancies are often filled with the same workers as they move rapidly between low-wage jobs. This means that if there are fewer vacancies in a labor market snapshot taken in the wake of a mandatory wage increase, it may reflect greater job stability among low-wage workers *not* job losses.

Though the data are hard to generalize at the national level, because municipalities keep incomplete and inconsistent records, Luce estimates that "as of mid-2004, as much as three-quarters of a billion dollars was redistributed from firms, city governments, and consumers into the paychecks of low-wage workers, at an average of $3,000 per year per worker" (Luce 2009, 146). However, the net benefit to workers would be lower because of the loss of federal and state aid that accompanies the higher income. Still, on balance, workers benefit from living wages in two ways: they take home more in wages and enjoy increased job stability.

In addition to living wage campaigns, ACORN and the unions and CBOs that they partnered with have sometimes undertaken statewide minimum wage campaigns, which are structured in broadly similar ways to living wage campaigns. (Indeed, at ACORN, Jen Kern oversaw both kinds of campaigns.) Minimum wage laws often affect many more workers than municipal-level living wages and are harder to overturn. In the period of study, this was a relatively rare occurrence, with only three states seeing a raise in their minimum wage, but in the years since several states have increased their minimum wages through the legislature or by ballot initiative. The first wave of states to do so in 2007 included New York, Ohio, Missouri, Colorado, and Arizona. ACORN founder Wade Rathke claims that the living wage and minimum wage increases combined "in states where ACORN was the central driver" resulted in "$6 billion in wage increases to approximately 5 million low-wage workers" (Rathke 2009, 57). Lisa Ranghelli of the National Committee for Responsive Philanthropy found that between 1995 and 2005, the monetary benefit to workers from both living and minimum wages was more than $2.2 billion (Delgado 2009, 268).

Also in 2007, Congress voted to raise the federal minimum wage from $5.15 per hour to $7.25 per hour. Living wage activists felt that the federal action was due to their successful, sustained efforts at the state level. During the midterm

election of 2006, living wage advocates put raising the minimum wage on the ballot in six states: Arizona, Colorado, Michigan, Missouri, Montana, and Nevada.
Jen Kern reflects that the state-level work did have a policy payoff at the federal
level in 2006–2007.

> We got six ballot initiatives on the ballot in 2006 and all six passed.
> Two of those states produced senators [Jim Talent D-MO and Conrad
> Burns D-MO] that tipped the balance of the Senate, and neither would
> have won if not for the people who turned out to vote for the living
> wage. People were voting for the living wage at higher rates than they
> were voting for those candidates, and they know very well that they
> would not have been elected without that legislation on the ballot.
> We've made major political changes and had an impact on the capacity
> of these groups on the ground so they can organize other campaigns.[10]

Along with the monetary benefits to workers, ACORN and their partners always
viewed building their own organizations as a part of the benefit of pursuing living wage campaigns. Jen Kern asserted, "We don't just think poor people should
get programs, we think they should join ACORN and get a collective voice to
contest for power in their own community" (Luce 2009, 147). Although there
is no way to quantify exactly how much living wage campaigns contributed to
the incredible expansion of ACORN as an organization in the 1990s through
the first decade of the twenty-first century, it is the case that in 2009, ACORN
had "opened offices in more than one hundred cities in the United States and
[seen] membership balloon out to more than 500,000 members" (Rathke
2009, 59). And a part of that expansion was "certainly" due to the living wage,
according to Luce (Luce 2009, 147). It should be noted that the movement to
increase worker wages continued to persist and win in localities after the demise
of ACORN. In 2014, Alaska, Arkansas, Nebraska, and South Dakota voted to
increase their minimum wages through ballot initiatives that passed with strong
public support. The same year, the cities of San Fransisco, Oakland, Seattle, and
Chicago also opted to increase the general, municipal minimum wage through
local legislative action.

It is important to pause here and point out that amid all of the policy success
of the living wage as well as the 2007 increase in the federal minimum wage, two
claims that are regularly made about potential negative effects of wage increases
have been thoroughly debunked. First, it is not the case that wage increases at the
bottom of the labor market disproportionately accrue to teenagers (Allegretto,
Dube, and Reich 2011, Pollin, Brenner, and Luce 2008). Second, it is also not
the case that a living wage causes industry migration or other dramatic economic effects. It may be the case that in some cases, living wages cause small

disemployment effects (Ropponen 2011), but there is little evidence that this occurs consistently and, as indicated above, these effects may not reflect loss of jobs as much as loss of vacant positions due to less churning in the low-wage market. It is also important to point out that raising wages does mean that businesses incur extra costs. However, from what researchers can tell, that increase in cost is so minimal that it is easily absorbed by small price increases (about a penny on average) and rarely leads to job losses (Pollin, Brenner, and Luce 2008). Additionally, several studies by Robert Pollin and the Economic Policy Institute have found that though there are costs to implementing living wage laws in a locality, the benefits to the working poor substantially outweigh the costs (Shoenberger 2000, Allegretto, Dube, and Reich 2011, Dube, Lester, and Reich 2011).

Pollin, writing in the *Nation* about a living wage ordinance passed in Los Angeles, explained that, though "blustering politicians" often caution that raising the wage floor will cause job loss and industry migration, in the case of the Los Angeles wage law, there was no empirical evidence that there would be significant negative consequences to business or workers. In fact, Pollin and Luce found that the ordinance raised the pay of 7,600 full- or part-time workers by $3,600 as well as guaranteed them access to more affordable employer-provided health insurance—all at a cost of about "1.5% of the total annual budget of the average affected firm. Indeed, for about 85% of the firms involved, the total annual increase in costs [was] less than 1% of their budgets" (Pollin 1998). On balance, then, it seems that living wages make a difference in the paychecks of the lowest paid workers and do not unduly burden business or cause industries to uproot.

However, some other criticisms of the living wage do hold water. Stephanie Luce observes that living wage ordinances cover a relatively small number of workers, because a typical ordinance applies only to firms that receive contracts or economic development assistance from a city government. And even living wages the movement has won are not enough to bring a worker out of poverty, especially since many low-wage workers are involuntarily part-time. To meet the federal poverty line for a four-person family, a worker would need to earn $10.63 an hour and work forty hours a week, fifty-two weeks a year. But this official poverty line—$22,113 a year for a family of four—grossly underestimates the real cost of living. The living wages won in the last twenty years vary from $9.50 to $17.78 (if health benefits are not provided) and include no guarantee of hours (Luce 2012).

In addition, even though workers get a raise, it is often not enough to lift them out of poverty. This seems especially true for those workers who are supporting children (Pollin, Brenner, and Luce 2008).

Another significant and surprising limitation of living wage legislation is that once passed, these laws face problems of implementation. A brief on the living wage by the Economic Policy Institute states: "Regarding implementation and enforcement, there have been problems for living wage ordinances from the very beginning. Even after adopting the first living wage ordinance in Baltimore, it took many months, rallies, public hearings, complaints, and fines before some firms started to obey the law" (Chapman and Thompson 2006). As of 2002, when only eighty-two ordinances had been passed, Stephanie Luce found that the implementation of 10 percent (eight) of the ordinances was blocked or retroactively repealed by state legislatures claiming that municipalities have no authority to pass such laws; and 52 percent (forty-two) had been narrowly implemented, which means that city administrators wrote up rules to determine coverage and apply the ordinance, but there was no system of oversight and no requirement for affected businesses to report compliance with regulations. That means that up to 62 percent of the ordinances passed by 2002 may have been completely ineffective. Yet few municipalities have considered revised legislation, and in most cases the advocates, activists, and coalitions that spearheaded the original legislation moved on to address new issues, not always returning to the un- or underimplemented living wage legislation (Luce 2005).

In an interview that I conducted with Luce, she extends her political analysis of the difficulties that face living wage ordinances once the campaigns have been won:

> After the laws are passed, governments are doing little to enforce the ordinances. They are not devoting the staff time or resources to monitor and enforce. This is sometimes due to ideological opposition to the ordinance within city administration, sometimes due to pressures from employers who are opposed, and sometimes due to a fear on the part of city leaders that they cannot hire new people to enforce the law due to downsizing pressures and budget issues.
>
> So, it seems that those officials most vulnerable to democratic accountability—city council members, county board—are most likely to follow the majority wishes of the electorate and pass the ordinances. Those higher up—state reps, federal level—are less subject to democracy and more accountable to monied interests. [They] are not as quick to pass the ordinances but do so under growing pressure. Those insulated from democratic accountability, like city administrators, are not enforcing the laws.[11]

At the local level, the outcomes of living wage campaigns are thus somewhat mixed. At the level of the movement as a whole, it is clear that while the work of the movement has mattered for federal policy, the idea of a living wage was never incorporated into the national political agenda. While living wage activists consistently claim that "in addition to specific outcomes for covered workers . . . the living wage movement has had a larger impact on how the term is used and perceived by the general public" (Luce 2009, 147), it is not at all clear that this is so. Between 1994 and 2004, the coverage of the living wage movement in national papers, represented in my study by the *New York Times* and *USA Today*, was quite low: the *Times* gave the movement a peak of thirty stories in 2002, when New York's own ACORN branch launched a municipal living wage campaign. In addition, although when polled, overwhelming majorities support raising the minimum wage and approve the idea of a living wage, there is actually very little national polling data on the topic. While organizers have commissioned polls in specific cities, national pollsters such as Gallup, Rasmussen, and Public Policy Polling have never asked a question on the living wage, and no questions about the living wage have been included on the well-respected, annual research polls used by scholars such as the General Social Survey and the National Election Survey. This absence is significant because pollsters try to ask questions about issues they perceive to be politically salient. This means that while the living wage as an issue has significant latent popularity, it is nevertheless not regarded as politically salient by pollsters or political decision-makers.

We shall see that in the case of marriage equality, as the issue was more often covered in national newspapers and officials began taking positions on the topic in their public statements, pollsters began to include questions about marriage on the short list of topics affecting the national political agenda. The absence of the living wage from this mainstream public discourse has been an impediment to its ability to change the discussion and thus, potentially, the politics on the issue of a living wage.

There is no question that the living wage movement has been successful at organizing some low-income people, building many enduring organizations, pressuring legislators, and moving its preferred policies through municipal and state legislatures. What is less clear is how these accomplishments should be evaluated. If power means only the power to influence behavior in discrete moments of decision, living wage campaigns have built and continue to build that kind of power. However, if power is also the ability to influence the political agenda of the public and to shape public understandings, then the living wage movement has not, so far, succeeded in bringing these aspects of power to bear. How might a movement advocating for people who are relatively marginalized in our politics achieve other kinds of power? The marriage equality movement, which emerged and grew over the same time period as the living wage, provides insight into this question.

3

A Tale of Two Movements

Marriage Equality

In the previous chapter, I set the stage for comparing the living wage and marriage equality movements, noting that the two emerged during the same time, each out of larger and older movement sectors not only addressing different issues, but more importantly, holding disparate conceptions of power and distinct *organizational structures, organizational cultures,* and *interorganizational environments* that led to divergent preferences regarding institutional *venue choice* and political *tactics.* The last chapter focused on telling the tale of the political emergence, ideology, structure, strategy, and outcomes of the efforts of the living wage movement between 1994 and 2004. This chapter explores the marriage equality movement in the same terms, telling the tale of how same-sex marriage came to be seen as a political issue and, in remarkably short order, also came to be politically accepted on the short list of issues of perennial importance in America's national politics.

The Political Emergence of Marriage Equality

In 1994, the issue of marriage equality was virtually unheard of—indeed, the term would have been incomprehensible even to most politically engaged citizens. By 2004 marriage equality had become a political issue that engaged the leaders of both political parties, mobilized a powerful and hostile countermovement, provided endless fodder for pundit commentary, captured the sustained attention of the general public, incited religious turmoil in many Protestant denominations, frequently appeared on state ballot initiatives, and became the subject of a potential amendment to the United States Constitution. The issue of marriage equality was thought to have such a profound impact in American politics that the presence of eleven referendums seeking to ban marriage equality was blamed for swinging several key states into the "red" column in November 2004, handing President George W. Bush a narrow re-election. Though that interpretation of poll data has been disputed by many analysts, the idea of "values voters" turning out to bar gay people from marrying and vote the Republican ticket still has the status of conventional wisdom. How could an issue emerge from obscurity to become a cornerstone of the political landscape within a decade?

The advent of marriage equality as an issue of national advocacy took even its eventual supporters by surprise. Although the first recorded attempt for people of the same sex to secure the right to marry was in 1969,[1] the first stirrings of the contemporary marriage equality movement began in the late 1980s. The AIDS crisis brought issues of kinship for hospital visitation, child-custody arrangements, and inheritance rights to the fore. In 1989, public scholar and political journalist Andrew Sullivan wrote a cover story for the *New Republic*, "Here Comes the Groom," in which he suggested that "the way to tackle the issue of unconventional relationships in conventional society is to try something both more radical and more conservative than putting courts in the business of deciding what is and is not a family. That alternative is the legalization of civil gay marriage" (Sullivan 1989).[2]

In 1990, Joseph Melillo and Patrick Lagon attempted to get a marriage license in Hawaii. They described their motives in apolitical terms: "We were just two guys in love who wanted to get married," Melillo recalled. "It's unfortunate it's all gotten so political."[3] However, gay marriage did not really get political until 1993, two years after Dan Foley, an ACLU attorney, filed suit against the state of Hawaii on behalf of Melillo and Lagon as well as two other couples who had been denied the right to marry in *Baehr v. Lewin*. Although the circuit court ruled against the three couples, Foley won on appeal to the state supreme court. The judge unexpectedly agreed with Foley's argument that same-sex marriage is a matter of equal protection under the law, meaning denial of the right to marry could be considered gender discrimination under Hawaii's constitution. Absent the state's ability to show compelling state interest in perpetrating such discrimination, the current law, it was ruled, could not stand. The Hawaii state supreme court remanded the case to the circuit court to determine whether a compelling state interest could be found for denying people of the same sex the right to marry. Given the history of gay rights litigation in general and same-sex marriage litigation in particular, Foley's success was astonishing.

Both organized gay rights groups and conservative religious organizations took notice. In 1996, the *New York Times* reported:

> Until the state Supreme Court ruled partly in their favor in May 1993, they had little attention and support from gay groups, which were busy fighting other battles and divided on the issue of gay marriage. Some gay-rights advocates still argue that the campaign to legalize such

unions diverts attention from more important issues, like AIDS. Nor did civil rights groups, like the American Civil Liberties Union, support them before the victory. The couples did much of the fund-raising for their lawyers' fees themselves, at dinners and barbecues.[4]

With the unanticipated acknowledgment from the court that marriage equality might credibly be seen as an issue of equal treatment under the law, Lambda Legal Defense and Education Fund began to help with the case and one of its lawyers, Evan Wolfson, became co-counsel along with Foley. An organization called Hawaii Equal Rights Marriage Project began to raise money for court costs from donors all over the country.

Advocates and allies of gay rights were not the only people struck by the credence that the Hawaii state court had given the Foley argument. Conservative citizens of Hawaii were up in arms. In response to the rapid mobilization in support of equal marriage rights, a countereffort led by state legislators resulted in laws declaring that procreation is the basis of marriage, so same-sex marriage could have no legitimate basis and was therefore illegal.

In 1994, the year after the Hawaii Supreme Court challenged the legitimacy of heterosexual-only marriage rights, a commission on "Sexual Orientation and the Law" was established by conservative legislators to advise the state on public policy that might satisfy the legal requirements now facing them. The commission came back to the legislators with a recommendation that they could find no compelling state interest that countered the *Baehr* decision and that comprehensive domestic-partner legislation ought to be drafted in order to give same-sex couples most of the benefits of marriage. Conservative legislators and activists of both parties were greatly disturbed by the commission's report and attempted to mobilize a more forceful legislative response before the circuit case that was scheduled for the fall of 1996 could be heard. They called again for an amendment to the state constitution that would counter *Baehr*. However, the state senate of Hawaii remained deadlocked on the issue (Chauncey 2005).

Hawaii was not the only state preoccupied with the possibility of same-sex marriage in this period. After the surprising 1993 ruling, other states and the federal government began to watch the legal and political processes in the fiftieth state with interest and, in most cases, alarm. Two Alaskan men filed a parallel suit in 1994 (*Brause v. Bureau of Vital Statistics*) and dozens of state legislatures, taking notice of the preferred pathway of gay rights advocates, attempted to ban same-sex marriage in state law before suits could be brought. The federal government took a similar tack: President Bill Clinton signed the Defense of Marriage Act (DOMA), a law that declared that "the word 'marriage' means only a legal union between one man and one woman as husband and wife, and the word 'spouse' refers only to a person of the opposite sex who is a husband or a wife,"[5] into law on September 10, 1996. In a positively cinematic turn, September 10 was also the day that the *Baehr* trial began in Hawaii's circuit court. In the end, the court decided that the state had no compelling interest in barring same-sex marriage, but the DOMA decision at the start of the trial nullified the effect of the ruling. Still, the decision did give activists hope and put fire into the belly of the new marriage equality movement.

During the late 1990s the momentum of the movement continued to build. In 1997, three gay couples in Vermont filed suit against the state for denying them the right to marry in *Baker v. Vermont*. The trial judge, Linda Levitt, dismissed the case. However, the plaintiffs appealed, and the Vermont Supreme Court ruled, like Hawaii's, that same-sex couples were entitled to "the common benefit, protection and security that Vermont law provides opposite-sex married couples." Alaska's high court issued a similar ruling in *Brause v Alaska*. Whether common benefit requires marriage or some other "equivalent" legal status was a question left by the court to the legislature in "cognizance of the popular reaction against 'judicial activism' in the forgoing Hawaii and Alaska cases" (Goldberg-Hiller 2002, 5). The courts did have reason to be concerned, as Gerald Rosenberg has argued: it is difficult for courts to hand down decisions focused on social change when public opinion is not with them (Rosenberg 1991). And it was clear that public opinion did not favor altering the legal institution of marriage to include partnerships between people of the same sex in the 1990s. Indeed, between 1995 and 1998 an astonishing thirty-three states where same-sex marriage challenges *had not* yet been brought preemptively banned gay marriage, in most cases, through referenda (Goldberg-Hiller 2002).

In 2000, when Vermont courts followed Hawaii in ruling that the state had no compelling interest in preventing couples of the same sex from entering into legally recognized unions, the legislature followed the "equivalent legal status" route, creating civil unions as an intermediate status that could apply to couples of the same sex. Many advocates for marriage equality like Wolfson and legal scholar Jonathan Goldberg-Hiller regarded the advent of civil unions as a throwback to the separate-but-equal jurisprudence of *Plessy v. Ferguson*. In an interview I conducted in 2008, Wolfson argued, "We are not fighting for 'gay marriage.' Headline writers use that terminology, but what we're fighting for is the end of exclusion of same-sex couples from marriage. So the subject of the struggle is the freedom to marry.... Now, civil unions, *that* is gay marriage. It is another form of status for gay people. That's exactly what we're *not* fighting for."[6]

Though not on the terms that the advocates of marriage equality wanted, the Vermont decision offered a compromise legal designation for couples of the same sex who wished to have their relationships recognized.[7] Civil unions also represented a policy position attractive to political elites, especially those in the Democratic Party, who were reluctant to appear intolerant of gay people or insensitive to their individual rights, but also nervous about embracing gay marriage, which a majority of the public clearly opposed. The relief of Democratic elites and social moderates over this compromise is evident in the mainstream political discourse of the time. *USA Today* quoted Joe Lieberman, then a candidate for vice president:

> I have friends who are in gay and lesbian partnerships who have said, "Isn't it unfair that we don't have similar legal rights to inheritance, to visitation when one of the partners is ill, to health care benefits?" And that's why I'm thinking about it. My mind is open to taking some action that will address those elements of unfairness while respecting the traditional religious and civil institution of marriage.[8]

A letter to the editor in the *New York Times* from a resident of Middletown, New York, states the appeal of civil unions in a similar way:

> As a citizen and Christian, I support whatever reduces promiscuity and encourages commitment, be it between heterosexuals or homosexuals. If lawmakers are convinced that marriage by definition is a union for the procreation of children, and therefore not appropriate for homosexuals, perhaps they could support a commitment ceremony that would legally give gay couples the same tax, insurance and other benefits that come with marriage. If not, I can only assume that those who refuse are either motivated by intolerance or lack the generosity this would require.[9]

In May 2003, Massachusetts took the step that Vermonters were not ready for in 2000: after the state Supreme Court decided in *Goodridge v. Department of Public Health* that a parallel and unequal legal status for gay couples was unconstitutional, Massachusetts began issuing marriage licenses to same-sex couples.

Not everyone in the state was pleased with the decision. Indeed, public opinion was not with the court and neither were many of the elected lawmakers. The Republican governor, Mitt Romney, encouraged an attempt by conservative state legislators from both parties to amend the state constitution to prohibit marriage by people of the same sex, as Hawaii did in 1998. However, due to an onerous and lengthy amendment process in Massachusetts, which requires a constitutional convention as well as approval by voters through referendum, opponents were never able to marshal enough support to pass an amendment.

In the same year, the U.S. Supreme Court signaled that the long debate about whether gay people had the same legal standing as their straight peers regarding their sexual relations, should be settled nationally on the side of equality. In the landmark decision *Lawrence v. Texas*, sodomy laws were invalidated, and the majority found that gay citizens, like all others, were entitled to a constitutional right to privacy, overturning the 1986 *Bowers v. Hardwick* decision, which held that homosexual sodomy was beyond the scope of constitutional protection. Delivering the majority opinion on June 26, 2003, Justice Anthony Kennedy stated in introductory oral comments:

> To say the issue in *Bowers* was simply the right to engage in certain sexual conduct demeans the claim put forward, just as it would demean a married couple were it to be said that marriage is simply about the right to have sexual intercourse. The laws involved in *Bowers* and here are, to be sure, statutes that do prohibit a particular sexual act. Their penalties and purposes though, have more far-reaching consequences, touching upon the most private human conduct, sexual behavior, and in the most private of places, the home. The statutes seek to control a personal relationship that is within the liberty of persons to choose without being punished as criminals. (Carpenter 2012, 258)

Although the Court did not explicitly address gay marriage, legal scholar Dale Carpenter notes:

> The Court's opinion in *Lawrence*, despite protestations to the contrary, was at root a verdict about the content of morality in a world where gay men and lesbians were no longer at the fringes of life and culture. It was a judgment that gay sex, too, might lead to—and might be an integral part of—lasting relationships. The opinion implicitly recognized that gays might aspire to formal recognition—marriage—although Justice Kennedy remained carefully agnostic on that issue. Gay sex was not constitutionally protected merely because a free society must allow people to do objectionable things in the exercise of their own autonomy. It was constitutionally protected because it was normatively right, just as it was for heterosexual couples who might decide to marry. It was part of the good life.. . . The mainstreaming strategy had paid off. (Carpenter 2012, 260)

The "mainstreaming strategy" that Carpenter speaks of refers to the effort, quite controversial within the gay rights movement, to frame advocacy on behalf of gay people as a question of whether or not to grant fundamental rights to a group bearing an inherent and benign difference. The uptake of this strategy was neither self-evident nor uncontested. Instead, it was the result of an organizational culture that prioritized identity work, both internally and externally, under the pressure of a historical circumstance that necessitated a certain level of movement cohesion in order to facilitate literal physical survival.

Structure and Strategy: Organizational Culture, Organizational Structure, Interorganizational Environment, Venue Choice, and Tactics

Sociologist Mary Bernstein asserts that critics of "identity politics" and those who hold to the notion that there are some collectivities that are obviously and naturally "identity movements" often misunderstand the functions identity serves in all social movements as well as the differential strategic functions that identity can serve in some social movements. She writes:

> In order to mobilize a constituency, a social movement must draw on an existing identity or construct a new collective identity. . . . The Civil Rights movement drew on a black identity, whereas the labor movement had to create a worker's identity in order to mobilize. Identity may also be the goal of social movements, as activists "challenge stigmatized identities, seek recognition for new identities, or deconstruct restrictive social categories" (Bernstein 1997a: 537). . . . Finally, identity may be used as a strategy so that the identities of activists—their values, categories, and practices—become the subject of debate. Identities may be deployed strategically to criticize dominant categories, values, and practices (for *critique*) or to put forth a view of the minority that challenges dominant perceptions (for *education*). Such identities can be used to stress similarities with the majority for purposes of education or to stress differences from the majority for purposes of cultural critique. (Bernstein 2002, 539)

In her view, all social movements are identity movements. Movements must either use an existing identity or construct a new identity in order to mobilize a constituency. However, the role that identity plays in the way a group conceives of itself, structures itself, and strategizes political goals may differ.

Because most people who later come to identify as gay are not born into bodies marked as gay (as women are born into bodies designated female) or born into families that are already marked as culturally, ethnically, or racially gay (as African Americans are born into black families bearing "black culture"), nor are they uniformly or disproportionately present in one region, cast, or class (as southerners, Untouchables, or the poor are), the gay political project is necessarily one that begins with identity construction. The need for self-identification as a member of the group "gay" was symbolized by the practice of "coming out," or revealing oneself as gay to friends, family, and the world at large. Beginning in the 1970s, amid the feminist politics that declared the personal political, the practice of coming out was also politicized. It was not only a way for people to reveal themselves, but also a necessary part of identifying and mobilizing an emerging group of people with a certain set of political interests. Identity work, both internally focused group cultivation and externally focused group definition, was essential to the organizational (and intellectual) culture of gay rights groups (Bernstein 2002, Dugan 2008, Myers 2008). This identity focus does not mean there was or is consensus on what it means to be gay, either politically or personally, within the community or outside it, or even where those boundaries lie. On the contrary there is vigorous contestation, sophisticated theorizing, and constant reevaluation of the "oughts" of this identity work. However, for the gay rights movement, identity work itself is self-conscious and ubiquitous (Gamson 1995, 1996, 1997, Reger, Myers, and Einwohner 2008). The gay rights movement generally, and the marriage equality movement in particular, acknowledges that the self-conscious construction of identity is a condition of the possibility of organizing. Therefore, the process of identity construction (including ever-present contestation) is also used as a tool for empowerment, and the de-stigmatization of this identity is also held as a goal. In addition, movement actors deploy gay identity as a strategy for both public education and cultural critique.

This means that the *organizational culture* of the gay rights movement, unlike that of the living wage movement, has always been explicitly interested in and occupied by questions of identity. There has been a tension about the nature of this identity in the movement between "assimilationists" or "normalizers" and "liberationists" or "queers." This tension is based on the question of whether gay people as a group are and/or should present themselves politically as bearers of a fixed, "socially neutral difference" or whether instead they ought to use their difference to challenge what constitutes "normal" sexual/gender identities and behaviors (Wald 2000, Bernstein 2002, Vaid 1995, Warner 1999).

Social identity based on sexual orientation had been percolating in the United States at least since the establishment of the Mattachine Society and the Daughters of Bilitis in the 1950s. In those days, "homophile activists" did not make political challenges, but were instead engaged in "trying to persuade psychological and religious authorities (and themselves) that homosexuality is neither a sickness nor a sin" (Bernstein 2002, 541). At the time, self-identifying as "homosexual" was an inherently political act. People could be fired from their jobs, lose their homes, be attacked on the street with no recourse, or even be imprisoned for being perceived as engaging in "moral indecency" or "flagrant conduct" (Bernstein 2002).

In October 1979, gay rights activists organized the first march on Washington to raise awareness about discrimination and violence against LGBTQ people, and to demand public officials take notice. In response, six months later, a conservative religious coalition called Washington for Jesus hosted a national "March for Jesus" in April 1980, where a series of speakers, including Pat Robertson, denounced homosexuality, abortion, and women's liberation (Diamond 1995). By the dawn of the 1980s, Bernstein observes, "in addition to the routine opposition that lesbian and gay organizations had always faced, they now faced a well-organized opposing movement" as well as an antagonistic presidential administration and a hostile American public (Bernstein 2002, 555). As gay rights activists began to make headway on some issues—for example, pressuring municipalities and states to add sexual orientation language to their antidiscrimination statutes, winning the right for gay organizations to be recognized, and getting the U.S. Public Health Service to drop the designation of homosexuality as a mental illness—organized opponents pushing *specifically* antigay initiatives began to coalesce (Bernstein 2002, Stein 2012).

The combination of federal government unresponsiveness, a mobilized countermovement, and the AIDS crisis created a perfect storm of dangers that seemed to come to a head in 1986 when the U.S. Supreme Court ruled in *Bowers v. Hardwick* that the U.S. Constitution did not grant "a fundamental right to engage in homosexual sodomy" (*Bowers v. Hardwick* 1986). Instead, the majority opinion, authored by Justice Byron White, dubbed the very idea that gay people had a right to privacy in their sex lives as "at best, facetious" (*Bowers v. Hardwick* 1986). Gay rights activists took the decision as a slap in the face, especially since it was coming at a time when the national government was providing virtually no information, research, care, or support to individuals and communities across America that were being devastated by AIDS. By 1985, over 15,000 cases of the disease had been reported in the United States and there were, as yet, no treatments. The "AIDS cocktail," composed of three or more potent antiretroviral medications, was still ten years from being developed (Petro 2013). Urvarshi Vaid remembers, "At the outset, AIDS presented a pair of political dilemmas to gay and lesbian activists. How were we going to get a response from an administration that did not care about us? And how were we going to motivate and mobilize a community that was largely in the closet and invisible?" (Vaid 1995, 72). The answer to this question was to "institutionalize, nationalize, and aggressively pursue the mainstream" (Vaid 1995, 72).[10]

By the 1980s there was a small, but established, gay rights movement sector, a handful of organizations that had been pressing a political agenda aimed at reducing job and housing discrimination, recording and punishing violent crimes motivated by homophobia, and backing gay-supportive candidates for public office. For example, Lambda Legal Defense and Education Fund was founded in 1973 (after having to sue for the right to incorporate, Cain 1993), and the National Gay Task Force (to be renamed the National Gay and Lesbian Task Force in 1985) was founded the same year. In 1980, the Human Rights Campaign opened its doors.

In terms of *organizational structure*, these national groups tended to be centralized, public interest groups located in a major cities like New York, San Francisco, or Washington, DC. Staffs were generally professional and often did not have on-the-street organizers whose job it was to mobilize members. Instead of dues-paying members, who have constant contact with staff, most national gay rights organizations have a donor model where supporters open their wallets relatively regularly, but gather only occasionally at (fundraising) events to show that they back the cause, otherwise participating very little in campaigns. In this model, the members of the larger gay community are constituents in a broad and shallow sense, having little necessary contact with or direct say in the priorities of the professionalized organizations. Given the disincentive to be an "out" gay person in the 1970s and 1980s this organizational model makes sense.

In the early 1980s, several organizations on this model, as well as many founded to deal with particular community needs, like the Gay Men's Health Crisis (GMHC), would come into existence. In addition, some groups built on more direct organizing and action models, most notably the attention-grabbing ACT UP, would play an essential role in creating and taking advantage of various kinds of political opportunities, contributing novel tactical innovations that would become indispensable tools during the late twentieth-century struggle for survival (Stein 2012).

ACT UP, which would become famous for its piercing slogans (e.g., Silence = Death) and effective direct actions, was formed in 1987. The pickets, "die-ins," marches, and guerilla theater that the group enacted, aiming to bring attention to the fact that people were dying, changed the face of gay activism with creative, in-your-face public strategies that were designed to be impossible to ignore (Ingram, Bouthillette, and Retter 1997). In 1988, AIDS activists across the country called for Nine Days of Action, which were autonomously authored and carried out by various local groups. One action, designed by ACT UP's New York Women's Committee, took place at Shea Stadium, where activists bought out blocks of seats on all three sides of the U-shaped stadium and, dressed in black T-shirts, unfurled large banners printed with messages to raise awareness about AIDS. One activist, Maxine Wolfe, recounts her memory of the event this way:

> It was the most amazing thing because we had made these banners with a black background and white lettering. We had six long rows in each area and each row had a set of banners, and we only opened them up

when the visiting team was up because we did not want to upset the New York Mets fans. At a certain point, I do not remember what inning it was, the first banners opened up. They started at the top of the group and they were always three lines. And the first one opened up and it said "Don't balk at safe sex." And then across the stadium, opposite them, in the seats above the other field, three banners rolled open and they said "AIDS kills women," and then in the center, behind home plate, the next three opened up and they said "Men! Use condoms."

And then, people from ACT UP got so into having these banners that people started swaying back and forth, up and down, and the visual effect was incredible because it was at night, totally dark, and the lighting from the ballpark totally reflected the white letters of the banners. An inning and a half later, we opened the next set of banners. They said "Strike out AIDS," "No glove, no love," and the final one said "SILENCE=DEATH" and it had a huge triangle and ACT UP! This was on C-Span. (Ingram, Bouthillette, and Retter 1997)

However, ACT UP, an organization that differed from the large, centralized public interests groups with its loose, autonomous, networked structure, was an eye-catching part of a massive mobilization that occurred. In fact, for the first time, gay people that did not think of themselves as particularly political were getting involved, and organizations were making space to incorporate the newly active volunteers.

AIDS, probably more than any other external threat, mobilized huge numbers of formerly apathetic gay men and lesbians. Not everyone became "politically" involved, but many helped to raise money, worked on the AIDS Quilt [which was presented during the 1987 National March on Washington for Lesbian and Gay Rights], or volunteered as "buddies" for homebound people with AIDS. AIDS significantly affected which issues the movement targeted as well as policy outcomes. While lesbians had always been concerned with family policies, particularly child custody, such issues were largely ignored by the movement. With the advent of AIDS, family policies, such as domestic partnership, access to sick or dying partner, and inheritance became critically important to gay men. (Bernstein 2002, 559)

The experience of AIDS facilitated a focus on family issues. While reproductive freedom, child custody, and the legal rights and obligations partners had toward each other had always been an important part of lesbian activism, gay men did not turn their attentions to such issues until AIDS vividly displayed the legal insecurity of the familial bonds that shaped their lives. The heartbreaking experiences and stories of people being barred from the hospital as their partners lay dying, or being kicked out of homes that legally passed from their deceased partner's control into the hands of unsympathetic biological families, caused gay advocacy groups to concentrate new efforts on winning kinship rights. This was when the turn to "coordinated efforts to achieve the rights and privileges accorded married couples" began climbing closer to the top of the gay rights agenda (Bernstein 2002, 559).

The most prominent national gay rights organizations were making some strides, both in terms of gay identity and in terms of policy, but it is important to note that the movements' leading organizations were rife with intraorganizational and, often, sector-wide challenges regarding what constitutes a "gay community" in the face of race, gender, and class differences (Vaid 1995). The reality of the gay rights movement was that the *interorganizational environment* was rife with conflict, mitigated at the time by the need to mount an effective response to the AIDS crisis.

Even though the danger of AIDS kept the movement from fracturing completely, it was still the case that the people who were speaking for "the" gay community tended to be the people who were already relatively demographically advantaged: predominantly middle- and upper-class white men. Lesbians and people of color felt that both their gay identity work and its political translation needed to be stitched together at the intersections of marginal identities acknowledging the constellation of issues that impacted their lives, not homogenized into a faux-universal category, which primarily represented the concerns of relatively well-off white gay men (Boykin 1997, Schroedel and Fiber 2000).

Jean Schroedel and Pamela Fiber write, "The gender hierarchy that existed within the heterosexual world was replicated within the homophile movement. Lesbians were expected to fill traditional women's roles within groups—coffee making and secretarial tasks" (Schroedel and Fiber 2000, 99). For this reason, though lesbians and gay men often worked cooperatively on certain issues, they tended not to work together in the same organizations (Phelan 1989, Taylor and Whittier 1992). In addition, their policy priorities were often different from those of gay men, with lesbians caring a great deal about abortion rights (which some gay men have claimed is "not a gay issue"), quality child care, access to healthcare, and the sexual exploitation of women in pornography. After the AIDS movement formed, advocacy organizations for "the gay community" rarely addressed lesbian-specific sexual precautions, like dental dams, that could be taken in order to practice safer sex (Schroedel and Fiber 2000). Up until the mid to late 1980s, lesbian and gay organizations were largely separate. These two groups were unified by their experience of social and legal stigmatization and subordination, but in tension because of the reality of the way sex and gender differentially impacts people's lived experience.

Gay people of color also found that their interests and concerns were not well represented by the flagship gay rights organizations. The National Coalition of Black Lesbians and Gays was founded in 1978 in order to "combat racism within the lesbian and gay movement and homophobia within African American organizations" (Bernstein 2002, 557) and played a key role in organizing the march on Washington in 1979. However, unlike the other national organizations for community support and political action mentioned here, it faded from the national scene in 1986. Presently, there are no national organizations that work specifically on issues facing black lesbians and gays. The lack of a strong and consistent voice was felt most keenly during the height of the AIDS crisis, which disproportionately affected gay people of color (Cohen 1999).

Still, the AIDS crisis sustained pressure on organizations to work together in order to obtain resources and save lives in short order. Urvashi Vaid, a longtime activist for gay liberation, writes eloquently about the felt necessity of the time:

> Homophobia required gay people, nationwide, to create an AIDS-specific movement. We chose to focus on AIDS rather than on homophobia and racism, even though these were the causes of the governmental and societal paralysis. Today, there is broad acknowledgement among gay activists that the degaying of AIDS was a conscious political choice made by gay organizers in the mid-1980s. (Vaid 1995, 75)

So, while the Human Rights Campaign, ACT UP, the National Gay and Lesbian Task Force, Lambda Legal, Gay Men's Health Crisis, Queer to the Left, and the many other organizations that populated the gay and queer advocacy movement sectors had differing political orientations and worldviews that led to conflicts that flared within and among local grass-roots groups, there developed norms of interorganizational communication (and silencing) and cooperation (and shaming or intimidation) that stopped the nationally focused organizations from becoming dysfunctionally sectarian (Rimmerman, Wald, and Wilcox 2000, Bernstein 2002, Farrow 2012).

However, there was quite a bit of tactical diversity in the movement. Mary Bernstein notes that "several distinctly new mobilization patterns appeared in response to *Hardwick*" (2002, 560). Unlike the living wage movement, which was expert at pressure politics in legislatures, the gay rights movement was largely shut out of access to legislators and administration officials, the channels often utilized by professionalized interest groups. Due to the inability to act effectively within electoral politics, gay politics became both more mobilized at the grass-roots level than it had been before and more militant overall. By the early 1990s a gradual turn away from direct action and toward interest-group

politics began, accelerating with the election in 1992 of self-declared gay-friendly
Democrat Bill Clinton, who had courted the centralized and wealthy portion of
the gay rights movement with a promise to end the ban on gay people serving
in the military. With what seemed increasing access to Washington, DC, elites,
ACT UP, and other organizations favoring insurgent tactics like direct action
began to lose influence within the movement, and the more professionalized
organizations, which had knowledge and experience with interest group and
electoral politics, redoubled their efforts in those political venues.

It should be noted that before Clinton's presidential campaign, ending the
ban on gay people serving in the military had not been anywhere near the top of
any national LGBT organization's agenda. In fact, many in the gay rights community, particularly those who identified as politically left, were affronted by the
notion that the movement should spend resources on such a conservative issue
(Rimmerman, Wald, and Wilcox 2000, Vaid 1995). But, as in the case of marriage equality, which was to emerge on the heels of the gays-in-the-military push
in the early 1990s, "internal dissent . . . notwithstanding, many activists jumped
on the . . . bandwagon" and mobilized around the opportunity for a significant
political win (Bernstein 2002, 566). However, it wasn't just about wining favorable policy, but also and more importantly about winning a legitimated place in
the polity. If gay people could serve openly in the military, then it would be much
harder to argue that gay people were not equal citizens.

However, Bill Clinton and the gay rights community were to be handed
a spectacular defeat on the military issue in 1993, when Congress, backed
by public opinion, drafted and passed a policy commonly called "Don't Ask,
Don't Tell" (DADT), which technically lifted the ban on gays serving in the
military, while mandating that those who served remain closeted. There would
be another stinging defeat in 1996, when Clinton, who had presented himself
as a friend to the movement, signed the Defense of Marriage Act (DOMA),
which stated that the federal government would not acknowledge same-sex
marriages, even if they were performed legally within particular states, and that
no state would have to honor the marriage of such couples performed outside
its borders.

While the institutional mediation of movement challenges and claims does
matter (Mucciaroni 2008), it is not completely accurate to think about movements as entirely characterized through or bound by a single institutional framework. This is especially true since HRC, National Gay and Lesbian Task Force
(NGLTF), and Lambda Legal are all multi-issue organizations and put different
emphasis on different advocacy issues over time.[11] Still, it is fair to say that in terms
of *venue choice*, the marriage equality movement had most of its initial success in
the courts. However, as the 1990s wore on, it is inaccurate to characterize the marriage movement's strategy as strictly limited to that institutional domain because

at the same time that the court struggles were going on, the increasingly large, professionalized gay rights organizations were also raising money for candidates friendly to their policy preferences. That means that while the courts produced marriage equality as a viable issue and yielded the marriage equality movement's only early victories, the strategy of the major gay rights organizations was always multidimensional, interfacing with a number of political institutions and processes, fundraising for campaigns and elections, lobbying legislators, and providing research, data collection, and public education. In addition, while the national organizations have been indispensable to the marriage equality movement, it is also the case that they have not been pioneers in the marriage equality movement, they came to the issue only after independent activists had significant wins.

It is also the case that there has always been a lot of state-level movement activity. This is largely because antigay marriage groups were mobilized at the state level, proposing restrictive state legislation and fielding referenda that would nullify favorable court rulings, so proponents of marriage equality had to answer those challenges in the states. In this way, the venue choice of the marriage movement was dynamic.

Although each movement evidenced predominant institutional pathways in terms of their venue choice, both the living wage and marriage equality movement also devoted resources and developed tactics in other institutional arenas. Since the American political system is federated, movements often must develop venue and tactical repertoires at more than one level of government and with more than one type of political institution. This is generally to the benefit of political challengers because, as Gary Mucciaroni points out, "Jurisdictions differ dramatically in public support for gay rights; general political ideology; size, social diversity, education levels, and resources of the gay and lesbian community; political party competition; and opportunities available for citizens to vote on gay rights through the initiative process" (2008, 218).

Outcomes

In the early 2000s, marriage equality felt like a losing issue. Thirty states adopted constitutional amendments banning same-sex marriage and an additional eight states passed legislation limiting the definition of marriage to a union between one man and one woman. Bill Clinton, a Democrat who came into his 1992 presidential term with gay-friendly policies near the top of his agenda, was handed two stinging defeats. In addition, a highly organized religious right wing used the very notion of same-sex marriage as a wedge issue in the ongoing political contest that Patrick Buchanan dubbed the "culture war" at the Republican National Convention in 1992. Moreover, during the decade of study, public support for marriage equality

Table 3.1 **State Constitutional Amendments Banning Same-Sex Unions, 1994–2012**

State	Year	Type of Ban
Alaska	1998	Marriage
Nebraska	2000	Marriage, civil union, domestic partnership
Nevada	2002	Marriage
Arkansas	2004	Marriage, civil union
Georgia	2004	Marriage, civil union
Kentucky	2004	Marriage, civil union
Louisiana	2004	Marriage, civil union
Michigan	2004	Marriage, civil union, domestic partnership
Mississippi	2004	Marriage
Missouri	2004	Marriage
Montana	2004	Marriage
North Dakota	2004	Marriage, civil union
Ohio	2004	Marriage, civil union
Oklahoma	2004	Marriage, civil union
Oregon	2004	Marriage
Utah	2004	Marriage, civil union
Kansas	2005	Marriage, civil union
Texas	2005	Marriage, civil union
Alabama	2006	Marriage, civil union
Arizona	2006 (2008)	Marriage, civil union
Colorado	2006	Marriage
Idaho	2006	Marriage, civil union
South Carolina	2006	Marriage, civil union
South Dakota	2006	Marriage, civil union, domestic partnership
Tennessee	2006	Marriage
Virginia	2006	Marriage, civil union, domestic partnership
Wisconsin	2006	Marriage, civil union
California	2008	Marriage
Florida	2008	Marriage, civil union
North Carolina	2012	Marriage, civil union, domestic partnership

Source: National Conference of State Legislatures, http://www.ncsl.org/issues-research/human-services/state-doma-laws.aspx.

Table 3.2 **Same-Sex Marriage Made Legal
through Legislative Action as of May 13, 2013**

State	Year
Hawaii	1994
Illinois	1996
Delaware	1996
Pennsylvania	1996
Minnesota*	1997
West Virginia	2000
Wyoming	2003
Indiana	2004

*Same sex marriage made legal through legislative action on May 13, 2013.

Source: National Conference of State Legislatures.

was quite low, with an average of 33 percent of respondents supporting marriage equality across nineteen national polls in 2004 (Silver 2013). Americans also rejected the idea of marriage equality each of the eighteen times that they were asked to decide on the issue between 1994 and 2004 (tables 3.1–3.3).

Civil Unions, *Lawrence v. Texas*, and Marriage Equality in Massachusetts

During the decade between 1994 and 2004, amid the overall policy drubbing, the marriage equality movement did have three key policy successes. In 1999 the Vermont Supreme Court ruled in *Baker v. Vermont* (1999) that "the State is constitutionally required to extend to same-sex couples the common benefits and protections that flow from marriage under Vermont law." Instead of extending marriage rights, the Vermont state legislature developed a parallel status called civil unions, which became legal on April 26, 2000. This invention of a new policy accommodation to deal with the legal and political question of equality successfully raised in the national conversation by the marriage equality movement is an important milestone. Civil unions came into being in Vermont, and subsequently became the favored policy option for moderate Democratic candidates, not only because of the state supreme court's ruling. Instead, both ordinary Americans and the political class increasingly recognized the need for laws that could accommodate basic equality for gay people.

Table 3.3 **Ballot Measures Limiting Legal Recognition of Same-Sex Unions**

State	*Year*	*Text of Ballot Measure*
Hawaii	1998	The proposed amendment is intended to make it absolutely clear that the State Constitution gives the Legislature the power and authority to reserve marriage to opposite-sex couples.
Alaska	1998	This measure would amend the Declaration of Rights section of the Alaska Constitution to limit marriage. The amendment would say that to be valid, a marriage may exist only between one man and one woman.
California	2000	Only marriage between a man and a woman is valid or recognized in California.
Nebraska	2000	A vote "*FOR*" will amend the Nebraska Constitution to provide that only marriage between a man and a woman shall be valid or recognized in Nebraska, and to provide that the uniting of two persons of the same sex in a civil union, domestic partnership or other similar same-sex relationship shall not be valid or recognized in Nebraska.
Nevada	2000 (2002)	The proposed amendment, if passed, would create a new section to Article 1 of the Nevada Constitution providing that, "Only a marriage between a male and female person shall be recognized and given effect in this state."
Utah	2004	Shall the Utah Constitution be amended to provide that: (1) marriage consists only of the legal union between a man and a woman; and (2) no other domestic union may be recognized as a marriage or given the same or substantially equal legal effect?
Oregon	2004	Only marriage between one man and one woman is valid or legally recognized as marriage.
Oklahoma*	2004	This measure adds a new section of law to the Constitution. It adds Section 35 to Article 2. It defines marriage to be between one man and one woman. It prohibits giving the benefits of marriage to people who are not married. It provides that same sex marriages in other states are not valid in this state. It makes issuing a marriage license in violation of this section a misdemeanor.
Ohio	2004	Be it Resolved by the People of the State of Ohio: ... Only a union between one man and one woman may be a marriage valid in or recognized by this state and its political subdivisions. This state and its political subdivisions shall not create or recognize a legal status for relationships of unmarried individuals that intends to approximate the design, qualities, significance or effect of marriage.

(continued)

Table 3.3 **Continued**

State	Year	Text of Ballot Measure
North Dakota	2004	Marriage consists only of the legal union between a man and a woman. No other domestic union, however denominated, may be recognized as a marriage or given the same or substantially equivalent legal effect.
Montana	2004	Montana statutes define civil marriage as between a man and a woman, and prohibit marriage between persons of the same sex. The Montana Constitution currently contains no provisions defining marriage. This initiative, effective immediately, would amend the Montana Constitution to provide that only a marriage between a man and a woman may be valid if performed in Montana, or recognized in Montana if performed in another state.
Missouri**	2004	Shall the Missouri Constitution be amended so that to be valid and recognized in this state, a marriage shall exist only between a man and a woman?
Mississippi	2004	This proposed constitutional amendment provides that marriage may take place and may be valid under the laws of this state only between a man and a woman. The amendment also provides that a marriage in another state or foreign jurisdiction between persons of the same gender may not be recognized in this state and is void and unenforceable under the laws of this state.
Michigan	2004	Amend the state constitution to provide that "the union of one man and one woman in marriage shall be the only agreement recognized as a marriage or similar union for any purpose."
Louisiana**	2004	Proposing an amendment to the Constitution of Louisiana, to enact Article XII, Section 15, relative to marriage; to require that marriage in the state shall consist only of the union of one man and one woman; to provide that the legal incidents of marriage shall be conferred only upon such union; to prohibit the validation or recognition of the legal status of any union of unmarried individuals; to prohibit the recognition of a marriage contracted in another jurisdiction which is not the union of one man and one woman; to provide for submission of the proposed amendment to the electors and provide a ballot proposition; and to provide for related matters.
Kentucky	2004	Are you in favor of amending the Kentucky Constitution to provide that only a marriage between one man and one woman shall be a marriage in Kentucky, and that a legal status identical to or similar to marriage for unmarried individuals shall not be valid or recognized?
Georgia	2004	Shall the Constitution be amended so as to provide that this state shall recognize as marriage only the union of man and woman?

(continued)

Table 3.3 **Continued**

State	Year	Text of Ballot Measure
Arkansas	2004	Proposed amendment to the Arkansas constitution providing that marriage consists only of the union of one man and one woman; that legal status for unmarried person which is identical or substantially similar to marital status shall not be valid or recognized in Arkansas, except that the Legislature may recognize a common law marriage from another state between a man and a woman; and that the Legislature has the power to determine the capacity of persons to marry.

*Only amendment that establishes criminal penalty for issuing marriage license in violation of the statute.

**On the ballot prior to November presidential election.

Source: National Conference of State Legislatures, Ballot Measures Database, http://www.ncsl.org/legislatures-elections/elections/ballot-measures-database.aspx.

This was due in large part to the heated public debate on the topic that had been ongoing for nearly six years in 2000. The marriage movement pursued the equality argument in U.S. courts, but successfully expanded the "scope of conflict" to include the public in general, which, though the strategy did not result in immediate approval, did yield serious and sustained attention that eventually resulted in the issue's acceptance onto the short list of topics regularly discussed in American politics. This acceptance set the stage for the slew of policy victories that the marriage movement has won in the second decade of the twenty-first century.

In addition to civil unions in Vermont, in 2003, the U.S. Supreme Court struck down the legality of sodomy laws in the six-to-three decision of *Lawrence v. Texas*. While there was no discernible uptick in national news discourse about same-sex marriage after the Vermont decision, *Lawrence* made quite a splash, in part because it was decided at the beginning of the 2004 presidential campaign season in which the candidates took different stands on the issue. Though neither George W. Bush nor John Kerry favored same-sex marriage, Bush declared his support for a constitutional amendment banning gay marriage and Kerry claimed to want to leave the matter up to the states. Thus same-sex marriage was declared an electoral wedge issue, which made it imminently newsworthy during the following year. In 2003, the number of news stories on same-sex marriage in the *New York Times* was more than six times what it was the year before (212 stories vs. 34) and in *USA Today* there were ten times as many (20 vs. 7). Underscoring the newsworthiness of same-sex marriage in the election year, Massachusetts legalized same-sex marriage, eschewing the creation of an intermediate status, in May 2004. In addition, there were same-sex marriage bans on the ballot in eleven states on Election Day 2004, all of which passed by comfortable margins. It was widely speculated after the election that if not for same-sex marriage, Bush would not have retaken the White House. Though this speculation proved questionable,[12] there was nevertheless an outpouring of regret and recrimination against the marriage equality movement, not only from disappointed Democrats, but also as a form of self-criticism within gay rights organizations.

It might be difficult to recall, as more and more states legalize same-sex marriage through legislative action, that only ten years ago the issue was seen as a political loser for liberals and an ace in the hole for conservatives. In that short amount of time, the politics of same-sex marriage had shifted significantly, and, as of 2014, the liability in electoral politics has changed hands. It is now cultural conservatives who wish to avoid the topic of same-sex marriage for fear of alienating political moderates and young people, while support for same-sex marriage has become a litmus test issue for Democratic candidates hoping to raise funds and votes (Izadi 2013).

Possible Alternative Explanations

I have argued that the disparate notions of power and the different strategies of engagement with the general public are key to understanding the differential impacts of the living wage and marriage equality movements during the decade of their emergence. However, there are other factors in play that are worth considering as alternative explanations. In the following I confront four potential explanations that attribute the relative successes of these two movements to causes having nothing to do with their divergent conceptions of power and their opposite regard for engagement in mainstream public discourse.

"But the Gays Are Rich"

The first and most straightforward alternative explanation for the political subsistence of the living wage movement and the political acceptance of the marriage equality movement is a simple matter of resources. Perhaps the marriage equality movement simply had more resources than the living wage movement. Maybe both gay organizations and gay individuals have more money to bring to bear to pursue their policy preferences?

The resource mobilization theory of social movements teaches that resources are both tangible and intangible. They include financial resources, powerful organizations, skilled leadership, preexisting social ties, dense personal, social, and political networks, collective identity, and the oppositional consciousness, or the sense that the group is oppressed and deserves to be treated better legally, structurally, and interpersonally (Zald and McCarthy 1979, McAdam 1999, Mucciaroni 2008).

If we compare the resources of the marriage equality and living wage movements across these dimensions, we are presented with a picture that is not very clear cut. First, neither gay people nor gay organizations are as rich as people often think. In fact, during the period between 1994 and 2004, gay organizations were no richer than the labor organizations funding living wage initiatives. While many opine that "gays and lesbians as a group are not as disadvantaged economically as groups represented by other social movements" (Mucciaroni 2008, 34), it is not clear whether and to what degree this is true. Gay people are, on the whole, no richer than the general population, given that gay people are randomly distributed through the population. This means that there are many more working-class people than gay people, and most gay people are actually working class. However, it is also the case that those people who are most likely to "come out," self-identify as gay, and politically support gay causes are also more likely to be affluent. This is for two reasons. First, as Kay Schlozman, Sidney Verba, and Henry Brady have shown, the more affluent are generally more likely to be politically active (Schlozman, Verba, and Brady 2012). And second, affluent gay people are more likely to move in social circles in which homophobia is stigmatized and gay identity is accepted.

In addition, there is evidence that even affluent gay people are not as well off as their straight counterparts. M. V. Lee Badgett writes that "the paucity of available data for large numbers of lesbians and gay men has made comparisons of income by sexual orientation difficult," and studies of gay men and lesbians in the 1980s tended to use biased samples, such as the demographic profile of those who subscribed to gay and lesbian magazines, a group that tends to be more affluent, as representative samples of the population at large (Badgett 1995, 729).

Using pooled data from the General Social Survey between 1989 and 1991, controlling for education and experience, Badgett estimates that lesbian women earn about 18 percent less, on average than do their heterosexual peers and gay men earn about 7 percent less, on average, than their heterosexual counterparts (Badgett 1995). In addition, these numbers may slightly underestimate these ratios because there are good reasons to believe that "the willingness of respondents to identify themselves as gay or lesbian to an unknown interviewer [varies] along income lines and within income groups," in such a way that people who are less educated and lower-income are less likely to admit to a stigmatized social identity.

Although there are great limitations to the data that are available on poverty and sexual orientation, some studies that use extrapolations from U.S. census data (which provides information about same-sex households), the National Family Growth Survey, and several state health information surveys have provided some information on the differential impact of poverty on GLBTQ people. According to a study by the New York–based Queers for Economic Justice, children in same-sex couple households have poverty rates twice those of children in heterosexual married couple households. Lesbians, in general, have higher poverty rates than gay male couples or heterosexual couples. Gay male couples who include a black partner or an unemployed partner or have children under the age of eighteen also have poverty rates that exceed those of married heterosexual couples. In addition, same-sex couples who live in rural areas have poverty rates that exceed those of their heterosexual peers as well as poverty rates that are twice those of same-sex couples who live in metropolitan areas. Poverty in the LGBTQ community also differs dramatically by race. Black gay male couples report a median income that is $23,000 lower than white gay males, and black lesbians report median incomes that are $21,000 lower than those of white lesbians (Queers for Economic Justice 2007).

For transgender people, the situation is even worse. One of the few large-scale surveys of transgendered Americans, including a national sample of 6,450 people, conducted by the National Center for Transgender Equality and NGLTF found the following:

> Respondents were four to five times more likely than the general population to live in extreme poverty, with an annual household income of less than $10,000 at all levels of educational attainment. Those surveyed were twice as likely to be unemployed; 26 percent had lost a job because they were transgender, though if you factor in not being hired in the first place or denied a promotion, that number rises to 47 percent. A full 90 percent of respondents reported harassment or other mistreatment in the workplace. The statistics for transgender and gender nonconforming people grew even worse when race is factored in, with transgender people of color faring worse than white participants across the board. (Grant et al. 2011, 2–3)

Organizational Resources

But what if we consider instead the resource level of the leading organizations in each movement? In doing so we find that the organizations at the forefront of each movement had comparable resources during the decade of their emergence.

Comparable data on the operating budgets of the organizations involved in the living wage and marriage equality movements are difficult to find. In addition, since ACORN was not a nonprofit organization (though many of its affiliates were), it was not required to file public disclosure of its budget with the IRS, so there is no available record of its funds from 1994 to 2004, the time period I focus on in this study. Press accounts of ACORN's overall budget are available, but only in 2009, after the revelation of the embezzling scandal that was the start of the troubles that would prove fatal for the organization. In a 2009 interview with the Associated Press, Brian Kettenring, the deputy director of national operations at ACORN said that the group's budget was $25 million per year (Theimer and Yost 2009). Founder Wade Rathke wrote in a 2009 essay that ACORN and its affiliates combined raised and spent "over $100 million" per year (Rathke 2009, 52). This may seem quite a discrepancy, but given that ACORN had hundreds and by some press reports over one thousand affiliates[13] and often worked in partnership with unions, particularly SEIU locals, on living wage campaigns, the organizations' financial resources may well have reached or exceeded Rathke's estimate. In addition, HUD disclosed that it had given ACORN $42 million in grants between 2000 and 2009, and a House Oversight and Government Reform Committee report, spearheaded by Republican representative from California Darrell Issa, claimed that ACORN received $53 million in federal funds between 1994 and 2009.[14]

Of course, not all of those funds would be dedicated to the issue of the living wage. ACORN was a multi-issue organization that did work on many issues concerning low- to moderate-income people, including predatory lending and affordable housing, Hurricane Katrina relief, voter registration, and gun control. As Gary Mucciaroni writes, "It is difficult to ascertain how many resources social movement organizations devote to advancing their goals on particular issues, because they generally budget resources according to organizational activities and functions that cut across issues" (Mucciaroni 2008, 43). So there is no way to accurately estimate what portion of ACORN's operating funds were devoted to the living wage; however, if we take attention that the organizations themselves pay to their different issues as a proxy (Mucciaroni 2008), we can infer that living wage was one of ACORN's top priorities (Fisher 2009, Atlas 2010).

Like ACORN, the three national organizations most involved in the marriage equality movement are multi-issue organizations. Of the three, the Human Rights Campaign devoted the greatest proportion of its attention to marriage equality, with 35 percent of its press releases devoted to the topic between 1995 and 2005 (Mucciaroni 2008, 5). HRC's 1999 annual report stated that the annual budget of the organization, including its foundation, was $15,264,956; by 2004 the budget reached $27,210,974, and in 2009, the year for which we have press reports on ACORN, HRC's budget was $35,828,496.[15] For the National Gay and Lesbian Task Force, marriage was the second most attended issue following workplace discrimination and fairness issues. In 2000 NGLTF had a budget of $4.4 million; however, the organization saw its budget decline to $3.4 million in 2002 (Haider-Markel 2002). According to the 2010 NGLTF annual report, total expenditures for programs were $6,060,336. Lambda Legal Defense and Education Fund reports that in 2011 it spent $8,431,888 on programs, with an annual budget of $11,939,618.[16] This rough comparison paints what is for many a surprising picture. It is not clear that the marriage movement was any wealthier than the living wage movement between 1994 and 2004, or indeed up until the dissolution of ACORN in 2010.

Declining Union Power Dooms Labor Politics

A second possible alternative explanation for the differential success of the living wage and marriage equality movements asserts that the decline of union power has stalled labor politics in general and gravely constrained the living wage movement, in particular. While it is certainly the case that union power has been declining since the 1980s, I would argue that the relatively limited reach of the living wage movement between 1994 and 2004 was not due to the decline of unions. Rather, the decline of unions was instead one of the symptoms of a lack of engagement with the general public and a lack of attention to resonant public speech, which has been a characteristic of the labor movement broadly, including the living wage movement.

The decline of unions as a powerful political force and the disappearance of an institutionalized journalistic labor beat did make the political environment that the living wage movement entered into more difficult than it would have been in an earlier decade of the twentieth century, but these difficulties did not prevent the purposeful development and consistent deployment of resonant discourse on work, labor, wages, and the American dream. Rather, labor opted out of such lofty discussions in favor of local policy struggle. This choice was based on the worldview and skill sets of labor activists, particularly those in the living wage movement, and it left a prime power of social movements—namely, the power to *create* new political understandings through the use of resonant public discourse over time—off the table.

Longtime AFL-CIO president George Meany explicitly articulates the internally focused reasoning of the labor movement: when he was asked, in 1972, whether he was worried that the proportion of workers who were union members was decreasing, he said:

> I don t know. I don't care.... Why should we worry about organizing groups of people who do not appear to want to be organized? If they prefer to have others speak for them and make decisions which affect their lives, that is their right.... The organized fellow is the fellow that counts. (Kelber 2005)

This is indicative of the labor movement's orientation toward organizing, which places emphasis on shoring up advantage for those already inclined to be involved and ignoring the rest. This tendency helps explain why labor activists have tended not to focus resources and energy on attempting to change public ideas about the significance of their issues.

What If Raising Worker Wages Really Will Have Negative Macroeconomic Effects?

A third alternative explanation is rooted in doubt about the efficacy of wage floors in general. However, based on the balance of empirical evidence the perception that raising wages to a level that pulls workers above the poverty line will automatically kill jobs and raise the cost of production seems to be just that—a perception that holds a great deal of sway, but is based on inconclusive evidence. Nevertheless, it is a perception that has become increasingly prevalent over time. This belief in the negative relationship between increasing wages and increasing economic stability and prosperity is not evidence of a world-historical phenomenon, it is the result of a discursive one. The now-dominant view that wage floors inevitably result in negative economic consequences is not conclusively supported by most economic research, and was not the consensus position of economists before the late 1980s.[17] The increased prevalence and influence of this view has not been the result of new evidence-based discoveries, but instead a change in the dominant understanding of what is at stake, what ought to be guarded against and what supported, as well as which trade-offs are acceptable. These changed ideas are the result of the articulation and use by economic conservatives of a consistent and resonant public discourse touting versions of trickle-down economic theory as commonsensical, articulations that remain resonant even in the face of dubious, or even contradictory empirical evidence.

Gay Politics Is More Culturally Salient Than Labor Politics

A final alternative explanation for the differential impact of the marriage and living wage movements is that perhaps the early 1990s cultural moment was just more receptive to gay politics than to labor politics. However, as the foregoing discussion shows, there is no evidence that this is the case.

It is, however, also important to consider that the fact that gay identity crosscuts other kinds of salient demographic categories like race, class, gender, ethnicity, and nationality, is a double-edged sword. On the one hand, the crosscutting nature of the identity means that affluent, connected people are as likely to have gay people in their families and acquaintance as anyone else and for that reason may be more likely to be sympathetic to movement perspectives and more motivated to act as political allies. However, there are some undeniable disadvantages that also arise from the fact that gay identity cuts across other demographic categories. First, the gay, lesbian, bisexual, transgender, and queer population group is very small, estimated to be between 3 and 10 percent of the population. Second, the tiny population is also geographically dispersed, especially prior to adulthood. And finally, GLBTQ people are still an unpopular minority, whom it is still legal to discriminate against in housing and employment in more than half the states in the United States. In addition, it is still the case that the families that gay people are born into may be hostile to the practices and identity that GLBTQ members develop as they grow up. Although it is possible that the next generation of GLBTQ kids may find their families relatively more receptive to them on average, the current and previous generations of gay adults have often found

> [g]ay identity [to be] routinely stigmatized as aberrant, perverse, and immoral. This means that many gays are to some degree "closeted," hiding their sexual orientation from family, friends, and coworkers. Moreover . . . gays are usually isolated from one another until adulthood. . . . Politically . . ., these experiences undermine the formation of common political identity and discourage people from mobilizing to achieve common goals. (Wald 2000, 13)

Given a pop culture environment that has had more and more representations of gay people since the late 1990s and the frequency with which those who live in urbane, secular settings exist in easy community with affluent gay people, it is tempting to commit a post hoc fallacy regarding the marriage movement and imagine that it was always already successful. However, the fact is that "to be openly gay, to run organizations that are recognized as legitimate, and to engage in overt political action on behalf of gay causes, are all possible today, but would not have been so a generation ago" (Wald 2000, 12). It is also the case that GLBTQ people who are not urban and affluent may not live in social contexts that are much different than those of a generation ago.

A Gay "Politics of Respectability"

However, it must be admitted that marriage equality activists deliberately deployed a "politics of respectability"—which dictates that in order to counter the negative views of the dominant group, members of the oppressed minority must aggressively adopt the manners and morality that has been deemed virtuous by that group (Higginbotham 1993). This practice has created the *misperception* that most gay people are upper-middle-class (white) people with "virtually normal" (Sullivan 1996) styles of self- and gender-expression who seek to be in long-term, monogamous relationships. This portrayal is not a comprehensive one and may not even be particularly representative of the incredibly diverse GLBTQ community. The deliberate overrepresentation of the most well-off, socially, and sexually normative gay people as the face of marriage politics has been a deliberate choice by marriage equality activists, one that radical critics within the GLBTQ community have found problematic because respectability politics tends to normalize one segment of the population and mark another portion for what Cathy Cohen has called "secondary marginalization" (1999).

All political coalitions must navigate endemic cleavages. One common strategy for navigating these cleavages is to practice respectability politics. Respectability politics confers some strategic advantages; however, critics argue that this kind of politics allows the images and interests of the most assimilable parts of the population to stand in for, and therefore obscure, the whole. Instead, respectability politics can reinscribe discrimination against the nonnormative and enforce invisibility upon the most marginal members of the minority population, while doing little to challenge the logics and institutions that structurally disadvantage all members of the population. In this way, respectability politics can actually make conditions for the most vulnerable members of excluded populations (often those who are browner and poorer) *worse*, both materially and in terms of social and political standing.

These fault lines are not easy to overcome, and when a social movement sector is able to act in concert despite the inevitable cleavages where people's multiple identities intersect, it is quite an accomplishment. In the case of the gay rights movement, it is questionable whether the divergences in viewpoint could have been overcome without the clear danger that HIV/AIDS posed, even given the reality of an initially unresponsive federal government and a mobilized, hostile, and electorally influential countermovement. This overwhelmingly and overtly hostile political environment created an interorganizational environment in the gay rights movement generally, and in the marriage equality movement that grew out of it, that operated in concert, even in the face of vigorous disagreement.

Though the marriage equality movement was not operating under the necessity of saving lives, the gay rights movement sector had learned how politically important it can be to appear unified, and the major national organizations, all of which had grown larger, more professionalized, and more powerful during the fight against AIDS, threw their weight behind marriage equality, albeit with varying degrees of enthusiasm, by the end of the 1990s (Vaid 1995). In an August 3, 2004, interview with the *San Francisco Daily Journal*, Evan Wolfson said of the interorganizational conflict that persisted in the gay rights community: "Even if people don't completely agree with what I say, when they hear the bigotry from the other side they invariably move closer to my position."

The triumphant distancing from bigotry in this pronouncement ought to be tempered by the fact that the gay people who have represented the marriage equality movement in public are overwhelmingly middle- to upper-class white men and women practicing a combination of a "politics of respectability" and good old-fashioned interest group politics (which requires vast sums of money).

It must be noted that people whose only mark of difference and only lack of demographic privilege is their sexual identity are at a relative advantage over those who exist at and advocate for concerns that spring from the intersection of marginalized or marked identities. However, it must also be admitted that movements generally reproduce the hierarchies of privileges that exist in the outside world within the boundaries of their movements. At times, this primacy of the relatively privileged has been an explicit political strategy. The term "politics of respectability" actually originates from the study of African American politics,[18] and the practice of putting only the most "unimpeachable characters" forward to challenge oppression has been standard movement practice.[19]

Underlying the observation of the relative privilege of the most prominent members of the marriage equality movement, though, is often a sense that gay identity has never really been that big a barrier to success, including political success, for the otherwise advantaged. This is a retrospective rationalization that is simply incorrect. As recently as the 1980s, there was no way to be both openly gay and politically powerful. You could be in politics, but neither "out" nor advocating for gay rights. Or you could advocate for gay rights, but not from an influential public position in politics and usually at great personal cost. Remember, up until the 2003 *Lawrence v. Texas* Supreme Court decision, even middle- to upper-class white gay men could be arrested in many states for having sex with their consenting adult partners inside their own homes—not to mention having little recourse in enduring a host of indignities and injustices, both legal and customary, including being fired, denied custody of children, attacked, or killed in retaliation for a sexual difference that was prosecuted as grave moral deficiency. This is not to say this group is not, these days, *relatively* advantaged. They are. However, the fact that one can easily slip into thinking (wrongly) that this relative advantage is the *obvious* and *self-evident* reason for the success of the marriage movement is actually the *result* of deliberate movement efforts to alter the public understanding of what it means to be gay, rather than the cause of movement success.

The marriage equality movement did not merely take advantage of a relatively more gay-friendly political environment in the 1990s—there is little evidence that the political environment was gay friendly in the 1990s, and quite a lot of evidence that it was no more gay friendly in 1994 than it had been in 1974. Instead, the movement endeavored to *create* a friendlier political environment for its issue through the repeated and consistent deployment of culturally resonant discourse over time.

I want to be quite clear on the following point: I am not making the argument that successful movements are those that take advantage of serendipitous cultural resonances between their issue(s) and the prevailing ethos of a particular time. Instead, my claim is that movements can actually *change* the politics surrounding their issue through the disciplined use of resonant arguments over time. It is important to use the decline of the union movement as a way to highlight and underscore the difference between these two possible hypotheses, because based on an analysis driven by the first reading, the preexisting friendliness of the political environment toward unions and gay people is decisive regarding their success; in the second, which is the one I wish to advance, it is not. That is because on my analysis, movement actors can take an unfavorable political environment and make it more favorable to their issue over time.

Conclusion

In the preceding two chapters, I have painted a picture of the political genesis of the living wage and marriage equality movements. With a deeper understanding of these two movements, let us now revisit the question that animates this book: how could the legal battle for the marriage rights of a tiny percentage of a commonly maligned group of Americans capture the imagination of the American public, compel a new rubric for elite position taking, and influence the outcomes of numerous political elections both local and national, while the regionally dispersed push for living wages, popular with the public (when people are aware of the issue), which won numerous policy victories in local legislatures all over the country, remains politically obscure, never rising to the level of the national agenda?

In the following chapter, I examine the concept of resonance, which is a key term in the explanation of political acceptance, the phenomenon that has facilitated the differential impact of these two movements. The resonance of political arguments makes a difference in the uptake of issues in a democratic polity. Using a combination of insights from three thinkers not normally read together, Aristotle, Pierre Bourdieu, and Hannah Arendt, I piece together a definition of resonance that helps to specify the symbolic power that scholars and laypeople alike have accorded the concept.

4

The Discursive Architecture
of Resonance

"Resonance" is a term that political observers employ often, but most of the time it is with little specificity. Additionally, few have attempted to answer the question: what makes an idea or argument resonant? The decision-rule implied is: we know it when we hear it. But there is more that we can learn about what makes discourse resonant. I argue that resonant frames combine existing understandings of the way things are, through commonplace logics of the way things work or relate, with new arguments about what is significant or what is to be done. Resonant arguments, and the frames that they combine into, are able to influence people's political understandings and social imaginations more forcefully than other kinds of information and evidence because they inhabit a special discursive space in which background notions, common logics, and new ideas are aligned in a harmonious way.

My choice of the term "harmonious" as a key descriptor of resonance is not only a rhetorical flourish, but is also a nod to the definition of resonance in the physical sciences. That definition is: the tendency of a system to oscillate with greater amplitude at some frequencies than at others. This phenomenon, which occurs widely in nature, means that some points of relation between a force and an object facilitate a great range of movement, while requiring the output of little energy, while other points of relation between force and object require a large expense of energy, while garnering a very slight range of movement. The first kind of force-object relation is described as resonant, while the second is not. Interestingly, the second more frictional relation, which does not produce resonances, has no name and is instead considered the normal state of things. The same can be said of resonance in discourse. Arguments may covary or, extending the analogy, oscillate together along a preexisting harmonic parameter set by *endoxa*, or they might not. Those arguments that do so are resonant.

But how are resonant arguments made? What do they consist of and what accounts for the especially harmonious way certain ideas fit together? The following chapter explores the theoretical underpinning of what I call the architecture of resonance. In it, I review the existing literatures in sociology and political science that make use of the term. I then present my own theory, which pulls together insights from Aristotle, Pierre Bourdieu, and Hannah Arendt.

Because resonance can only be assessed in relation to background understandings of the way things are (*endoxa*) and common-sense logics about the way things relate, it is essential to have a functional understanding of those background understandings, which we often refer to as culture. Thomas Rochon defines culture as "the linked stock of ideas that define the set of commonsense beliefs about what is right, what is natural, what works. These commonsense beliefs are not universal, but are instead typically bounded by time as well as space" (9). For the political scientist, these cultural understandings are important not because they exist, but because the content of these cultural notions conditions and prescribes the way political agents think, speak, and act. Even more significantly, these cultural understandings can and do change over time, and political change often follows. Rochon goes on to observe that "the process of cultural change involves the introduction of contention into how events should be viewed" and further, that "cultural change is completed only when the new values are no longer highly controversial, when they have been accepted as a normal way of thinking" (16).

Gamson's Dialectic View of Resonance

Political challengers introduce contention in a way that facilitates an effective hearing by making resonant arguments. The literature on social movements provides some discussion of how to understand the relationship between culture, resonance, and political change. Sociologist William Gamson provides one of the most attentive and influential descriptions of this relationship, putting forward two related concepts that he calls "cultural resonance" and "narrative fit" in an essay that attempts to explain how researchers can determine "movement impact on cultural change" (Gamson 2006). He writes:

> Not all symbols are equally potent. Some metaphors soar, others fall flat; some visual images linger in the mind, others are quickly forgotten. Some frames have a natural advantage because their ideas and language resonate with a broader political culture. Resonances increase the appeal of a frame by making it appear natural and familiar. (Gamson 2006, 122)

However, this convincing diagnosis of what resonance *does* cannot give us a precise idea of what resonance *is* or, put differently, how resonances are constituted.

Gamson posits that one can identify resonance by examining "the dialectic between cultural themes and counterthemes [that] are linked with each other so that whenever one is invoked, the other is always present in a latent form, ready to be activated with the proper cue" (122). However, I argue that a dialectic view of the components of cultural resonance is too limiting. Dialectics is not a good way to examine public discourse, because public discourse has no telos. There is no ultimate end of public discourse and the relation of what the public is talking about at the moment, in a particular context at a particular time, is contingent and contestable. Instead, I would describe public discourse and the political understandings that emerge from it in Arendtian terms as an "unending activity by which, in constant change and variation, we come to terms with and reconcile ourselves to reality"—a term whose practical meaning is not "the world as it really is," but rather, "the world as we understand it at the moment" (Arendt 1994, 307–308).

Additionally, the notion that discourses are organized around themes and opposite counterthemes implies too neat a relation. While it is true that frames are competitive, it is not the case that they must operate along the same or even parallel lines of logic in order to seem comparable. This is because discourses do not consist of opposites, but fields. In fact, in chapter 5, I show that political challengers stand a better chance when they can redefine what is at stake rather than trying to prove that their opposing argument is more correct or more righteous than the one that is already dominant. In such a contest, what already seems usual, especially backed by the material and other resources of political actors who already have power, will, as Schattschneider observed, almost certainly prevail. Instead, political challengers will have better results if they are able to create a resonant argument that makes the dominant and commonplace interpretation seem a less accurate description of reality, and therefore less relevant to the redefined problem. In other words, the point is not to directly overcome the opposing argument, but instead to change the way that the problem is commonly understood by ordinarily competent members of the polity, thereby changing the range of options thought to be possible and commonsensical.

Of narrative fit, the second component of discourse that makes certain frames ripe for uptake in politics in Gamson's theory, he writes, "Frames provide a narrative structure which leads one to expect certain kinds of future events.... A poor narrative fit with unfolding events that cannot be ignored places the burden of proof on those frames that must make sense of them; with a good narrative fit, unfolding events carry the much easier message: 'I told you so' " (Gamson 2006,

124). Like his definition of cultural resonance, this attentive description of narrative fit is enlightening but ultimately too limiting.

While Gamson acknowledges that any theory seeking to explain why certain frames succeed and others fail "must be based on an epistemology that recognizes facts as social constructions and evidence as taking its meaning from the master frames in which it is embedded (124)," his account still remains wedded to the notion that some kinds of discontinuities between narratives and facts "cannot be ignored." However, it is clear from the ways that political debates play out in practice that there is nothing predetermined about what can be ignored. The set of accepted "facts" is contested. Demonstrably inaccurate information may be treated *as though* it is fact in public discourse, even after repeated and thorough technical debunking. Likewise, even when factual bases are shared, people will freely interpret the same facts to fit their preferred narratives regardless of any discontinuity that might appear obvious to others. For example, discourse on the viability of a living wage is bounded by predominant understandings about what it means to be business-friendly and pro-economic growth, including the mainstream assumption that there is a zero-sum relationship between paying workers well and employing workers at all. That this bit of orthodoxy has repeatedly been called into question empirically has not stopped the anxieties and arguments that flow from it from being taken for granted in mainstream discourse.

As Stephen Skowronek contends: "Political actors are continually seeking out what is culturally resonant and using it for their own purposes" (2006, 387). Indeed, that is what rhetoric is for, according to Aristotle, the theorist with the most systematic definition of the structure and function of rhetoric referenced in political science. Aristotle writes that rhetoric is the ability "to observe the persuasive about 'the given'" (Aristotle 1991, 37). In order to be persuasive, a speaker must have a deep understanding of "the objectives and values of human life" (Aristotle, 57). These insights are equally valid whether one believes, as Aristotle did, that the objectives and values of human life are given by nature, or, as modern social scientists are more likely to, that the objectives and values of human life will depend upon one's particular historical location and cultural lexicon. In this conception, commonly held values set up linguistic hedges that constrain persuasive discourse. These boundaries are neither impenetrable nor static. Yet they are rhetorically sticky, providing the glue of intelligibility and the foundation for resonance that is required for shared political meaning.

Reassociating Old Ideas with New Purposes

I develop a theory of resonance that avoids the limitations of dialectical reason, instead combining the insights of three disparate thinkers: Aristotle, Pierre

Bourdieu, and Hannah Arendt, through a lens that I borrow from Stephen Skowronek, into a philosophically pragmatic view that resists the need for telos to organize our thinking about political change. Instead, I posit that what Ann Swidler has called "culture in action" will and must create new opportunities for the recombination of ideas and purposes over time in both familiar and surprising ways (Skowronek 2006, Swidler 1986). I share Skowronek's view that ideas and purposes are not intrinsically linked, but are instead practically linked in the context of their own political place and time. The connections between ideas and purposes are made by participants in the polity as they articulate their favored political understandings and outcomes. These connections can and will be unmade and remade again in different constellations over time.

Putting the concepts of *endoxa*, commonplaces, and natality in relation helps us better understand what discursive resonance is and how resonant arguments can facilitate political change. These concepts, authored by scholars in different fields, unalike in the times and places that they inhabited and the political ideologies that they championed, can nevertheless be bought together, reassociated in a way that provides insights about how politics works. Specifically, I argue that bringing key concepts in their thought together reveals three elements of public discourse that are necessary for understanding the process of political change. The first is widely accessible and easily understood background beliefs about the way the world is, which are held in a particular time and place. *Endoxa*, unlike, for example, *ethos*, are easily observable in popular discourse. They are the corpus of truisms, idioms, clichés, and advice that are commonly used to describe people's experiences in the world. *Endoxa* are a source of cultural wit and wisdom, and the ideas embedded in them are constitutive of our understandings of how things are even when we find them disagreeable and challenge the veracity of the claims made (e.g., often contested, yet persistently common beliefs like "Boys will be boys").

"Commonplace," a minor term in Bourdieu's *Outline of a Theory of Practice* (1977), is one that I highlight in order to describe the common connections or lines of argument that people within the same polity at the same political time make between ideas present in the *endoxa*. The last term is natality, the condition of the possibility for action in Hannah Arendt's *Human Condition*, but also a major component of her less-well-known essays on political understanding (Arendt 1994). Natality is the capacity of human beings to bring new things into the world, to invent, to act in ways and for purposes that are not predictable and cannot be exactly replicated. Public discourse is constituted by the corpus of these elements of speech and understanding in relation. And, I submit, when the relation between these terms changes, what we believe to be self-evident, possible, probable, or desirable changes too. This process creates new understandings, which seem, at the same time, familiar. And this newness that seems familiar is what we mean when we say that a concept is resonant. Resonant frames pull

Table 4.1 **The Elements of Resonance: Marriage Equality**

	Endoxa *Cultural Wit and Wisdom*	*Commonplace* *Common-sense Logics or, Lines of Reasoning*	*Natality* *New Ideas, Interpretations, and Arguments*	*Resonant Idea*
Marriage equality	Marriage is about "true love" and creating familial ties.	You can't chose whom you love and there are all kinds of families.	Sexuality is innate, not a choice. And same-sex attraction does not nullify the desire to pursue the happiness of family life.	Some people find true, unchosen love with members of the same sex. It is unfair to deny them the right to pursue the happiness of family life with their true love through marriage.

Table 4.2 **The Elements of Resonance: Living Wage**

	Endoxa	*Commonplace*	*Natality*	*Resonant Idea*
Living wage	Hard work should be rewarded.	A better life through hard work is the American dream.	America no longer rewards hard work and that is not only unfair, but a betrayal of the American dream.	Hardworking people deserve to be rewarded for their effort. It is unfair that they should be denied a decent living and a chance at the American dream of a better life.

together old ideas and new purposes using commonly intelligible logics, bundling together distinct and sometimes disparate ideas in a discursive package that seems to go together in a natural way.

For example, content analysis of the discourse on the living wage and marriage equality shows that the most resonant frame in the marriage equality discourse is that love makes a family and that different families deserve the same equal treatment before the law and respect as persons. This frame contains several resonant arguments that combine in a harmonious way, combining the wit and wisdom of *endoxa*, a commonplace line of reasoning, and a new interpretation of the meaning of these familiar ideas (table 4.1).

The most resonant argument in the living wage debate is that full-time workers deserve a living wage. The components of this resonant argument break down as shown in table 4.2.

The "Reassociation of Ideas and Purpose"

Since I am studying contemporary American social movements, it is important to try to understand the current American political *endoxa*. Mid-twentieth-century interpretations of American political thought by political theorists like Louis Hartz (1955) and sociologists such as Gunnar Myrdal (1944) attempted to describe a single tradition of American political thought anchored in and ultimately guided by the normative and institutional conceptions of classical liberalism. However, in the late twentieth century scholars interested in the causes and appeals of oppressed peoples took issue with the story of America as a nation of liberals-at-heart yearning to actualize their true convictions over the petty, clannish, and finally recognizably misguided temptations of racial, sexual, class, and other axes of domination.

In his work *Civic Ideals* (1997) Rogers Smith convincingly debunks the 1950s-style "consensus theories" through an exhaustive examination of prominent figures and political movements in American history, arguing that there are three distinct categories of American ideals in competition over the course of the country's political development. Though liberalism has its place as an anchor of American political thought, he argues, so too does republicanism (defined as the cultivation of community bonds) and what he terms the "ascriptive tradition" (the defense of social, especially racial, hierarchy).

Stephen Skowronek enters this debate with the keen observation that traditions of thought and action are not only not singular—it is unlikely that any plural, democratic culture produces and maintains its institutions and practices with consistent reference to a single ideological source—but are also not at all static. In other words, political actors neither rely on only one source of corrective ideas nor consciously and deliberately shift their allegiance and advocacy among several distinct categories of thought. Instead, Skowronek asserts, ideas and purposes may be formulated and reformulated, mixing, matching, changing, or exchanging many different elements of common belief and original thought in order to suit the political needs and salve the political tensions of a given political time.

Skowronek's observation makes intuitive sense. After all, ideas do not move through time of their own accord as entities eternally pronouncing the intent of the original speaker or reminding new generations of the initial political context. On the contrary, the connection between ideas and purposes, the meaning of a particular concept, and the political actions connoted and denoted are matters of discursive negotiation, the ongoing public discussion of how issues and events relate to our understanding of who we are (especially who is included in the "we"), what we are doing, and what, if anything, we ought to change.

To be clear, the practice of political speech that allows actors to improvise connections between concepts is not reducible to the concept of "spin," which I take to be the disingenuous and cynically received[1] manipulation of facts to suit particular ends. Instead, the "reassociation of ideas and purposes" that I examine references the "reconstruction of meaning" that can take place in political dialogue (Skowronek 2006, 388). Skowronek identifies it as a "creative act of first order significance," one that changes the implications and import of the original idea as it combines with and changes the significance of purposed and accomplished actions (Skowronek 2006, 388).

Notions embedded in *endoxa* live in the present according to their continued usefulness as stories that tell us something about who we are, what we ought to want, and what we ought to do. Indeed, taking up old ideas, asserting their meaning and utility, and finding contemporarily relevant and pragmatic purchase in their principles and implications are the conditions for their continued existence in the political world. To a large extent, the capacity for inherited ideas, ideals, and values to remain defining across time is due to the fact that political actors are "free to pick and choose," appropriating "sources of authority in bits and pieces, stylizing and combining ideas to make their purposes resonate" (Skowronek 2006, 388). Skowronek focuses on the structural and discursive constraints that condition the success of charismatic leaders, while I am more interested in the way that the boundaries of intelligible public discourse also enable the generation and acceptance of the politically new. This quality of the discursive environment, what Emile Durkheim might have called a discursive fact, creates a field of discourse that is at once practically bounded and potentially infinite.

The complexity and contingency of political discourse can, however, be oversold. While there are many moving parts in the activity of discourse, it is not the case that it exists in a terrain too "wild" to be mapped (Habermas [1996] 2000, 307).[2] It is perfectly possible to diagram the ways that ideas and purposes are associated and reassociated over time. The tricky part is deciding what standard to use in accounting for the essential elements of relation between political ideas and purposes. I contend that Aristotle, Bourdieu, and Arendt provide us with three essential terms for the identification and evaluation of resonant discourse.

Aristotle: Translating *Endoxa* into Persuasive Speech

In his three books on rhetoric, Aristotle lays down the foundations for an analytical typology of speech. At the outset, he is careful to set rhetoric apart from

dialectic argumentation and scientific proofs. Unlike the latter two forms of argumentation, rhetoric is not a form that must proceed via syllogism or indeed in any
other particular fashion. Instead, Aristotle considers rhetoric an art that like any
other art has guiding principles, but leaves practitioners free to find the appropriate strategies for filling in the form, giving it shape and meaning. Otherwise
there is no art, but only rules empty of substance. This means that rhetoric is
the "ability in each [particular] case, to see the available means of persuasion"
(1355a). The available means of persuasion are located in *endoxa*—those ways
of observing, describing, and interpreting the world that are generally understood to be common, familiar, and usual. Explained in this way, *endoxa* could be
misunderstood as mere boundaries or limiting aspects of thought and action.
However, *endoxa* are not only a limit, but also the foundation of innovation. The
reality of the new, in political discourse (as in any other case), is that it does not
appear afresh out of the ether; instead, it is constructed from existing knowledge,
understandings, and beliefs.

Rhetoric is built from *endoxa* and takes the form of an *enthymeme*. An
enthymeme is an argument that leaves the premises unstated because they are
considered obvious and commonsensical. Aristotle contrasts this form to the
more scientific syllogism, which is an argument based on deductive logic that
requires all premises be explicitly stated and subject to proofs. Enthymemic
rhetoric is suited to communication in mass publics because it is broadly accessible. Syllogisms are ill suited to mass communication about complex topics for
several reasons. First, syllogisms not only follow the form of deductive logic but
require conclusions that are certain. Politics is a realm of opinion and contestation and certainty is rarely on offer. Second, even when syllogisms might be
possible in politics, they would require specialized knowledge that cannot reasonably be expected from the general population. It is also important to note
that while syllogisms are suited to making correct claims, enthymemes are suited
to making resonant claims. This is because an enthymeme can weave together
endoxa, commonplaces, and natality in a single statement, whereas syllogisms
require a chain of connected logical reasoning, often requiring specialized
knowledge not available to ordinarily competent persons.

I do not make the distinction between syllogism and enthymeme to valorize
the former and condemn the latter. As Aristotle pointed out, different forms of
argument are appropriate to different topics and different ends. Syllogistic discourse is well suited to science, where the community of interlocutors has been
trained to a high level of specialized knowledge on a narrow range of subjects
and the ends are best satisfied by technical accuracy and logical correctness. It
is, however, ill suited to politics, where the community of interlocutors is broad
and diverse, having general knowledge and expertise in a variety of areas and the
determination of the ends is precisely what is at issue. For politics, rhetoric and

its formal vehicle of argument, the enthymeme, are the proper tool for the task at hand.

Aristotle goes on to point out that the rhetorical translation of endoxa can be accomplished using three modes of speech. These three main modes of speech, or *pisteis*, are identified as *logos*, or logic, *pathos*, or emotion, and *ethos*, or character. To be clear, rhetorical argument in the mode of logos is not the same as a syllogism. While syllogisms always proceed in a deductive fashion from stated premises to certain conclusions, rhetorical argument via logos may proceed inductively from evidence to probable (though not certain) conclusions or even abductively, from observation to the simplest or most economical conclusions. A rhetorical use of *logos* may involve the introduction of statistics to prove a point or rely on the testimony of scientific authorities to explain some observed phenomenon, but such claims must still be judged according to various criteria brought to bear by the audience, not by the single standard of logical certainty.

Of the three modes of persuasion *ethos* is the one Aristotle spends the most time exploring because it is the least self-evident. That a speaker might persuade by logic or by moving the audience into a particular emotional state of mind is easy to understand, but how is it that the speaker can create a disposition toward belief (in both the message and the messenger) in the audience? Aristotle contends that competent rhetoricians are able to do so by presenting themselves as a certain kind of person—the kind of person who is trustworthy, fair-minded, and wise—through their speech. I should take a moment to dally on this point, because it might appear that *ethos* is a characteristic of the speaker and not of the speech, but that is not the case. Persuasion by *ethos* is a form of argument in which the speaker is able to convey a certain kind of character to the audience, but this character is created *in speech*, not outside or antecedent to it. In addition, this persuasive character is pieced together based upon the *endoxa* or commonly held notions extant in a particular time and place.

Aristotle expands on this point in book 1 of *The Rhetoric*:

> There is persuasion through character whenever the speech is spoken in such a way as to make the speaker worthy of credence; for we believe fair-minded people to a greater extent and more quickly [than we do others] on all subjects in general and completely so in cases where there is not exact knowledge but room for doubt. *And this should result from speech, not from a previous opinion that the speaker is a certain kind of person.* (1356a; emphasis added)

Argument by *ethos* requires that speakers be able to present themselves as "worthy of credence," something that rhetors can show by demonstrating that they have "practical wisdom," "virtue," and "goodwill." The quality of goodwill, or fair-mindedness, combined with commonplace wisdom that can be shown in the manner of argument is what gives credence to a particular argument and credibility to a particular speaker, especially in those instances in which general opinion is not settled on the matter and there is room for doubt. This is the case with most controversial political questions. When deciding such questions then, logic does not necessarily satisfy the argument, as a proof is often devoid of the kinds of nonrational, yet profoundly influential considerations that may enter into making judgments. Likewise, appeal through emotion alone is often ineffective because such appeals work as amplifiers. The amplification of emotion is useful to persuaders only if a fact or story can be relied upon to produce predictable and similar emotional responses in most members of the audience. This kind of appeal works best in instances in which common opinion is already settled and all the speaker has to do is point to the agreed-upon norm and invoke the affect that usually corresponds to situations like the one being spoken about. In cases in which first premises and goals are not shared, *ethos* becomes a decisive mode of argumentation because the speaker must rely on his awareness of "the objectives and values of human life," which often provide additional premises that are held in a particular society and time to be significant and enduring enough to help decide tough cases (Aristotle 1991, 56).

Examples of the Modes of Speech and Their Best Uses

There are many cases in which political discourse cannot proceed deliberatively, with the audience of judges weighing the quality of evidence of one against the other. Premises and ends may not be generally agreed upon, the evidentiary referent of one side may not have any standing for the others (as in the case of particular religious texts or philosophies), or there may exist a simple mistrust of the motives and intentions of the party attempting to persuade.

For an example I turn to the abortion debate. This debate has become intransigent in American political life largely because those on either side of the issue believe that they share no common ground—their premises about when life begins and their goals concerning which entity deserves legal protection, woman or fetus, do not seem to overlap. It is important to note that this divergence, though seemingly fundamental is, in large part, an artifact of discourse, specifically, the way that the "pro" and "anti" positions have been characterized as irrevocable in mainstream political speech. An examination of political attitudes on the subject shows quite a bit more nuance to the positions of members of the polity than the stalking horses of "pro-life" and "pro-choice" lead one to believe. The authors of a Pew Research Center analysis released on October 3, 2005, put it this way, "While activists on both sides describe abortion as an issue on which there is no middle ground, decades of polling have shown public opinion on abortion to be anything but black-and-white." In fact, in every survey that Pew has conducted since 1989 more than two out of three respondents have rejected overturning *Roe v. Wade*. However, opinion on who should have access to abortion and at what stage of pregnancy it is permissible is highly dependent on circumstances, and differences in question wording can produce huge effects. Generally speaking, while there is little support for making abortion illegal, there is wide support for a range of restrictions on abortion. Pew reports, "Polling in recent years has shown large majorities favor such measures as mandatory waiting periods, parental and spousal notification, and a prohibition on late-term abortions."[3]

However, despite the range of opinion that exists in the polity the pro-life and pro-choice positions are constructed, not only rhetorically, but by and through the efforts of grass-roots organizers on either side, as well as in relation to the legal framework and institutional consequences that have been codified in response to their challenges, to be static, decisive labels that signify inflexible positions. This is not to say that the pro-choice and pro-life constructions have no practical effect. They do provide very real boundaries surrounding discussion and action in regard to this issue.

Likewise, there are plenty of examples of those cases in which the same happening provokes strong yet various emotional responses, making appeal through the amplification of the audience's emotional state, or *pathos*, ineffective. Take the case of a traumatic event such as the myriad school shootings that have taken place in the first decades of the twenty-first century, most affectingly, the slaughter of twenty first-grade children and six of their educators at Sandy Hook Elementary in Newtown, Connecticut in December of 2012. According to a poll conducted on April 23 of the following year by the Pew Research Center, 60 percent of Americans believe that it is more important to control gun ownership than to protect the right of individuals to own guns. However, a sizable and vocal minority of Americans, 32 percent, think that protecting the right of individuals to own guns is more important than controlling gun ownership.

The proportions of this divergence of opinion have been stable since the 1980s and were unchanged in the wake of the Columbine shooting in 1999, the Amish schoolhouse shootings in 2007, or the tragedy at Virginia Tech the same year. Anyone with exposure to any news outlet witnessed the affecting scenes in the aftermath of these events, but the occurrence did not change the stable and opposing positions extant in the polity. Instead, the emotionally evocative spectacle served to reinforce the preexisting views that were already present among citizens. Gun control activists who held up the events as examples underscoring their policy positions, relying on the emotional stimulus inherent in the occurrences to make their case, would fail to persuade. Rather, the fact of the event merely reinforces preexisting and diverse sentiments about its meaning.

Ethos is the most powerful mode of persuasive speech because it can change the domain of decision-making in a political disagreement. That is, argument by ethos can allow the speaker to change people's ideas about what is at stake without seeking to break down or correct their premises about what counts as the good life. This is because, for ethotic speakers, the force of the argument comes from their capacity to cultivate belief or trust in their ability to be a good judge in tough cases. The ethotic speaker can say, "We should be concerned with *this* rather than *that*," using his knowledge of the "objectives and goals of human life" as demonstrated in speech as his evidence. Knowledge of the objectives and goals of human life cannot be presented as authored by the speaker, but derives its persuasive potency from the fact that it is a resonant translation of *endoxa*. This ability to translate gives the speaker a special kind of credibility with the audience who shares the same background knowledge about what is generally considered valuable in their place and time because it means that the audience doesn't have to trust that you know what is right in every instance; they can instead trust that you know how to decide in tough cases. Argument by *logos*, on the other hand, assumes the terms in which the question is posed, while argument by *pathos* uses those terms to try to evoke an emotional response in the audience.

In these tough cases, which are common in politics, the kind of argument with the greatest chance to persuade, to move people to a new way of thinking or a new point of view, is the one that relies not strictly upon the projected outcome of the controversy if it is decided one way or another, but just as much on the audience's impression of the speaker as equipped with the tools for good analysis and judgment. Importantly, these tools cannot be limited to the idioms of a particular group; they must be accessible to the majority. This is because, when deciding a hard case, it is just as important to trust the information and analysis of the speaker as it is to know the material facts of the situation. Aristotle reminds us that political trust is, at some basic level, based upon affinity, the invocation of a particular (broad or narrow) we, who understand things to be a certain way. I argue that this is true whether the audience of judges, who in a democratic society are all the members of the public, are able, in their final judgment, to agree with the speaker or not. Of course, the finality of any one member of the public's judgment is a fiction; whatever subjects are considered worthy topics of discussion, whether they have been formally decided or not, are in play, available for the consideration and reconsideration of the polity and therefore vulnerable to reformulation, reassociation, and re-presentation by speakers intending to persuade.

Logos, Pathos, and Ethos in Movement Discourse

In the contemporary debate on marriage equality the various logical arguments for and against allowing two individuals of the same sex to enter into a state-sanctioned union often proceed in parallel, neither beginning from the same premises nor ending with the same goal. Likewise, while emotions run high in regard to the topic, the emotions of those who favor the change in policy and those who oppose it seem diametrically opposed, in part because they are motivated by disparate evaluations of American social and political history, different opinions about what's at stake for the majority of the polity, and distinct interpretations of consequences and goals.

In a 1996 *New York Times* editorial, Lisa Schiffren, a former speech writer for Dan Quayle, wrote:

> The Hawaii courts will likely rule that gay marriage is legal, and other states will be required to accept those marriages as valid. Considering what a momentous change this would be—a radical redefinition of society's most fundamental institution—there has been almost no real debate. This is because the premise is unimaginable to many, and the forces of political correctness have descended on the discussion, raising the cost of opposition. But one may feel the same affection for one's homosexual friends and relatives as for any other, and be genuinely pleased for the happiness they derive from relationships, while opposing gay marriage for principled reasons. "Same-sex marriage" is inherently incompatible with our culture's understanding of the institution.... A society struggling to recover from 30 years of weakened norms and broken families is not likely to respond gently to having an institution central to most people's lives altered.

What is at stake in this formulation of the debate is society's very foundation—a foundation that according to the speaker's premise is rooted in heterosexual marriage and other values lost as the norms of social practice have been assaulted by the forces of "political correctness" over the last several decades. This battering of tradition, according to the author, has resulted in negative consequences, indeed, a public struggle that transcends our private affection for relatives and friends with what she clearly considers unfortunate lifestyles. The presented goal here is to persist in, or even return to, a more traditional way of life, one that would ostensibly produce better outcomes for everyone. The last, though, goes without saying and certainly without argument. In fact introducing an argument for this assumption would actually weaken her rhetorical position because it would open up questions about the correctness of the premise instead of putting the onus of explanation on the alien, indeed commonly "unimagined," and concordantly unmentioned, premise(s) that underlie the idea of same-sex marriage. The reason this might work is that the author is plausibly banking on the prospect that a sufficient proportion of her audience will tacitly accept the assumption without having it explicitly stated or argued for.

In addition to defining the public aspect of the problem in a particular way, the speaker attempts to show herself to be fair minded in this passage. Not by explicitly declaring herself to be wise and even-handed, for such an assertion is persuasive to no one—as any writer of fiction knows, the skillful practitioner is able to show instead of tell. Here, Schiffren attempts to show herself to be fair-minded by acknowledging with sympathy the complicated feelings that attend associations among diverse people. Still despite our real and complex personal feelings, the unspoken part of her argument goes, sentiment is a private matter. The issue that should be of general concern is whether the society that we are all familiar with, that we all either do or should cherish, can stand the degradation of this traditional, indeed foundational, institution that undergirds the good life. Interestingly, from Schiffren's point of view she is making an argument from *logos*, or by calling on logic. She is making what she presents as a definitional distinction between personal or private attachments and the principles that ought to inform public policy. It is through making the claim for this logical distinction, as opposed to a distinction based in *pathos*, that the author attempts to create the impression of fair-mindedness, enabling her to credibly project the character that argument from *ethos* demands. This example demonstrates the fact that an individual statement not only can have many valences in terms of interpretation, but also work from more than one basis of persuasive argumentation. Indeed, the most effective arguments are able to incorporate several modes of argumentation into a single utterance. With this presentation she shows the audience that hers is not an argument about acrimony toward a particular person or group of persons, but instead one about social sustenance, the preservation and ever resuscitation of a way of life that, the narrative argument implies, we all benefit from and ought to value.

An example of a common pro-gay marriage formulation takes a very different tack, beginning from completely different premises and highlighting entirely dissimilar consequences and goals. However, the premises and goals are still presented as usual, enduring, subscribed to by all of us. This *New York Times* editorial, also written in 1996, presents the following case:

> Chances are that Americans will look back 30 years from now and wonder what all the fuss was about. . . . Opponents of same-sex marriages invoke religious tradition and family values. Allowing same-sex couples to marry, they assert, would somehow diminish the meaning of marriage for heterosexuals. These arguments, uncomfortably similar to those raised in resistance to repealing miscegenation laws a few decades ago, cannot obscure the entrenched anti-gay bigotry underlying much of the public dialogue. Nor can it disguise the fundamental unfairness

of government denying a whole class of citizens the important benefits
that flow from civil marriages.

The basis of this argument is exactly opposite the one above. Here, the interpretation of American history as tending toward increasing social tolerance is
what is at stake. The last thirty years of social and political history are seen as
building toward progress, not breaking down cherished institutions. Unfairness,
based not on an imperative that might be justifiable, the sustenance of our way of
life, but only upon petty bigotry, is the fundamental issue that the author wishes
us to consider. The goal is to be, as the reformers of the African American civil
rights movement were, on the "right side of history."

This author invokes a universally understood interpretation of history from
the black civil rights movement in order to make himself seem fair-minded, not
a partisan ideologue. We are charged, the author asserts, to be the ones who
recognize the necessity of justice and concede what is deserved to the "whole
class of citizens" being unjustly denied. By invoking antimiscegenation laws as
the congruent paradigm for viewing anti-gay marriage efforts, the author casts
himself as a righteous and apolitical dissenter in that if his analogy holds water,
then he is not on the side of "liberals" or "conservatives," but simply what is right
or, even more stirringly, what is American. After all, what is more American
than progress? In this way we see the author weave together an argument from
pathos or emotional appeal (what we all know is right), while also using *ethos* as
a modality of persuasion. The future-oriented reference to the passage of time
and the change in views that comes with it combined with the invocation of
the miscegenation laws that bared interracial marriage until the 1960s is also an
instance of showing instead of telling. It calls upon the reader to remember that
we have heard this story before and we know who the good guys are. Even more
importantly, we know how it must end if we are to become who we already know
ourselves to be as Americans.

To finish out the paragraph, the author emphasizes civility, both its valence as
a governing ideal for interpersonal interaction as well as the older definition that
implies the obligations of political society and citizenship. We have chosen in the
past to be uncivil, the author reminds us, but we have learned our lesson and are
now equipped with the wisdom to see through the "disguise." In this way, he calls
not only on the nostalgia of the audience, but also evokes a sense of comfortable
progress, a progress without uncertainty or risk because the end is both already
known and already known to be just.

There is still another line of argument that is worth considering, one that is vig-
orously made in left, queer circles, which is against marriage, including same-sex
marriage, because it is seen as a conservative, even regressive institution, which
is at best irrelevant and at worst detrimental to advancing social justice. This

perspective was and is less commonly forwarded in the mainstream media, but there have been moments of its emergence, especially in the mid-1990s before coverage of gay marriage reached its peak of influence on the national political debate. This left, antimarriage argument is distinct from the other two in terms of its basis, what it identifies as the public trouble, and the consequences reported.

In the following passage, editorialist Frank Browning questions one of premises on which the most common opposing arguments are based, that is, the health and efficacy of traditional heterosexual marriage itself. He writes:

> I suppose it's a good thing for gay adults to be offered the basic nuptial rights afforded to others. We call that equal treatment before the law. But I'm not sure the marriage contract is such a good plan for us. The trouble with gay marriage is not its recognition of our "unnatural unions." The problem is with the shape of marriage itself. What we might be better off seeking is civic and legal support for different kinds of families that can address the emotional, physical and financial obligations of contemporary life. By rushing to embrace the standard marriage contract, we could stifle one of the richest and most creative laboratories of family experience. We gay folk tend to organize our lives more like extended families than nuclear ones. We may love our mates one at a time, but our "primary families" are often our ex-lovers and our ex-lovers' ex-lovers. The writer Edmund White noticed this about gay male life 20 years ago; he called it the "banyan tree" phenomenon, after the tree whose branches send off shoots that take root to form new trunks. Nowhere has the banyan-tree family proved stronger than in AIDS care, where often a large group of people—ex-mates and their friends and lovers—tend the sick and maintain the final watch. Modern marriage, by comparison, tends to isolate couples from their larger families and sometimes from friends—especially if they are ex-lovers. And a nuclear family with working parents has often proved less than ideal in coping with daily stresses or serious illness.[4]

First the author places himself in the existing debate by affirming the commonplace idea that equal treatment before the law is always a good thing. However, he attempts to further the argument by asserting that while juridical inclusion in the institution of marriage is morally right, it might also be practically dysfunctional. He then states that the problem of marriage does not rest in the allowance of "unnatural unions," which the author smartly deigns to even engage on the way to his more interesting point, which is that the institution of marriage itself is flawed. This is a beginning in *logos*, but unlike the argument that Schiffren uses, this argument is complex, making several connecting claims instead of a simple distinction. Here the argument is that traditional marriage is not big enough to hold the complexities of modern life. Although this appeal is meant to hail publics other than gays, namely anyone who feels that the tension between the way institutions have been traditionally arranged and their ability to meet the exigencies of daily life, the bridge between gay "banyan tree" families and failing traditional families is rickety with connections that are not necessarily obvious. In addition, such an argument seems to dismiss or set aside the aspirational meaning people invest in marriage even as they simultaneously and readily recognize its practical limitations (Swidler 2001). This misstep is where many rhetorical arguments in the mode of *logos* fail, by assuming that arguments that are *logical*—reasoned in accordance with the principles of logic—are always identical to and synonymous with arguments that *make sense*—that is, help us understand who we are (and want to be) in the world.

Browning suggests that contemporary marital love is isolating and shows its fragility when families are at their most vulnerable, but he doesn't include an example of how gay families and "regular" families are vulnerable in many of the same ways. Put differently, the argument needs to be crafted so that gays and straights are explicitly and intelligibly under the banner of the same vis-à-vis contemporary organization of personal and familial security.

Browning appeals to the cultural specter of AIDS, the devastating impact of which was, in 1996, fresh in the minds of most people who had lived in or around gay urban communities, but had not yet become an experience often shared beyond those publics. It is the case that AIDS awareness in America was at its peak in the mid-1990s, having exited the closet of the disease-that-shall-not-be-named and become, through the creative and effective efforts of gay activist organizations like ACT UP, the cause célèbre of worldly schoolchildren, artists, politicians, and the otherwise hip and famous, but the familial challenges that the disease presented might easily be due to the particular circumstances of gay people who were, at the time, often estranged from their nuclear families.

The author does attempt to point out similarities in negative outcomes for all kinds of modern families by pointing out that most families must struggle to make ends meet and provide care to dependent children, parents, or seriously ill family members. His strongest volley in this direction is when he points out that if there are only two responsible adults in a household and they are both working, as well as isolated from a larger community of supportive intimates, their challenges will be many and difficult to surmount. After this assertion Browning invites the reader to consider attending to what he argues is the general weakness of the nuclear family and try something new. This should be the focus for the new domain of decision-making that he proposes, essentially arguing that marriage reduces social isolation and provides security, but not enough to solve the problems that we all encounter regardless of sexual orientation and diverse familial arrangements.

In this passage, the author puts himself in positive relation to the equal rights side of the gay marriage debate, but does not, as the other two arguments do, appeal to any kind of commonplace value or set of values to situate himself as a credible speaker. In this way, Browning misses the opportunity to make an argument from *ethos*. Instead, Browning gives us a well-thought-out, but seemingly particular, take on a social issue. The argument makes no appeal to a generally accessible and resonant interpretation of history. It makes no appeal to commonly held emotional interpretations, and keeps the reader who considers themselves outside Browning's groups of reference at a great distance. The frame of this argument, if we were to strip away the content, is not, as it was for the previous arguments respectively, "For the sake of a healthy society, we must all do what's right (even if it is personally painful)," or "Let us learn from our past mistakes and live up to the demonstrated greatness of America to overcome petty prejudice," but instead, "If you think about it, our cherished institution doesn't work that well, especially for my minority. Why not chuck it and start anew?" You can see the disadvantage.

To be fair, the kind of argument that Browning wants to make—establishing oneself as credible while demonstrating a commitment to a particularity that the speaker has no intention of collapsing into a narrative of ultimate similarity ("we're all human, after all"; "we're all Americans") is the most difficult kind of argument to make persuasively. And perhaps the evidence of the difficulty is in the delivery, which appears, in terms of persuasive modalities of argument, quite unmoored. As stated above, Browning's argument requires more than one logical step to grasp its basis, and even if an ordinarily competent reader grasps the starting point, it is difficult to ascertain what principle is then at stake. This makes argument from both *pathos* and *ethos* very difficult, and since the author employs neither form it is highly unlikely that people attuned to generally accessible ways of thinking about the good life will find what the author presents to be resonant with their own attitudes, understandings, and observations.

By keeping his frame of reference contemporary, his reference group particular, and emphasizing the need for a potentially radical response to a new and perhaps frightening problem, Browning gives people who don't already agree with his way of seeing the world little to use for anchor. Without appeals to history, tradition, goodness, rightness, the roots of civilization, American identity-affirmation, or any other principles that are generally considered to transcend particular circumstances, his argument is at a disadvantage because it seems to be concerned with issues that are less weighty and more distant from general concern. The proportion of old to new is out of balance, and the appeal to the general is outweighed by education about the particular.

While the speaker does use some knowledge of the contemporary *ethos* of individual frustration in the face of institutional indifference to craft his argument, he does not draw upon a historical or principled narrative to root his position. While his argument is valid and accurate, this is a rhetorical mistake. When the orator asks society to make a choice between reproducing itself as it is or producing some seemingly significant change, the most successful appeal must "put itself in the right" (Bourdieu 1977, 22) by making claims to the principles that help organize popular understandings of ourselves in the world, not merely matters of logical or practical convenience.

By themselves, experienced as a single iteration, none of the preceding arguments from mainstream discourse are likely to persuade a conflicted listener, let alone those who avow a particular ideological label such as liberal, conservative, progressive, or queer. However, what is important here is that these appeals attempt a similar tone, each making claims not only about the way society should be, but also observations about the way things already are. In addition to exhibited cultural wisdom and goodwill, persuasive speech attempting to utilize the principles of *ethos* must establish the speaker as a reliable observer of reality. The main way speakers can do this is by demonstrating their ability to precisely identify the workings of the usual, in the same argument in which they are able to show even-handed facility in integrating the new.[5] Even those who are not persuaded to the position that the speaker is trying to advance can be convinced, through the presentation of the issue, about whether the topic is of immediate public importance or a matter of private dispute. That is why public persuasion requires the *political acceptance* of an issue as worth consideration by the mass public.

For challengers, persuading the national audience to grant their cause such consideration is a win in and of itself because it means that the ordinarily competent citizen finds their claims intelligible and worthy of attention, even if not agreement. Even when public opinion is not sympathetic to challenger claims, responses to those claims that validate what challengers believe is at stake, introduce an element of risk for the status quo because they raise the issue from the presumptive background ether of "goes without saying" to the deliberative platform of contestability.

Bourdieu and the Habits of Practice

The sometimes controversial French sociologist Pierre Bourdieu is best known for his work *Distinction,* in which he parses the relationship of the individual subject to social structures such as those conditioning the family, the workplace, and the state. He is often read as a rigid structuralist, detailing a social logic that is essentially deterministic, in which individual responses to social situations can always be predicted by investigating the norms present in their social class. For this reason, some scholars read (or simply dismiss) Bourdieu as denying the empirical variety of social experience present within and between classes and, even worse, not adequately attending to the question of agency (Honneth 1995, Swartz 1997). I believe this to be a misreading. Bourdieu himself denies being a strict structuralist, claiming that to focus on the "structure of signs, that is, the relationships between them, at the expense of their practical function" is to miss out on a large chunk of meaning. Indeed, it is this rejection of linguistic structuralism that causes him to reject discourse as a fruitful site of analysis outside its connection with cultural practices. Of course, discourses are deeply embedded in cultural practices, but because Bourdieu thought of studying discourse as identical with Saussurean structuralism, he missed that discourse, and the changes it can catalyze, provides a way out of habit. This is because discourse is the vehicle that political actors can use to change common understandings, thereby providing a reason to change common practices. Discourses that shift the domain of decision-making through using rhetorical arguments do so not by highlighting rational inconsistencies, which only goes so far, but instead by providing new practical understandings.

Still, it is fair to say that Bourdieu is more interested in how and why people reproduce social structures (especially those that create negative consequences for those in their social position) than the ability of actors to alter the structures in which they find themselves. But in putting together his detailed analysis of how practice becomes habit, he also develops a less explicit account of how habits can be broken and reconstituted in new ways. For Bourdieu, habit and invention are not polar opposites. In fact, they are not easily separable. Instead, they are two aspects of the same reproductive process, that is, the way that people live out their lives in the contexts in which they find themselves. It is true that reproducing old habits is more common than innovating new practices, but even when people practice centuries-old rituals, these reproduced practices are deliberate, not automatic. All practices take place "in-play," necessitating a series of strategic choices by the agent—choices that inscribe the familiar activities with presently relevant meaning.

Those who have been long socialized in the environment where a particular activity takes place, what Bourdieu terms the *habitus*, know their position in-play by experience. With the (often implicit) knowledge of their place in the daily social world of activity, actors are able to make choices about what they will do, determine what they are responsible for, decide who is like or different and what is owed to either, as well as a whole host of other judgments. Bourdieu (1977) calls this everyday knowledge that guides practice "practical mastery" or "competence." Interestingly, for Bourdieu, this practical mastery is not primarily expressed in language. Indeed, actors often will not have immediately articulable reasons for all their competent habits of practice. Bourdieu hypothesizes that language entails a different kind of competence, which is underlined by a "repertoire of rules," a necessarily formalized system of intelligibility that competent practice does not require and that may even confuse or frustrate it.

Bourdieu does not make much of the way that language can frustrate practice, but he does describe how important it is to habit, ritual, and tradition that actors misrecognize their new reproductions as identical with the old. Otherwise, the illusory yet foundational tie between what is usually done and what must be done now becomes visible, weakening the authorizing power of the *habitus* and creating the potential for instability and the attendant opening for new explanations, activities, and even the development of new commonplaces.

Bourdieu misses that language is the most potent tool that one can use to point out and highlight differences between the meaning of the habit of yesterday and the necessity of the practice of today. Over time such interruptions can create ruptures in the tenuous and misrecognized link between habit and necessity. Bourdieu argues that when the tether between the two is broken, the result is a "reflection on practices, which impose new meanings" and create new opportunities for action (1977, 20). This effect, which can have a great impact on the individual level, can also alter the commonplaces present in society if it takes place in the mass public.

The ability to improvise is essential for meeting "the challenges of existence." Indeed, it is a talent that seems to belong to all sentient creatures to some degree. Otherwise survival, not to mention the peculiarly human inventions of language, sociality, and politics, would be quite impossible. There simply isn't a rule or norm to govern every case. Luckily, Bourdieu notes, we do not require a one-to-one congruence between rules and socially intelligible and/or appropriate behaviors and speech (Wittgenstein 2001). In fact, "However close [analysts] may come to decoding the logic of practices . . . , the abstract diagram which has to be constructed in order to account for that logic is liable to obscure the fact that the driving force of the whole mechanism is not some abstract principle . . . , still less the *rules* which can be derived from it," but is instead the *sense* of the way things are usually done or the way people ought properly to interact (15). This sense, according to Bourdieu, is "a disposition inculcated in the earliest years of life and constantly reinforced by calls to order from the group" (15). It is this sense of things that underlies the concept of resonance. It is from this pool of common knowledge that rhetoricians must draw their persuasive ammunition; it is the figurative ground upon which the new, if it is to be accepted, must be built.

Those concerned about the tendency of some scholars in the structuralist tradition to oversimplify complex and variable human interactions into rigid categories that attempt to totalize individual experience are often wary of the claim that a single standard of social "sense" can characterize any society, especially a modern plural one. This is a valid worry. As Nancy Fraser (1990), Michael

Dawson (2001), Michael Warner (2002), and Melissa Harris-Perry (2004) have shown, mass publics contain sub- and counterpublics who may have standards of speech and behavior that are very different than those maintained by the dominant group(s). Still, Bourdieu's improvement over previous scholars of the commonplace, like Aristotle, is that he does not seek to provide a catalog of all possible norms. Instead, he makes an argument at the typological level: whatever the point of reference (in my family, in my neighborhood, in my country, or simply among people like me), such standards *always* exist, and the scope and variety of the application of that standard will *never* be completely codified in rules or laws. Instead, what the *habitus* inculcates in people born into it is "strategy generating principle[s] enabling agents to cope with unforeseen and ever-changing situations" (Bourdieu 1977, 72).

Bourdieu shows us how common logics allow people to translate *endoxa* in specific ways, connecting ideas with purposes. He has something to say about how people can successfully make these connections. The most successful players in the political game can use social mores to their advantage if "the values they pursue or propose are presented in the misrecognizable guise of the values in which the group recognizes itself" (Bourdieu 1977, 22). Even when the actor improvises in a way that takes her out of established norms, in order to put herself in the right and prove to be the kind of speaker the audience ought to give credence, increasing the likelihood that she will be able to persuade people to her view, she must seem to honor some aspect of the groups ethics. By "falling into line with good form, [s]he wins the group over to [her] side by ostentatiously honoring the values the group honors" (Bourdieu, 22). Bourdieu points our attention toward the way that the common logics arising from the *endoxa* connect agents to structures, not causing them to behave in lockstep with preexisting scripts, but instead causing them to act in the context of what is commonly understood to be possible, true, just, or what have you. He notes that the most successful actors accomplish their discursive and practical aims precisely because they use intelligible commonplace logics that "put them in the right," in relation to *endoxa*.

In Bourdieu's description of practice, recitation is not the same as reproduction. Agents work to make their practice "regular" by reference to a set of shared norms that they have learned in the *habitus*. He argues that "strategies aimed at producing 'regular' practices are one category, among others, of *officializing strategies*, the object of which is to transmute 'egoistic', private, particular interests . . . into disinterested, collective, publicly avowable, legitimate interests" (Bourdieu 1977, 40). He goes on to explain that "political action proper can be exercised only by the effect of officialization and thus presupposes the *competence* . . . required in order to manipulate the collective definition of the situation in such a way as to bring it close to the official definition of the situation and thereby to win the means of mobilizing the largest possible group." Of course, there is often more than one official definition of events, and the "closeness" that Bourdieu speaks of may be accomplished by either bringing the challenging definitions nearer to official ones, dragging official definitions into proximity of challenging concepts, or a bit of both.

As Skowronek has noted, a particular discourse may be authorized by refer- ence to a venerable thinker, principle, or ideology and also may be put to con- temporary use for a project quite different from the original. This gives actors the power to "impose a definition of the situation, especially in the moments of crisis when the collective judgment falters." Political actors may also do the opposite, either deliberately or by mistake. That is, it is also in actors' power to demobilize the group with regard to a particular concern by "disowning the person [or people] directly concerned, who, in failing to identify [her] particu- lar interest with the 'general interest'" reduces her concern "to the status of the mere individual, condemned to appear unreasonable in seeking to impose . . . private reason" (Bourdieu 1977, 40). In order to figure out what kinds of speech and action will meet the criterion of the reasonable and public as opposed to the unreasonable and private, one must bring to bear "a whole body of wisdom, say- ings, commonplaces, ethical precepts . . . and, at a deeper level, the unconscious principles of the *ethos*" (Bourdieu 1977, 77).[6]

The speaker is dealing not with rules as much as an entire common-sense world that, though not objective in terms of being materially represented, is treated as objective because it is endowed with a "consensus on the meaning . . . of practices and the world" (Bourdieu 1977, 80). It is the commonplace world with which the persuasive speaker must wrestle, and it is in regard to this world that her strategies must be applied. Clifford Geertz puts the matter this way:

> The unspoken premise from which common sense draws its authority [is] that it presents reality neat. If common sense is as much an interpre- tation of the immediacies of experience, a gloss on them, as are myth, painting, epistemology, or whatever, then it is, like them, historically constructed and, like them, subjected to historically defined standards of judgment. It can be questioned, disputed, affirmed, developed, for- malized, contemplated, even taught, and it can vary dramatically from one people to the next. It is, in short, a cultural system . . . and it rests on the same basis that any other such system rests; the conviction by those whose possession it is of its value and validity. (Geertz 1983, 76)

Bourdieu, like Skowronek, reminds us that the new, in order to be recog- nized as such, must in some sense fit with what we already know (or think we know) about how things are or the way the world works. It is this harmonious congruence between familiarity and newness that can give certain speech a resonant quality. Successful rhetoricians are able to authorize both themselves and their words through the use of already-believed notions in order to win credence for themselves and the association between ideas and purposes that they advocate.

While Skowronek is particularly interested in the movement of ideas across time, and Aristotle in their mode of expression, Bourdieu makes an argument about what constraints an actor is under when improvising a new connection between what is already known or believed and what might come to be known and believed. In the next section, Hannah Arendt helps us to understand the particular necessity and efficacy of this potential newness in politics.

Arendt, Publicity, and Natality

In order to be stable the world must be familiar, but in order to survive the circumstances of fate we must be able to adapt. Likewise, political change can be stimulated when a speaker proves herself to be the kind of person wise enough to decide whether and how to adapt in tough cases. The rhetorician is able to do this through the use of resonant speech. We are often able to identify and even celebrate new ideas, but they reach the pinnacle of their influence on our practical, daily experience when we cease to recognize our new orientations as such. When we begin to act in our conversations as though new relationships of intelligibility are common, usual, and familiar, then they become founding ideas of their own and we repeat them, no longer challenging their basic constitution even if we question the rightness, appropriateness, or effectiveness of the purposes they champion, the activities they imply, or the policies that they occasion.

Arendt writes, "The human condition comprehends more than the conditions under which life is given to man. Men are conditioned beings because everything they come in contact with turns immediately into a condition of their existence" ([1958] 1998, 9). In this assessment Arendt seems to echo Bourdieu, though they are not two thinkers normally placed side by side. Still, while Bourdieu is focused on the question of how regularity is (re)produced, Arendt attempts to convey the necessity and efficacy of newness in the political world of action. Interestingly, she begins her explanation of natality, or newness, with the acknowledgment of humankind as a "conditioned" species. However, she argues this conditioning is, somewhat paradoxically, endlessly dynamic. She explains, "In addition to the [material] conditions under which life is given to man on earth, and partly out of them, men constantly create their own, self-made conditions, which, their human origins and their variability notwithstanding, possess the same conditioning power as natural things" (Arendt [1958] 1998, 9). Everyone has the capacity to act, but only some acquire the authority to do so. Authorization can be conferred by law, institutions, social position, or in other ways, but in each case, this authorization is rooted in interpretations of the way the past persists and functions in the present. In her essay "What Is Authority?" Arendt writes:

> The loss of tradition in the modern world does not at all entail a loss of the past, for tradition and past are not the same, as the believers in tradition on one side and the believers in progress on the other would have us believe. . . . With the loss of tradition we have lost the thread which safely guided us through the vast realms of the past, but this thread was also a chain fettering each successive generation to a predetermined aspect of the past. It could be that only now will the past open up to us with unexpected freshness and tell us things no one has yet had ears to hear. (Arendt 1993, 2)

Tradition defines the past in particular ways, but the past itself is open to be understood in a nearly endless variety of ways. Natality is possible because even though everything that "touches or enters into a sustained relationship with human life immediately assumes the character of a condition of human existence," these "conditions of human existence . . . can never 'explain' what we are or answer the question of who we are for the simple reason that they never condition us absolutely" (Arendt [1958] 1998, 11). It is impossible for things to condition individuals absolutely because "nobody is ever the same as anyone else who ever lived, lives, or will live" and "the new beginning inherent in birth" makes itself "felt in the world" through the newcomer's "capacity of beginning something anew, that is, of acting" (9).

It is important to note here that Arendt, like Bourdieu, does not understand the new to be the opposite of the old. Instead, the new is partially engendered by what has come before and still manages to emerge as something separate, unique, and full of original possibility. Arendt contends that observers of the political before the French and American revolutions had an inkling of the lack of opposition between tradition and novelty, but they were mistaken in that they did not believe that anything that emerged in the world of men could be truly unique, except perhaps people themselves. After the age of revolution though, a different problem of political apprehension manifested: the belief that the new, in order to be genuine, had to be wholly disconnected from the past. Arendt writes:

> Perhaps the very fact that these two elements, the concern with stability and the spirit of the new, have become opposites in political thought and terminology—the one being identified as conservatism and the

other being claimed as the monopoly of progressive liberalism—must
be recognized to be among the symptoms of our loss. (1965, 225)

The loss she speaks of here is a loss of a public-spirited perspective, one that
inculcates dispositions toward the political that are other than merely individu-
ally interested or based in personal values, but are instead focused on evaluating and improving the health of the political community. Arendt wishes to draw
attention to and resuscitate an American public spirit that she argues was inad-
vertently destroyed in the aftermath of the revolution. While I am sympathetic
to her cause, what is relevant here is only the awareness that Arendt argues, like
theorists concerned with the idea of public spirit from Aristotle to Montesquieu
have, that the old and new are not contradictory and indeed that any founding
moment must seem to advantageously and affectingly unite the two.

It is speech that creates and maintains the realm of the public, the only realm
of sociality in which politics can manifest. This is because the public is what we
hold in common and without the action of speech we would be unable to relate
and separate the world that mitigates, modifies, motivates, and conditions our
distinctly human experience. It is speech that enables the "public appearance" of
people and things in relation. Arendt writes,

> Each time we talk about things that can be experienced only in privacy
> or in intimacy, we bring them out into a sphere where they will assume
> a kind of reality which, their intensity not withstanding, they never
> could have had before. The presence of others who see what we see and
> hear what we hear assures us of the reality of the world and ourselves.
> ([1958] 1998, 50)

How, though, does the human characteristic of natality rely on public speech?
And how does the resonant quality of some public speech relate to the potential for natality in human action? Natality, means that "something new is started
which cannot be expected from whatever may have happened before" (Arendt
[1958] 1998, 178). Bourdieu makes a similar argument concerning the reproduction of regularity. The probable is a baseline for thought, action, and speech,
but the human capacities of free will and improvisation, combined with the
desire for particular outcomes, can and do motivate people to create variations
on the themes that they have learned in the *habitus* (Bourdieu 1977). Arendt
writes, "The new always happens against the overwhelming odds of statistical
laws and their probability.... The fact that man is capable of action means that
the unexpected can be expected from him, that he is able to perform what is infi-
nitely improbable" ([1958] 1998, 178). When the speaker improvises a connection between an old idea and a new purpose that she is able to frame as probable

using her knowledge of the dispositions present in *endoxa*, she is performing a profoundly inventive act, an act that only has its full impact in public speech because it is what enables people to hold the world in common and, in some cases, alter the common perception of the world we share.

Conclusion

This world we share is composed of the inert, material facts that lie around us, as well as the in-between that is constituted by the interrelated action of human-kind. "The physical, worldly in-between along with its interests are overlaid and, as it were, overgrown with an altogether different in-between which consists of deeds and words and owes its origin exclusively to men's acting and speaking directly to one another" (Arendt [1958] 1998, 183). Our basic descriptions of this in-between world we share are based on *endoxa*, but that baseline of wit, wisdom, and truism is only one of the tools that we use to interpret our experiences. Bourdieu reminds us that layered upon and embedded within the notions of *endoxa* are logics of practice that create meaningful, experiential, and agent-based contexts of action that can both reproduce usual habits and create opportunities for innovation. Arendt reminds us that the new is the hallmark of human action and highlights the ways that public speech is intimately tied to invention and intervention of the new.

Arendt, unlike Bourdieu, is most fascinated by the boundlessness that natality makes possible rather than the limitations that stability and sense-making require. Still, both Bourdieu and Arendt acknowledge that both aspects of human relation—boundless possibility and regular limitation—are necessary and constitutive of social reality, in general, and politics in particular. Arendt writes, "Limitations and boundaries exist within the realm of human affairs, but they never offer a framework that can reliably withstand the onslaught with which each new generation must insert itself" ([1958] 1998, 191). The insertion of the new is delicate business, and political challengers hoping that the new will yield their favored outcomes do well to cultivate tools that will help facilitate the inclusion of the particular kinds of newness that they desire. In politics, the most important of these tools is the rhetoric of public discourse, particularly aided by the sense of *ethos* that can be captured and conveyed through resonant speech. Public speech registers as resonant when *endoxa*, commonplace logic, and new ideas fit together in a harmonious way, such that beliefs about the way things are combine with commonplace logics about the way things work or relate and merge seamlessly with new arguments about what is significant or what is to be done.

As statistical analysis will show, resonance is rooted in pulling together each of these aspects of discourse, in the form of several linked arguments that nest inside a single frame that is deployed for a single purpose—combining familiar values, common concepts, and new ideas into presumptive wholes that can come to be taken for granted. Movements can use resonant arguments to help shift the domain of decision-making that is commonly understood as valid in regards to their issue. In this way, political challengers can advance their cause not only, or principally, by winning policy disputes, but also, and more importantly, by changing the public valuation of what is at stake and what is to be done in regards to their cause. In this way, the talk of movements can actually change politics, shifting the terrain of common understanding, public speech, and acceptable action in a direction that is more favorable to their preferred outcomes.

5

Political Acceptance and the Process of Political Change

Now that I have given a detailed account of these two movements during their emergence, as well as a theoretical explanation of the concept of resonance, it is possible to answer the question I first posed: what role does political acceptance play in the process of political change? Understanding political change requires us to pay attention not only to how discourse diffuses from elected officials and other elites down through news media to ordinary citizens, but also how new political discourses may effervesce from the bottom up. Other studies of the success of movements in political science ascertain the success of the movement from the number of favorable policies that advocates are able to win (Rimmerman and Wilcox 2007, Mucciaroni 2008). However, they miss a crucial aspect of social movement success, that is, the degree to which the framing of issues in public discourse during policy fights can affect the political understanding of issues and thus change the politics of what is at stake. It is for this reason that assessing whether a social movement has achieved political acceptance for its signature issues is so important. The degree to which a movement is able to win policy battles in the short term may say little about its ability to win a favorable political understanding of its issue in the long term. As we see with the living wage and marriage equality movements, the policy wins that a movement achieves in the short run can turn out to be pyrrhic if they are not successful at changing the political understanding of the issue through inserting resonant arguments and frames into public discourse.

This chapter proceeds in three parts. In the first, I engage the literature on political communications and social movements to discover what it can tell us about the place of public discourse in the process of political change. I show that while political communications has much to say about what frames are and how they may impact public opinion, most of the literature assumes a top-down communications process that does not account very well for possible differential effects based on frame resonance because they do not take public discourse seriously as a source of political meaning. The social movements literature has a different set of limitations that prevent it from adequately accounting for mainstream public discourse as an important factor in the assessment of frame resonance. The first limitation is that the social movements literature is biased toward resource-based and structural explanations. Second, even in the parts of the literature that take seriously culture, identity, and emotion, social movements explanations are almost exclusively focused on the mobilization of direct participants (and, sometimes, elite allies), nearly to the exclusion of the general public. Third, the social movements literature generally views media through an antagonistic rather than pragmatic lens. In the second part of the chapter, I expand on why the "socialization of conflict" is critical to political challengers. And in the third part, I offer a theory of discursive political change called *political acceptance*, which seeks to fill in these gaps and tell a different story about the place of discourse in the process of political change.

In the contemporary American political system, activists and advocates play a key role in highlighting how commonplaces or long-standing common-sense logics are connected to (or disconnected from) doxic values about what counts as the good life. Without their efforts, maintenance of status quo practices and policies is likely, even when those practices are widely believed to be unfair. This tendency toward the maintenance of status quo arrangements of power and privilege obtains for several reasons, the simplest being that most people value consistency and require good reasons to change. This is especially true for elected officials since their overarching interest is in having voters return them to their office. All things being equal, it is easier to win re-election in a political environment that does not deviate too much from the one in which election is first obtained (Mayhew [1974] 2004). Or as Doug McAdam puts it, political action by established polity members resists "changes which would threaten their current realization of their interests even more than they seek changes which would enhance their interests" or those of their constituents ([1982] 1999, 38). Therefore, the impetus for political change often comes from coalitions of people outside the office-holding elite.

It is important to note that this stimulation from the outside can be a boon for officials who may want to advance new policy, but feel unable to push for major change without a demonstrable grass-roots groundswell to legitimize and support their efforts. When it comes to promoting political change, all parties—activists, lobbyists, journalists, and elected officials—are acting under constraints. Still, as has been well established, those with access to resources like large sums of money, skills, professional political experience, and so on, are able to make their impact felt more swiftly and directly than grass-roots activists and advocates who must work through the slower and more indirect channel of the public sphere (Schlozman 1984, Schlozman, Verba, and Brady 2012).

Political challengers create the impetus for political change by connecting their concerns to the commonly understood principles, practices, and purposes that animate the lives of ordinary members of the polity. In order to do so they have to undertake two kinds of tasks, the first being practical and the second symbolic. Practically, political challengers must secure a platform to speak from and, symbolically, they must develop a political understanding that is likely to resonate with a large swath of the public. If advocates are able to accomplish these two things, then their issue has a better chance of persisting in the public sphere over time and eventually being accepted as a topic that deserves serious consideration and policy accommodation by the public and its governors.

For political challengers with limited regular access to monetary resources, official authority, or elite networks, this kind of political acceptance in mainstream discourse is the *only* way that they are able to acquire the kind of public authority and credibility that they need to make their case to the general public and challenge established arrangements of power and privilege. It is important that challengers are able to make such a public case because, as E. E. Schattschneider contends in his classic work *The Semisovereign People*, without the influence of public pressure the outcome of political contention is a foregone conclusion—whoever comes to the negotiating table with more power and resources wins. The public gaze, specifically the possibility that the public may side with the less powerful, is the element of political contest that makes bottom-up political change possible. This requires that political challengers be engaged with the public sphere through mass media.

Often politics scholars have been unwilling to investigate the terrain of mass-mediated communication and its content, mainstream political discourse, as a site rather than a symptom of political change. However, since newspapers, television, radio, and the Internet are the chief ways that citizens receive information about politics, it is important to become familiar with the contested and murky topography of the mass-mediated public sphere. Because my empirical analysis is based on the content of two national daily newspapers, the following overview focuses on that form of political communication.

The Top-Down Perspective of Political Communication

Although mass media receive quite a lot of criticism from all corners, much of it deserved, it is the existence of this apparatus, the arbiter of mainstream information and opinion, that can make it possible for the voices and ideas of marginalized people with relatively little access to official power to have great effect. Still, most of the time this is not what occurs. And while the increasingly anemic interest of most Americans in politics is certainly not all the fault of news media, it is the case that it may be a symptom of some systematic ailments of the press. These ailments include not only the widely acknowledged difficulty the press has in living up to the democratic hope for the fabled fourth branch, but also the professional expectations that have developed within the institution.

The scholarly literature on political communication has done a thorough job of tracing the paths that mainstream news discourse usually follows. If one were to imagine the flow of discourse in a shape, it would be a triangle, with ideational and policy content flowing from the top and down the sides to the base—from the White House, Congress or other top officials, through reporters and pundits, to interested citizens and finally the general populace (Bennett [1983] 2011, Bennett and Entman 2000, Schudson 1995, 2001, Entman 2004, Woodly 2008).

The triangular shape of public discourse is reinforced and maintained by the normal routines of reporting in the press and manifests in news content as elite bias (Parenti 1993, Jamieson and Waldman 2003). Longtime observers of political communication have noted that this elite bias is not necessarily the result of normative preference for the opinions of officials, but instead the consequence of a number of constraints and standard operating procedures that are characteristic of the modern press (Entman 1989, Gans 2005).

It is important to follow this symptom to its source because elite bias affects the news in at least three ways. First, the range of issues that the mainstream news media regard as newsworthy and from which they subsequently choose stories often determines which issues the general public comes to regard as politically important. Second, the way that media represents these important issues establishes which people are authorized to speak and which viewpoints are offered as germane to the explanation of problems as well as the alternative solutions that both elites and the general public come to regard as credible. Third, these two aspects, selection and representation, prescribe the contours of common national political discourses, constraining the practical and rhetorical options that are available to political actors who wish to influence policy outcomes (Iyengar 1991, Ansoblehere, Behr, and Iyengar 1993, Gitlin [1980] 2003).

Scholars of political communication have specified the mechanisms of elite bias in two main ways, expressed in "hegemonic" and "indexical" theories of political communication. Hegemony theorists like Todd Gitlin and Michael Parenti see the overabundance of news stories and news frames that originate with public officials in mainstream media as a symptom of the way that hegemony, as understood by Gramsci, functions in contemporary politics. Theorists who take this view contend that despite the appearance of conflict, elites have a relatively unitary interest in controlling the field of ideas that circulate in society. Therefore a main objective of elites is to underscore and preserve their political authority. Though the issue positions of elites may differ, they do not differ

very much on which issues they think are worth discussing. Political elites generally aim to protect the control they have over popular political epistemologies,
including the ideological range of political information that is produced and vali-
dated, thereby shaping and bounding public debate in a way that serves current
distributions of power.[1]

Some political communications analysts argue that indexical models of elite
discourse have more explanatory power. The indexical model emphasizes elite
conflict, arguing that the news acts as an "index" of elite dispute, playing up
divisions between one party and the other or between the White House and
Congress (or any elites that can be likewise opposed) as though all possible
relevant perspectives are contained within the DC Beltway (Mermin 1999).
Indexical theorists are more likely than hegemony theorists to recognize that
media coverage can avoid the blind transmission of official spin on news stories, especially when the American public regards the issues they cover as both
salient and controversial. However, they consider criticism of the frame(s) of
officials, especially high-ranking Washington officials, to be anomalous "interruptions." In this view, the emergence of public dissent into mainstream discourse is rare and counter to the normal course of discourse, a diagnosis that is
demoralizing for many scholars concerned with the democratic promise of the
press. Instead of functioning as investigators who unveil and clarify little-known
political truths, the press functions as referees of elite debate or merely as political announcers.

Robert Entman improves on these two analytics by offering a theory of political communication that combines insights from both. He describes the resultant
model as the "cascading network activation model of political communication"
(Entman 2004). In his cascade model, Entman argues that in normal political
communication, a story frame, or the way that a news story is to be told, extends
down from the acting administration to other elites, then spreads to journalists
who distribute the information they have received, complete with the definition
of the problem, stakes, and possible solutions, to the public. However, this does
not mean that the talking points that emanate from officials are transported and
delivered to the public untouched. Instead, each node in the cascade (administration, other elites, media, news frames, and public) functions, not as a unitary actor, but as a network of individuals, groups, and even institutions, which
interpret and evaluate the content that they have received from the proceeding
level according to its "cultural congruence." Cultural congruence, according
to Entman, is the "match between the news item and [the] habitual schemas"
that people who share the same political culture use as interpretive heuristics.
He contends that the closer the fit between the event and a regularly deployed
frame, the more easily the frame will pass from one level in the informational
cascade to the next with few challenges or modifications.

One of the virtues of Entman's model is that it highlights the importance of sequence; that is, the metaphor of the cascade emphasizes the hierarchal organization and evaluation of the voices present in the public sphere. In evaluating problems, arguments, and solutions, each level responds to the one above, ignoring or forgetting some elements and emphasizing others. The decision about what is worth talking about is made at each node in the cascade, but that first decision at the top constrains all the rest. The initial way of talking about the subject—the problem or puzzle, the interests involved, the criteria of evaluation—shapes subsequent debate, even when opponents seek to debunk the initial framing. Entman's model makes it clear that the original or, "first take" framing, usually the purview of the White House, circumscribes the scope of questions, problems, and arguments at each succeeding level.[2]

However, political communications scholars including Entman have much less to say about how discourses can percolate up, finding their way from the people to the White House. A cynic might say that we don't know how and why such reversals occur because they rarely do. In terms of the proportion of our news content that originates from nonofficials or political challengers, this is undoubtedly accurate. The dispersion of ideas from motivated grass-roots groups to the general public is much less than any democratic idealist would hope, but it nevertheless does happen. In contemporary politics, several of the issues that dominate the mainstream political landscape have their origin in the concerns of political challengers. In fact, most of today's "litmus test" issues are ones that emerged onto the political docket due to the efforts of organized groups of political challengers seeking redress from the powerful and challenging long-held assumptions about what counts as political and politically important. Affirmative action, abortion, gay marriage, and most recently immigration reform are all national political issues that rose to prominence because of the advocacy of political challengers.

It is the combination of the rarity of this democratic triumph and the influence such eruptions have on the political system when they do occur that ought to make these outlier cases interesting to political scientists. Understanding the conditions that facilitate the emergence and acceptance of new political issues onto the elite-dominated national agenda would add to our understanding of how politics works and, additionally, give us a window into how to increase the frequency and magnitude of these interruptions of insular official dialogue.

Social Movements Explanations

The literature on social movements provides some insight on the question of how grass-roots challengers are sometimes able to insinuate their causes into the national political agenda. However, the literature has three main weaknesses that prevent it from adequately accounting for public discourse as a resource: (1) social movements literature is biased toward structural rather than nonstructural explanations; (2) social movements explanations are too focused on direct participants and not enough on general public; and (3) social movements generally view media through and antagonistic rather than pragmatic lens. Beginning in the 1960s American scholars began to take contentious politics—bottom-up advocacy and activism outside established institutional politics—seriously as a subject worthy of study in democratic contexts. Before the sixties and the domestic upheavals the decade occasioned, social scientists generally explained political insurgency as an aberrant and irrational mob response to social psychological strain. This "classical model" of social movements proved inadequate after the black civil rights movement became a decisive force in mainstream American politics. During the 1970s a theory called "resource mobilization" became the dominant model for explaining political insurgency (McCarthy and Zald 1977, Tilly 1978). Resource mobilization theory asserts that political activities that erupt outside institutionalized pathways should be considered a rational tactical response to political systems that appear closed and unresponsive to aggrieved citizens. The theory is so named because its advocates argue that when it comes to contentious politics, the variable that determines whether a grievance will become politicized is whether challengers can amass sufficient resources from patrons, members, and allies to interrupt the ongoing elite political routines. Charles Tilly modified this framework by introducing the idea that movements might require more than resources to become organized and effective political challengers; they might also require opportunities to collect, direct, and deploy those resources. That is, those who wish to challenge status quo distributions of power might require the "political opportunity" to do so. Tilly argued further that political opportunities are not random, but are instead systematically distributed according to the sum of the differences between the strengths and weaknesses of challengers and elites, which determine the possible costs and benefits of collective action in any given society at any particular time.

The idea that movements are structurally related to the wider political environment in such a way that potential challengers respond to incentives for mobilization when they perceive that their chances for success are greatest is so simple and profound that it has become a ubiquitous concept in the study of social movements. In the early 1980s Doug McAdam articulated the "political process model" of social movement emergence, which adds to the notion of political opportunity the idea that movements require indigenous resources both material and cognitive, which are never, in the first instance, elite derived (McAdam [1982] 1999). Instead, McAdam argues that most of the population has access to "latent political leverage" that is derived from individuals' location in "various politico-economic structures." Quoting an insight from Marxist scholar Michael

Schwarts, McAdam clarifies: "Power relations define the functioning of any ongoing system; . . . the ability to disrupt these relationships is exactly the sort of leverage which can be used to alter the functioning of the system . . . [therefore,] any system contains within itself the possibility of a power strong enough to alter it" ([1982] 1999, 37). While acknowledging that politics is dominated by elites, the political process model emphasizes that when potential political challengers are organizationally ready to challenge ensconced political powers and psychologically or ideologically convinced that their efforts can make a difference, and the "structure of political opportunity" provides openings for their claims, they can create political change (Tilly 1978, Tarrow 1994).

McAdam's innovation is extremely helpful for understanding how nonofficials can launch a successful political challenge. But in his model the "structure of political opportunity" is doing quite a bit of work. Jeff Goodwin and James Jasper have argued that the concept has been used to explain so much that it has ended up being "tautological, trivial, inadequate, or just plain wrong" (2004, 28). Gamson and Meyer explain the problem thusly:

> The concept of political opportunity is in trouble, in danger of becoming a sponge that soaks up virtually every aspect of the social movement environment—political institutions and culture, crises of various sorts, political alliances, and policy shifts.. . . It threatens to become an all-encompassing fudge factor for all the conditions and circumstances that form the context for collective action. Used to explain so much, it may ultimately explain nothing at all. (Gamson and Meyer 1996, 275)

As Goodwin and Jasper point out, part of the difficulty concerning the utility of the concept of political opportunity is that social movement scholars have tended to want to develop "invariant and transhistorical theories," which are inevitably inadequate for studying the contextually contingent and dynamic phenomenon associated with political insurgency (Goodwin and Jasper 2004, 28).

Bias toward Structural Explanations

Goodwin and Jasper might argue that the unwillingness to incorporate analyses of political discourse as it is represented in news media into social movement theories is the symptom of a larger tendency to overemphasize structure in explanatory models (2004).

> The bias lurking beneath these problems is that "structural" factors (i.e. factors that are relatively stable over time and outside the

control of movement actors) are seen and emphasized more readily than others—and nonstructural factors are often analyzed as though they were structural factors.... A number of factors have been added to political opportunities in recognition of the influence of nonstructural variables—but without being accurately theorized as nonstructural. These include strategy and agency, which have to do with the active choices and efforts of movement actors as well as of their opponents and other players in the conflict, and cultural factors that deal with the moral visions, cognitive understandings, and emotions that exist prior to a movement but which are also transformed by it. (Goodwin and Jasper 2004, 29)

I hope to avoid this trap by taking the content of political discourse seriously as a contingent and dynamic source of meaning-making that is nevertheless stable over time as a category of analysis.

The concerns about political opportunity as an explanatory term are serious given that the definition makes no distinction between those opportunities that are the result of institutional realities, those that are created by advocates, and those that are serendipitous windfalls that advocates are able to perceive. While elite conflict over a particular issue may create fortuitous openings for political challengers, it is also the case that political challengers may incite elite conflict by politicizing an issue that generates salient attention in the press and the public.

This tendency is evident even in the most exemplary attempts to understand the impact of social movements on political change, such as the work of William Gamson. Gamson understands that you can "assess movement impact on cultural change through public discourse" (2006, 104). However, in his analysis he still privileges structure by separating "interests" from "symbolic interests," setting up a two-level structure of cultural change in which social movements do the work of connecting their constituents to decision-making authorities entirely separately from connecting their constituents to favorable framings in mass media. I argue, rather, that these two tracks are inextricably intertwined, and, in fact, social movements connect their constituencies to decision-making elites more effectively by going through the mass media. Gamson also claims that "some frames have a natural advantage because their ideas resonate with broader political culture" (2006, 122). In making this assertion, Gamson makes the mistake that Goodwin and Jasper warn of in treating a nonstructural factor-resonance—as though it were a structural factor. Resonance is not inherent to any particular topic; it is instead created in and through discourse. Therefore, an issue frame's greater or lesser resonance can result from the deliberate communicative efforts of social movements. Finally, like most social movement scholars, in focusing on movement organizations, Gamson forgets the public. In his model for measuring the impact of movements on cultural change the key explanatory variable is *organizational* acceptance. This is measured by whether and to what degree authorities consult, negotiate, recognize, or include social movement organizations as well as whether such organizations have "media standing," such that they become a "regular media source whose interpretations are directly quoted" (Gamson 2006, 115).

I would argue, rather, that the degree of a social movement's impact does not rest on the fate of an organization, but rather, the fate of a set of ideas and their political meaning. While organizations are indispensable in pressure politics (Baumgartner et al. 2009), it is also the case that an organization may fall away or become irrelevant even while the political understanding that it ushers into public discourse persists. These ideas cannot be stewarded from issue to policy without organizations that bring constituents to bear, but, from the viewpoint of the public, the audience who judges whether a new issue ought to be accepted onto the short list of topics that constitute the national agenda, it is not the organizations that matter, but the understandings that their interventions make possible. For example, most people can't name the myriad organizations of the second-wave feminist movement, but everyone knows what a "male chauvinist pig" is (Mansbridge and Flaster 2007).

Framing: For Participants Only

David Snow and Robert Benford adapted Irving Goffman's term "frame" to the study of social movements, arguing that much of the work that challenger groups do is about changing people's ideas about the connections between personal circumstances, political rights and obligations, and the responsibilities of governing institutions (Snow and Benford 1988).[3] In their definition, the term "frame" refers to "an interpretive schemata that simplifies and condenses the 'world out there' by selectively punctuating and encoding objects, situations, events, experiences and sequences of action" that allow individuals to "locate, perceive, identify and label" events in their lives or in the world at large (Snow and Benford 1992). In this way, frames can be used to make "diagnostic and prognostic attributions" (Snow and Benford 1992, 137). Snow and Benford also indicate the importance of frame resonance for its impact, stating that a frame's "narrative fidelity," or comportment with cultural "myths," is a significant factor in whether a frame will be mobilizing for movement participants (Snow and Benford 2000, 1988).

Relatedly, Albert Hirschman (1991) contends that in order to inspire people to engage in extrainstitutional politics, one must combat a "rhetoric of reaction," three default themes that discourage active involvement in politics.

These themes are *jeopardy* (we risk losing ground), *futility* (attempts to create real change always come to naught), and *perverse effects* (unintended negative consequences will likely outweigh desired effects). Together these discursive anchors set in motion a chain of reasoning that makes inaction seem the only prudent option. Movement organizers must counter these themes using frames that emphasize potential for change. "For each of these themes," write William Gamson and David Meyer, "there is a corresponding counter-theme making the opposite point about political opportunity. *Urgency, agency* and *possibility* describe a rhetoric of change" that is essential to mobilization efforts (Gamson and Meyer 1996, 286).

Even though the importance of cultural framing is acknowledged in the social movements literature, most of it, like the wealth produced by Gamson and Meyer, is focused on the mobilization of *movement activists* for insurgent protest. However, it is my contention that not only do the activists and advocates promoting new issues need to be exposed to a rhetoric that makes change seem possible, prudent, and right but *so too does the general public.* Because social movement scholars do not adequately address the efficacy of cultural framing efforts outside the context of internal mobilization, the framing literature falls short of its explanatory potential.

When social movement scholars discuss framing processes, they are almost entirely concerned with the production of "collective action frames," which either "underscore and embellish the seriousness and injustice of a social condition or redefine as unjust and immoral what was previously seen as unfortunate but perhaps tolerable" (Snow and Benford 1992, 137). When collective action frames are successful, they (1) establish the "we" and "they" of a particular grievance, (2) set forth convincing reasons why action is necessary, (3) and reassure people that acting is efficacious (Tarrow 1992). Tarrow refers to the accomplishment of this kind of framing as "symbolic mobilization" and remarks, "There is a paradox in the symbolic politics of social movements: between developing dynamic symbols that will create new identities and bring about change, and proffering symbols that are familiar to people who are rooted in their own cultures" (Tarrow 1998, 107). With this statement, Tarrow articulates the crux of the primary puzzle that political challengers face. However, he articulates it in reference to how social movements must mobilize participants across difference rather than in reference to how movements can mobilize favorable understandings of the stakes (and solutions) of the problem in the general public. Activists are engaged in a tricky business in which they must persuade not only their members, but also the general polity, to consider new aspects of political problems, how such problems are connected to common logics, as well as challenge entrenched notions about who particular groups are supposed to be and how they ought to behave, what they deserve and whether society and/or government is responsible for supplying them with the things they demand.

Tarrow acknowledges that frames ought to be flexible enough to be intelligible to a wide audience, quoting William Gamson's caution that "it is insufficient if individuals privately adopt a different interpretation of what is happening. For a collective adoption of an injustice frame, it must be shared by potential challengers in a public way" (Tarrow 1998, 111). However, the terminology and focus of his substantive concern leaves the reader with the impression that these two activities—the symbolic mobilization of members under a collective action frame and raising the awareness of the general public—neither easily fit together nor are of coequal importance. Appealing to both members and the general public is not easy, but focusing all mobilization efforts on developing collective action frames to woo members may often leave advocates short of the influence that they need to effect policy.

Tarrow is not the only social movements scholar who neglects giving external framing processes equal status with the strengthening of internal mobilization structures. McAdam, McCarthy, and Zald write:

> Framing processes are held to be both more likely and of far greater consequence under conditions of strong rather than weak organization.... Even in the unlikely event that system-critical framings were to emerge in the context of little or no organization, the absence of any real mobilizing structure would almost surely prevent their spread to the minimum number of people required to afford a basis for collective action. (1996, 9)

As the living wage examples shows, the reverse is, quite likely, also true. That is, even highly organized mobilization structures (grass-roots, professional advocacy, service groups) are unlikely to rally the minimum number of people requisite for influential collective action without developing "system-critical" frames that are accessible not only to members, but also to the general public.[4] I believe these tactics are nested one within the other and that ranking internal framing above external framing, instead of taking them to be coequal, is to misinterpret the political realities involved in political change.

The organization-focused, strategic approach of the living wage movement, while understandable (win where you can) is ultimately politically limiting because activists, often from a traditional labor organizing background, focus almost exclusively on recruiting members and pressuring officials, without taking the additional step of attempting to persuade the general public of the basic soundness and general applicability of their argument. Unlike gay marriage advocates, living wage activists have not been able to put the living wage into the context of *basic* and *inalienable* political rights. This is despite the fact that there has consistently been broad, bipartisan public agreement with raising the minimum wage and with the idea that people who work full time should not live in poverty.

There are reasons that this is especially difficult. Americans are ambivalent about intervening in labor markets even when they are convinced the state of affairs is problematic. This ambivalence makes the themes of jeopardy, futility, and perverse effects resonant, as I will show in the following chapter, even to those who support the notion that working people ought not make wages that leave them poor. The idea of a wage floor, especially a local wage floor (as opposed to a national minimum wage) is in deep tension with a free-market orthodoxy that declares that localities not only should, but must bend over backward for business in order to survive in the (inter)national economy. Opponents of the living wage often cast advocates as antidevelopment (which is nearly tantamount to anti-American) and argue that the idea of a wage floor as a solution is not only pie-in-the-sky idealism but also economically destructive. Furthermore, the orthodox argument goes, such measures will end up hurting the poor, precisely the people activists hope to help. A 2002 article by Stephanie Armour in *USA Today* headlined "Living-Wage Movement Takes Root across Nation" carries the most salient and resonant frame that appeared in public discourse regarding the living wage:

> The concern: higher wages will displace lower-skilled workers from the labor market because employers who pay more will demand more experienced hires. In cities such as New York, critics fear that higher wages will prompt employers to flee. A bill under consideration by the New York City Council would require city contractors and companies that receive sizable tax breaks to pay $8.10 an hour to employees who get health benefits, increasing to a maximum off $10 after five years. An estimated 80,000 workers would be affected. "We're trying to induce firms to stay in the city," says Katherine Wylde, President and CEO of the New York City Partnership, which represents businesses. "If New York needs the jobs, the idea is to make it as easy and streamlined for firms as possible. This is a mixed message."

It is important to note that this orthodoxy is still powerfully ascendant in public discourse and remains difficult to counter despite the fact that empirical studies repeatedly show that modest increases in the minimum wage paid to workers can almost always be absorbed by businesses with little to no job loss and minimal price increases (Brenner, Wicks-Lim, and Pollin 2002, Brenner 2004, Chapman and Thompson 2006, Pollin et al. 2008, Schmitt 2013). In addition, there is evidence that modest raises in wages for the lowest paid workers not only do not cost jobs or significantly increase prices, but can provide economic stimulus (Dube, Lester, and Reich 2011, Allegretto, Dube, and Reich 2011). Indeed, the fact that near-minimum wage jobs are becoming a larger proportion of the labor market (and are projected to become an even greater portion in coming years) has many economists worried about what that means for our consumer-based economy (Duke and Lee 2014). A 2013 survey of economists conducted by the University of Chicago's Booth School of Business showed that by a nearly 4 to 1 margin leading economists are now convinced that the overall economic benefits of raising the minimum wage and indexing it to inflation outweigh the potential costs to individual businesses.[5]

In examining the news discourse on the living wage, I found that arguments against it exhibit exactly the characteristics of the "rhetoric of reaction" that aims to protect status quo distributions of power, attempting to convince political elites and the public that living wage ordinances will put economic prosperity in *jeopardy*; that it is not business, but the iron law of supply and demand, that is to blame for low wages and attempts to alter this reality are *futile*; and that instituting wage floors in free markets will paradoxically cause higher unemployment and chase business away, leading to *perverse effects* for the poor.

For example, a 1996 *New York Times* article by Heather MacDonald of the Manhattan Institute titled "Living Wages, Fewer Jobs" makes the arguments this way:

> Minimum wage jobs (which in New York City generally means between $5 and $6 an hour) provide a vital entry into the labor market for the least skilled and educated workers. If an employer is forced to double the salary for a position, he will demand and find a more qualified applicant. Why should he hire a high school dropout for a security or maintenance job when he can now get a better educated and trained person who suddenly finds the $12-an-hour job attractive? The increased competition for jobs with city contractors will squeeze unskilled workers out of the labor market and possibly onto the welfare rolls. To pay for a "living wage" law, New York would face two choices: slashing services for which it uses private contractors and nonprofit groups—including low-income housing, AIDS services and foster care—or cutting back in other areas, like education, libraries and transit. Either way, the poor would suffer most.... There is no legislative shortcut to creating good jobs at decent wages. The best role for the city is to lower taxes and improve the overall quality of life, then let businesses create jobs and encourage their workers to acquire the skills that would earn them a better living.

According to this argument, there is no action that government can take to ensure that people do not have to work for wages that leave them in poverty. Taking any direct action to alleviate poverty-level wages will only put economic prosperity in jeopardy and is, in any case, futile because it is an attempt to use government policy to alter, on this popular account, neither a social nor political problem, but instead an unfortunate, but natural, economic reality. An implicit premise of this argument is that we are to understand economics not as politics, but as science, putting the results at a remove from political resolution. The worst implication of all, however, is that raising the wage floor to a level in which people who work full time could afford to support themselves at or above the poverty level, will, on this telling, actually hurt the people that it is meant to help more than anyone else because they can least afford to be driven out of work and have services cut in order to pay for the increased wages of a set of slightly more skilled workers (who are either not currently participating in the labor market or will develop more mobility because a greater variety of jobs will pay a decent wage).

This argument against the living wage (and against minimum wages in general) has been very powerful despite the fact that it appears to be completely untrue. Raising the federal minimum wage has never caused catastrophic economic consequences and no municipality or state who has raised their wage floor above the federal minimum appears to have experienced significant disemployment effects. Proponents of this argument generally do not have empirical examples of the theoretical doom higher wages might cause, but the boogey man of old economic orthodoxy nevertheless holds an enormous amount of sway.

This is, in part because empirical findings on the positive effects of living wages are somewhat mixed. While a survey of the literature on wages in economics reveals that disemployment effects due to wage floors are either not present or not large enough to be discernible to most people, there is quite a bit of ambiguity about whether current wage floors help either low-wage individuals or poor families escape poverty (Card and Krueger 1994, Card 1992, Neumark and Wascher 2000, Dube, Lester, and Reich 2011). This may be for a variety of reasons, chief among them that the wage rate required to lift a family out of poverty might require quite a large increase.

In order to counter the ambivalence that arguments asserting the potential jeopardy, futility, and/or perverse effects of wage floors living wage advocates need to change the *doxa* about *what* and *who* counts in assessments of economic prosperity. That is to say, the commonplace understanding that supports the status quo would have to change by linking new interpretations of economic prosperity to existing values such as fairness, equal opportunity, individual responsibility, human rights, the American dream, and justice, among other possibilities, in resonant ways. Thus far, living wage advocates have been less successful in, indeed, as my interview data show, somewhat resistant to, creating and promoting a rhetoric of change to the general public that conveys the *urgency* with which the problem of poverty-level wages must be addressed, the *agency* of not only recruited members, but ordinary voters, to demand economic policies that put their needs first, and most of all, the *possibility* that these fairer policies could be implemented without retarding economic development and betraying the ethos of prosperity that Americans hold in great esteem.

The tendency to privilege internal organization and member mobilization by activists and in the literature on social movements is understandable. From the perspective of advocates, members are the source of most of their resources and, more fundamentally, their reason for being. However, regardless of the conceptual centrality of membership to challenger organizations, the reality is that they exist in a wider political world that must acknowledge them and be able to understand their claims if they are to have any lasting impact. For that, challengers must craft their claims in resonant ways that will make their issues more likely to be accepted on the national agenda as it is articulated by elites and sanctioned by the general public.

Mass Media: The Wrong Villain

It is not that social movements scholars deny that attaining a hearing in public through mainstream media is important to movement success. Rather, it is that when social movements scholars do address the presentation of movement issues and goals to the general public, they tend to focus on the efficacy of the spectacle. For example, Gitlin writes, "What defines a movement as good copy [for mainstream media] is often flamboyance, often the presence of a media-certified celebrity-leader, and usually a certain fit with whatever frame the newsmakers have constructed to be 'the story' at a given time" (Gitlin [1980] 2003, 3, Gunderson 2008).

However, I would argue along with Lee Ann Banaszak (1996) that while staging spectacles may be useful for garnering one-time coverage, it is not usually conducive to persuading the general public to accept challenger claims about the political importance of new issues. Indeed, spectacles can actually decrease a challenger's credibility. As Robert Dahl cautioned more than half a century ago, there is a difference between being heard and being "heard effectively" (1956, 145). Securing an effective hearing entails more than the fact of making a noise, even when that noise is quite a loud one. An utterance may be theatrical, but such special effects do not necessarily impart, challenge, or influence political meanings unless they are accompanied by persuasive public appeals.

It is for this reason that the general dynamics of political communication need to be examined with a special focus on bottom-up pathways. This requires a serious engagement with mass media, a task that social movement scholars have undertaken only reluctantly.[6] Most seem to perceive mass media as getting in the way of the successful deployment of collective action frames. Tarrow writes that symbolic mobilization "has been rendered more complex by the barrage of information that competes with movement messages through books, newspapers, and especially the mass media" (1998, 107). Todd Gitlin, who wrote a book about the centrality of the media to the truncated fate of the "New Left" student movement of the 1960s, *The Whole World Is Watching*, introduces his study by establishing that mass media are the villains of his tale:

> The media bring a manufactured public world into private space.... They name the world's parts, they certify reality as reality—and when their certifications are doubted and opposed, as they surely are, it is those same certifications that limit the terms of effective opposition. To put it simply: the mass media have become core systems for the distribution of ideology.... One important task for ideology is to define—and also define away—its opposition. (Gitlin [1980] 2003, 2)

I believe the analysis of the social movements literature suffers from this adversarial analytical relationship with mass media because while news media may usually validate official ideologies, they are also the major institution of the public sphere, the only one that enables challengers with limited resources to get their claims noticed by the general public and responded to by elites. Also, the place of the Internet and social media in contemporary political discourse changes the balance of power, making it easier for political challengers to disseminate the frames and memes that they have crafted (Vaccari 2013, Groffman, Trechsel, and Franklin 2013).

However, the status of the Internet as a new node in news discourse does not overturn the hierarchy of political communication. Arguments that are deployed via the Internet still have to be filtered through traditional media to become significant parts of the national political conversation (Woodly 2008). In addition, the press is an institution that sincerely believes itself to have democratic responsibilities as information gatherers, questioners, and critics (Bagdikian 2004, Cunningham 2003). While it often falls short of its own aspirations, the picture the institution has of itself can be an important tool challengers can use both to encourage better practices and to call news organizations to account. Furthermore, journalists, editors, and even news organizations are at least occasionally allies to challenger groups, and they might be tempted to be so more often. In addition to or perhaps as a consequence of the tendency to regard mass media as a powerful nuisance or downright dangerous, the social movements literature on framing has tended to treat media content as a constant—a conglomeration of facts, ideas, normative affirmations, scandal, and so on, that is elite controlled, although sometimes tolerant of opportune and spectacular eruptions from the organized rabble. But this view of the mass media and the discourses that it contains limits the opportunities of social movements rather than expands them. Since, as I argued above, mass media are the major institution of the public sphere, it behooves scholars and activists to consider their uses.

The Socialization of Conflict

In order for political challengers to win a hearing from the public and to be able to demand the action of officials and other elites, they must successfully convince both groups that their problem is an issue that ought to concern the entire polity. That means groups must succeed at what Schattschneider has referred to as the "socialization of conflict." The socialization of conflict enables political acceptance and is crucial for the process of political change for several reasons. First, the socialization of conflict facilitates the politicization of the issues involved. As awareness of a particular conflict diffuses to a wider populous, the disagreement between the parties involved can no longer be treated as outside the purview of political negotiation. Second, the socialization of conflict facilitates the integration of the dispute into current aspects of law, policy, and governance, that is, the larger political environment. Third, the socialization of conflict creates the opportunity for the groups to vie for public authority and public favor. I employ public authority and public favor as distinct concepts. Public authority is a matter of right—that an individual or group is judged by the polity to be credentialed to speak and be heard in the public sphere. Public favor is a matter of agreement—that individuals or groups have succeeded in winning explicit majority support for their position. As the cases of the living wage and marriage equality show, the majority of the public may grant one without granting the other. In the two cases discussed herein, the American public disperses authority and favor separately, granting the former to gay marriage, but not the living wage and the latter to the living wage but not gay marriage. Finally, because the socialization of conflict brings disputes into the public sphere, facilitates politicization, and provides the opportunity to vie for public authority, it also creates the conditions under which political acceptance becomes possible.

Political acceptance is a theory based on the idea that public authority is a resource for political challengers because it allows them to broaden the "scope of conflict," which aids political challengers in gaining an "effective hearing" (Schattschneider 1975, Dahl 1956). Some scholars have argued that political challengers actually have a better chance at winning favorable policy when the scope of conflict remains narrow (Haider-Markel and Meier 1996). On this account, when opponents of gay rights are able to make the issue more salient, they win because the question then becomes one of "morality politics" in which religious groups, party competition, and partisanship are key determinants of success. When, on the other hand, the scope of conflict is kept narrow, advocates for gay rights can behave the way that any other interest group might, bringing to bear elite values, interest group resources, and past policy precedent (Haider-Markel and Meier 1996).

However, this analysis leaves out a crucial aspect of Schattschneider's political analysis. In *The Semisovereign People*, Schattschneider's ideas about the significance of the scope of conflict are tied to assessments of power. More powerful parties benefit from a narrow scope of conflict, while less powerful parties benefit from a broad scope of conflict. This is because, even when less powerful challengers are able to wring policy concessions from lawmakers who are either sympathetic to their cause or feel pressure from constituents to take a stance against the more powerful interest, those concessions can be dramatically weakened, go unimplemented, or be reversed—that is, unless a broader public conversation holds decision-makers to their word.

Schattschneider asserts that "at the root of all politics is the universal language of conflict" (1975, 2). He argues that all conflicts include two kinds of involved parties: the combatants and the audience, and as Schattschneider reminds the reader, "Nothing attracts a crowd so quickly as a fight" (1975, 1). Based on this premise, he develops three propositions. First, that "the outcome of every conflict is determined by the extent to which the audience becomes involved in it" (Schattscneider 1975, 2). Second, that the most important strategy of politics, any politics, is the estimation of both the actual and potential scope of conflict. No other single element of political contests is as influential and predictive as the degree to which the conflict has diffused into the awareness and concern of the larger polity. Third, Schattschneider proposes that in conflicts that are kept private, the relative strengths of participants can be ascertained in advance, and in such situations it is very likely that the stronger party will simply impose its will on the weaker. In conflicts that do not have a wider audience, the stronger party can accomplish this at relatively little cost.

However, when a conflict diffuses beyond the borders of direct involvement, the balance of power in the fight may change. The stronger side can find itself on shaky ground, not able to simply impose its will but forced instead to justify the positions the powerful group prefers in front of a concerned audience, opening itself up to all the uncertainties embedded in discussion, including doubt, dissent, and judgment. Conversely, "The weaker side may have great potential strength provided only that it can be aroused in the larger populous" (Schattscneider 1975, 4).

Of course, these are only possibilities. There is no evidence that American audiences have any particular preference for underdogs or that the stronger party is always corrupt or wrong and only needs to be revealed as such. On the contrary, the stronger can and do often bring their influence into the public sphere and utilize it to win over the polity. Also, citizens are not necessarily predisposed toward change and may support status quo policies and/or distributions of power for a number of reasons, including that they simply and genuinely prefer the position of the more powerful party. In other words, the socialization of conflict does not guarantee a win for the group that enters the contest with relatively fewer resources. What it does is give the weaker party a chance to make its case in front of a body of arbiters who may be persuaded that its claims have merit or even support their cause.

In this way, citizen observers are an integral, even determining, factor in political conflicts. "The crowd," Schattschneider writes, "is loaded with portentousness because it is apt to be a hundred times as large as the fighting minority and . . . it is never really neutral" (1975, 2). The crowd may overwhelmingly throw its support behind one party, split its support between them, or ignore the conflict altogether. Two of those three options give the weaker party an advantage it would otherwise not have, which are not bad odds. But the crowd is not beholden to either side. In fact, the general public may overtake the original dispute and terms of discourse, offering up nodes of conflict or concern that the contestants eschewed or tendering resolutions of their own. "So great is the change in the nature of any conflict . . . as a consequence of the widening involvement of people," Schattschneider argues, "that the original participants are apt to lose control of the conflict altogether" (1975, 3).

These variables make the "scope" of conflict or the number of audience members who are interested enough to develop a position on the problem, the most important overlooked X factor in the study of politics. The size, interest, and sympathy of the audience may serve to empower and protect one side while exposing and defeating the other. Taking the scope of the political conflict into account alters the political calculus that must be used to analyze the situation and to predict outcomes. More dramatically put, "The scope factor opens up vistas of a new kind of political universe" (Schattschneider 1975, 6), one in which the politically weak may wrest enough power to contest the claims of the strong, not only through the mobilization of fellow challengers to their cause, but also by persuading the crowd that their issue is one that deserves political consideration and redress.

It is important to note that the socialization of conflict is not automatic. While it may be true that a big crowd loves a good fight, it is also the case that constant and deeply divisive conflict may cease to have the titillation of spectacle and take on the brutal drudgery of civic war. The American polity does not seem particularly disposed toward accepting multiple new sites of political cleavage at once, and for that reason it is imperative for challengers that their issue seem to be both significant and solvable. Schattschneider argues that a look at the literature underlying America's conception of itself, such as the Federalist Papers, shows

> a long standing struggle between the conflicting tendencies toward the privatization and socialization of conflict.... A long list of ideas concerning individualism, free private enterprise, localism, privacy, and economy in government seems to be designed to privatize conflict or to restrict the scope or to limit the use of public authority to enlarge the scope of conflict.... On the other hand, it is equally easy to identify another battery of ideas contributing to the socialization of conflict. Universal ideas in the culture, ideas concerning equality, consistency, equal protection of the laws, justice, liberty, freedom of movement, freedom of speech and association, and civil rights tend to socialize conflict. (Schattscneider 1975, 7)

In Schattschneider's examples, these ideas seem to line up along ideological lines, with those principles that typically guide American conservatism tending to privatize conflict and the ideas that have steered American liberals seeming to enlarge conflict. But it is important to remember, as Steven Skowronek deftly points out, that these ideas are available to any political actor, whatever part of the spectrum her cause is seen to represent. While discourse affirming individualism might suggest policies that seek to privatize conflict, any of these principles may be rhetorically deployed in order to enlarge the scope of conflict (or disavowed to shrink the scope).

For example, privacy has been central to arguments about the right of gay men to have sex without the interference of the state. In the landmark *Lawrence v. Texas*, the Supreme Court ruled that sodomy could not be criminalized between two consenting adults acting in private. In a November 2003 poll conducted by the Pew Forum on Religion and Public Life, fully 80 percent of respondents agreed that "society should not put any restrictions on sex between consenting adults in the privacy of their own home," while a majority (55 percent) still maintained that homosexuality is a sin and nearly two out of three (59 percent) opposed gay marriage. Interestingly, that number was up from 53 percent in a survey taken shortly before the ruling, suggesting that respondents may have had increased sensitivity to the issue.[7] This suggests that most people's determination that an issue is significant and relevant to values generally acknowledged to be basic to the identity of the polity, does not necessarily correlate with individual polity member's agreement with or affirmation of the population that brings a challenge to the status quo.

The terms that advocates, journalists, and officials use to politicize an issue that may confer upon it the weight of generally acknowledged importance do not ensure approval, especially in the short term. In this case, advocates politicized the criminalization of sex between same-sex partners as a matter of discrimination *and* a matter of privacy. While the former often lines up with liberal concerns and the latter with conservative ones, in this instance, both work to enlarge the scope of conflict and underscore the importance of the issue, trumpeting the gravity of what is at stake. The public exhibited support for the claims made in regard to privacy and accepted the frame regarding equality without initially affirming it. However, the pairing of these frames has been repeated over and over by gay rights activists on a variety of issues, and polling shows that while Americans were reluctant to support gay marriage, they came to believe that gay rights issues were fundamentally civil rights issues. That is to say, the set of issues constituting gay rights in mainstream American political discourse, including what became the flagship issue, gay marriage, came to be generally regarded as *inherently* connected to the civil rights frame advocates repeatedly and consistently deployed, and therefore regardless of the personal agreement of individual citizens, the issue became generally perceived as *necessarily* connected to the principles of privacy, fairness, discrimination, and right invoked by the most common framing in mainstream discourse.

All of these principles belong to the short queue of key concepts that, if they are perceived to be credible, call for the attention of the polity. Charges of discrimination, lack of respect for privacy, and curtailment of liberty (among a few others) tend to enlarge the scope of the conflict, at least briefly, and though the direction of majority sentiment is not predetermined by a belief in the significance of the question, the challenger does secure a space in which it can make its case, which is more than it could hope for in a private dispute with powerful officials.

The phenomenon of political acceptance highlights the crucial relationship between the public meaning of discourse and the nature of persuasion in politics. Most of the literature on attitude change takes the psychological individual as the unit of measure. I wish to assert that political persuasion (as opposed to individual persuasion) is primarily a public and practical process. While individuals can be persuaded in the classical sense of experiencing an avowed change of heart and/or mind, public opinion research on priming and framing has shown that even when people do not change their personal attitudes, differences in the topics and frames discussed in mainstream discourse do change people's perception of issue salience and may also shift their policy preferences by persuading them that something they had not thought of is at stake. This general assessment of what is important and what kinds of options are commonly sayable and doable in public changes over time. That means that individual attitudes need not be the first element to shift in the process of political persuasion; public discourse can and often does change first.

As a resonant frame is frequently repeated in the media (priming), it may have a "framing effect," which causes people, not to change their minds, but to change the values that they apply for decision-making or position-taking in a particular instance (Chong and Druckman 2007). What I posit is that if we extend the time period of observation and the same frames and framing effect persist, the issue becomes generally regarded as *inherently* connected to the prevailing frame, and therefore the issue becomes generally perceived as *necessarily* connected to the principle invoked by the most common framing. I further posit that such a shift in the common perception of an issue is not automatic or inevitable but is instead a result of public contention over political ideas and social policy.

If challengers are able to socialize conflict and the scope of the contest continues to broaden, the terms of the conflict will become more familiar to a greater number of people. This will happen to an even greater degree if discourse about the conflict persists over a long period. This successful socialization of conflict is a rare phenomenon. But in the cases when conflict is both socialized and sustained, it is likely that the new issue, which paradoxically becomes familiar, will be accepted onto the short list of topics that the public, the press, and officials regularly discuss, debate, and take positions on. This acceptance creates the possibility that a new issue may not only win a place, but shift other issues around on what Lipset and Rokkan (1967) term the "hierarchy of cleavage bases" that characterize democratic politics. When audience members repeatedly and regularly identify an issue as a problem, relating it (favorably or unfavorably) to other political tribulations that they care about and have formed opinions about, then political acceptance has begun to occur. The discursive process reaches the threshold moment of acceptance when official elites take public positions on the new issue in question, offering opinions, calling on allies, and pitching policy options that seek to accommodate challengers in some measure, acknowledging that the problem that they have inserted into public discourse matters to the ever-present and surprisingly powerful interested public.

It is important to note that the argument for the distinction between political acceptance and public approval is not a scholarly rendition of the colloquial truism "Any publicity is good publicity." On the contrary, as I argued above, some publicity can be very detrimental to challengers. Often, moments of spectacle that seem to be disconnected from claims based on recognizable *doxic* values serve to discredit challengers and silence their voices in mainstream public forums. Rather, my point is that majority *support* is not essential to political acceptance. Instead, what is necessary is broad public *acknowledgment* that the issue is of consequence and worth discussing as a polity.

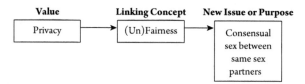

Figure 5.1 Linking Existing Values to New Purposes.

Given the nature of the contemporary public sphere, challengers have to be present for long enough and compelling enough in their speech to wrest the metaphorical microphone from those already bequeathed the mantle of routine pronouncement. This can only be done through the sustained repetition of and response to new ideas and policy positions that challengers manage to insert into mainstream political discourse. As I discussed in the previous chapter, the ability to present new claims credibly depends on whether the connection between old ideas and new purposes is likely to resonate with the values and understandings that are taken for granted in the general public. Again, this does not mean that those values and purposes need to map exactly onto previous political configu-rations. Quite the reverse: the trick to advancing a new issue is the union of old values with new prescriptions using plausible linking concepts (figure 5.1). For example, gay rights advocates were able to tie the commonplace American value of *privacy* from the invasive gaze to the protection of *consensual homosexual sex* using *fairness* as the point of linkage.

In democracies, the pressure of the public gaze can influence the awareness, public declarations, and policy actions of elites and the range of outcomes that come to seem possible. As Schattschneider argues:

> Private conflicts are taken into the public arena precisely because some-one wants to make certain that the power ratio among the private inter-ests most immediately involved shall not [automatically] prevail. To treat a conflict as a mere test of the strength of the private interests is to leave out the most significant factor. (1975, 37)

Furthermore, it is through frames and framing processes that new ideas, per-spectives, values, and policy options become (or fail to become) integrated into the wider political framework in such a way that the public begins to care about the issues at stake and officials come to believe that it behooves them to listen. Regardless of how organized and disciplined a movement is, without this inter-face with the wider political environment, its success may be temporary and lim-ited, as we see in the case of many living wage ordinances. This is because elites will always have more monetary, organizational, official, and human resources than challengers are able to squeeze from their members and close allies. As

Schattschneider writes, "Nothing could be more mistaken than to suppose that public authority merely registers the dominance of the strong over the weak. The mere existence of public order has already ruled out a great variety of forms of private pressure" (1975, 40). This means that in the public sphere, marginalized voices have a chance to influence the political behaviors and decisions of even the most powerful official elites and, I would add, even the ideologies that they hold inviolable, such as the current reigning orthodoxy regarding the support of "job creators" over workers in the pursuit of a prosperous economy. The only element that can make advocates equal to the ensconced power of elites and help widen the scope of political conflict to include the attention of those not directly involved is *public authority*.

Public Authority

Public authority is the influence of the people in determining what counts as the common interest.[8] The potency of this authority, as with its Latin root *auctoritas*, is in the ambiguity of the nature of that influence. It is, as classicist Theodor Mommsen famously put it: "more than advice and less than a command," it is precisely "advice that one may not safely ignore" (Arendt 1993). The source of that lack of safety is context dependent. The danger arising from ignoring authority might be physical violence, political repression, social stigma, or, as is most relevant to this project, the ability to exercise "voice" and receive an "effective hearing" in public discussion (Hirschman 1970, Dahl 1956).

In sum, public authority can only be conferred in public discourse and is a kind of authorization to speak that does not come from the state, other kinds of officials, or established elites. Public authority is not rules-governed and need not be conferred for rational reasons, but is instead conveyed through the attention, acknowledgment, and understanding of the general public as represented in popular discourse and public opinion.[9] If the public pays attention to a topic, acknowledges that the topic is both public and political, and understands the topic as a problem to be solved, then the public has authorized that topic as a subject for public discussion. Conversely, without such attention, acknowledgment, and understanding, no public authority can be conferred.

In formal, deliberative models of democratic politics, citizens are constructed as active participants, whereas in the empirically based models that have been produced in the literature on political communication, as well as the bulk of literature on public opinion, citizens are incorporated as either passive receivers or occasionally active interpreters of the political information and cues produced by elites (Lippmann 1922, Campbell et al. [1960] 1980, Zaller 1992, Druckman and Nelson 2003). Some scholars are attempting to move beyond these traditional configurations (Druckman and Nelson 2003, Chong and Druckman 2007), but few take ordinary citizens as originators of influential political thought or even as idiomatic gatekeepers who possess the ability to police the boundaries of discourse through their acceptance or rejection of topics and ideas.

In contrast, I argue that members of the political community, even one as demonstrably dispersed, divided, and inattentive as the contemporary American one, quite capably manage to accomplish both. Not only do grass-roots associations of people with minority and marginalized interests frequently articulate and mobilize around original associations of foundational ideas and new purposes, the general public also acts as a kind of ideational goalie for those new ideas, granting authority to some people and ideas and ignoring or denying others.

Even if citizens in our mass-mediated democracy are more like members of an audience than participants in a deliberative conversation, they are still gifted with an essential power—the power that all audiences have to sanction or reject what is presented to them. In political discourse as in a theater, sanctioning amounts to attention coupled with signs of appreciation and concern. In politics, this attention can be measured by the level of public awareness on a given issue, and signs of appreciation and concern can likewise be assessed by the direction and intensity of public opinion as it is recorded in surveys over time. Contrary to the dominant source of concern in the twentieth-century studies of political participation and public opinion, this is an ability that extends well beyond the voting booth and touches upon our daily experience of politics. Even those citizens who do not have the interest or time to participate in the myriad types of active engagement that make up democratic participation—such as joining political campaigns or issue advocacy groups or phoning a representative—still play a role in shaping the politics of the day simply because they are both originators and evaluators of what counts as good common sense.

Furthermore, there is evidence that Americans understand the nature of their civic duty to be collective and general. Kinder and Kiewiet's research on sociotropic voting has shown that when evaluating candidates according to economic factors, Americans do not base their decisions on their personal finances, but instead on the state of the whole economy as they perceive it (Kinder and Kiewiet 1981, DeBoef and Nagler 2005). As previous researchers have argued, this is probably not an altruistic endeavor, but instead a way to gage the chances of the individual by taking account of the health of the whole. For my purposes the point is that one of the most basic questions Americans tend to ask themselves when evaluating politics is this: Is this a problem that does or ought to concern everyone?

According to a July 2003 opinion poll conducted by the Pew Research Center, Americans tend to believe that "moral issues" rather than "strictly political" issues are the ones that require their closest attention. In the survey, those questions that the majority of respondents designated as "moral" rather than "strictly polit-ical" also received majority support for governmental intervention or a change in policy action. These issues include concerns not normally identified with "the culture war" or "family values," including healthcare and the death penalty.[10]

This is because, in a democratic polity, members of the public, whether its individual members wait to be given options to choose from during a vote or put their creative, financial, and other resources into advocating for issues and policies, are always important players. Contemporary representative democracy puts citizens in the peculiar position of making judgments on policies that they did not directly author and that they cannot directly enforce. But nonetheless, the mass public, as it is perceived through the admittedly imperfect devices we have devised to apprehend pervasive opinion and collective mood, is the arbi-ter of public authority, which is one of the most important political resources (figure 5.2). This is especially true for those seeking to dissent from or raise chal-lenges to status quo beliefs, policies, and institutions.

There are several steps advocates must take in order to gain public authority and win political acceptance. The first step to winning public authority is to gain a platform from which the group can disseminate ideas. The way to complete this step is through *exposure*. For people with few resources, this exposure can only be secured through emergence into mainstream public discourse through media. In the age of the Internet and new media, this emergence is not always direct. Mainstream media increasingly looks to political blogs and trending top-ics on Twitter or viral memes on Tumblr for the latest news. However, as influ-ential as these domains have become, the broadest audience of people is still reached through traditional print and television news.

The second step to obtaining public authority is to *craft an intelligible and con-sistent message*, one that plays up the qualities of an issue that will likely convince a general interest audience that the subject is urgent, immediately relevant and worthy of sustained public attention and consideration. This may seem cynically strategic, but given the limited number of items that can ever become a part of

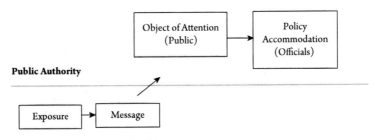

Figure 5.2 Discursive Model of Public Authority.

national political discourse and the fact that most of those items will be decided by official elites, it should instead be regarded as a pragmatic truth—one that does not automatically imply that groups will have to limit their speech to pandering and dissembling, but instead merely recognizes that challengers will not be successful if they develop messages that do not resonate with a political community wider than their membership. Message development in this case should not be thought of as advertisement for an issue, but instead clarification of the issue's importance in American political life.

Gaining exposure and crafting a resonant message confers authority to speak in the public sphere upon challenger groups. Social movement actors are given the opportunity to speak in press coverage, to ask questions or make demands of officials, and given greater access to the general public outside their membership. But this public authority is still only a tool to be used in the quest for political acceptance. Political acceptance must be earned by sustaining this effective hearing in mainstream public discourse over time. That is, to become a persistent *object of attention* by both officials and the general public. This third step is actually a kind of loop—officials may pay attention for a number of reasons: perhaps they have been looking for a grass-roots connection for an issue they already champion, or they have been seeking out an issue that can serve as a foil for a policy they advocate. However, the chief reason for public officials to remain interested in and take a policy position upon a new political issue is that they perceive public interest and attention to be piqued in such a way that they might pay a price for (or make gains from) their pronouncements and policy positions regarding the new issue. Likewise, mainstream media tend to put the spotlight on issues that officials have pronounced upon, and the political arguments that ensue are those the general public is most likely to encounter and form opinions about.

Once this loop gets going—with public interest piqued and officials pronouncing and arguing with one another, which argument in turn gets reported as news, galvanizing more or more intense public interest and causing officials to feel the need to take positions, which again get reported as news—then the issue is on its way to public acceptance. However, the crucial fourth step is sustaining this attention loop over a period long enough to prompt *policy accommodation*. This acceptance of new issues by a broad swath of the polity, won with the public authority that movement actors are able to garner with exposure and a resonant message, allows nonelite political challengers to become formidable voices in public debates with officials and other decision-making elites. Over time, this gives proponents of new arrangements of status quo power, the ability to shape public discourse in such a way that even when majorities disagree with the issue position of the challenger group, they accept the political salience of the issue and thus accord a place on the national issue agenda.

Political Acceptance in Mainstream Public Discourse

We have seen from the literature on both political communications and social movements that grass-roots political concerns do manage to emerge onto the pages of national daily papers and nationally broadcast segments in spite of the dense and familiar cascade of official-centered news from the top down (Bennett [1983] 2011, Gans 2005, Entman 2004, Drezner and Farell 2007).[11] In such an environment, emergence of new issues into mainstream politics is usually the result of an effort-filled and even painful process initiated by issue advocates. Dauntingly, as I argued above, a single story or even a month of stories that appear in mainstream media about a new political issue, or the *exposure* of that issue, is only the first step toward issue acceptance. In order to motivate the level of public awareness, concern, and elite response that is necessary for political change, the challenger group must leverage this exposure into *public authority*, which can then be used to share a resonant message with the general public that can help the group's issue become an object of sustained attention by the media, official elites, and the public. The result of these steps, if successful, is the incorporation of the new issue into the limited lexicon of regular political subjects that the public acknowledges as significant and that officials are charged to address, which is evidenced by *issue accommodation* in the form of both rhetoric and policies offered (but not necessarily adopted) by elected officials or other political elites.

As I have underscored, an issue's acceptance into political debate does not guarantee its approval, especially not in the short term. Indeed, public opinion may be largely set against the challenging claimants and their policy preferences, and elites may rail against the state of American politics, which demands such claims have to be considered. However, once both groups give their sustained attention to these newly politicized concerns, further development of opinion and policy on the issue is effectively sanctioned, giving challengers a regular and legitimated space to articulate their concerns, as well as more opportunities to advance their cause with multiple audiences (figure 5.3).

The final evidence of political acceptance is *issue accommodation*. This means that media, elites, and the public begin talking about a solution to the challenger-defined problem in policy terms, and officials may also offer and even pass policies meant to address the problem that the political challenger has raised. Often the issue accommodation offered is short of what challengers have demanded and may be tried at the municipal or state level in advance of national uptake. It can then be bandied about as a hypothetical solution by officials when they are taking positions. In order to witness evidence of this process, coverage

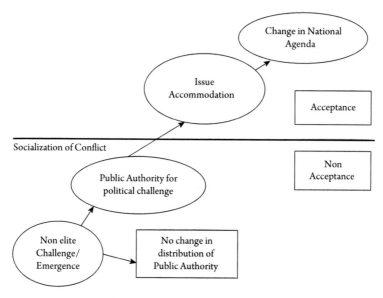

Figure 5.3 Discursive Model of Political Acceptance.

of an issue must continue over time, be accompanied by the repeated response of officials and established elites, and stimulate the persistent interest of the public in such a way that the policy environment is changed—not that the challenger wins, necessarily, but that options to placate the challenger become legitimate, simultaneously legitimating the challenger's issue.

It is important to acknowledge that there is a feedback relationship between exposure and acceptance that might seem confounding. It could be that the general public becomes interested in anything that receives sustained media coverage, at least enough to answer with an opinion when asked, and the presence of such opinions might compel elected officials to take rhetorical positions. However, this line of reasoning underestimates the power of interested citizens as active audience. It is not the case that people become interested in whatever issues mainstream media cover. Even when issues are covered with great intensity over a matter of days or weeks, it is not the case that members of the public or the public in the aggregate will follow the coverage or evaluate the issue as important. A recent example of a media frenzy that never created much concern in the general public is the coverage of the federal investigation that followed a surprise attack on an American consulate on September 11, 2012, in Benghazi, Libya. The attack resulted in the deaths of four diplomats, including the U.S. ambassador to Libya, J. Christopher Stevens. According to a September 16 poll conducted by Pew Research Center, the attack itself generated quite a bit of interest, with 43 percent of respondents claiming to follow reports of the incident very closely (Pew 2012b). However, the investigation that followed, with

much covered conflict between partisan elites as to whether the American public had been deliberately misled about the events leading to the attack, resulted
in much lower (and much more partisan) interest. A Pew poll conducted in
November 2012 revealed that only 28 percent were following news of the investigation (Pew 2013b). And, more generally, according to a CNN poll conducted
in December, a majority of the American public simply did not believe that the
Obama administration had been dishonest about the events that had transpired
(CNN 2012). In addition, while the Benghazi story was the only foreign affairs
story to appear on Pew News Interest Index "Top Stories of 2012" list, it was the
least attended story, with only 31 percent of respondents reporting that they had
followed the story at all (Pew 2013b).

Once there is a convergence of mainstream media coverage and public concern, however, official responses are inevitable. However, decisive action by
political officials that seems to answer the claims of challengers can end discussion about an emergent issue. This has very little to do with whether or not the
core problems raised by challengers in the debate have actually been dealt with
in good faith. For example, in the case of the living wage movement, while 120
municipal ordinances have been passed since 1994, there have been significant
barriers to implementation. As of 2002, when only 82 ordinances had been
passed, Stephanie Luce found that the implementation of 10 percent (8) of the
ordinances was blocked (some retroactively repealed by state legislatures claiming that municipalities have no authority to pass such laws), and 52 percent (42)
had been narrowly implemented, which means that city administrators had
written up rules to determine coverage and apply the ordinance, but there was
no system of oversight and no requirement for affected business to report compliance with regulations. That means that up to 62 percent of the ordinances
passed at this time may have been completely ineffective. Yet few municipalities
have considered revised legislation, and in most cases the advocates, activists,
and coalitions that spearheaded the original legislation moved on to address new
issues, rarely returning to the often defunct living wage legislation (Luce 2004).

Issues can also fade from public discussion even when there is intense interest
and vigorous elite position-taking, even while the topic remains a live issue in
resource allocation and governance. For example, outrage over the gross governmental negligence that led to the excruciating circumstances documented in
the gulf region after Hurricane Katrina in August 2005 caused the emergence of
many unusual topics in national debate. All of a sudden reporters, entertainers,
politicians, and ordinary people were talking to each other about the possibility of systemic racism; the existence and detrimental effects of nepotism in the
executive branch; and the persistence and growth of huge economic disparities
in America, topics that rarely rise to the level of mainstream national dialogue.
Activists and scholars who have been concerned about the consequences of race

and poverty on the life chances of America's marginal populations were hopeful that the mass attention to the issue would be sustained. Even the conservative *New York Times* columnist David Brooks was moved to write about stories like Hurricane Katrina (Brooks 2005). Scholars of labor and race Dara Strolovitch, Dorian Warren, and Paul Frymer wrote hopefully:

> While it is therefore unlikely that public policies in the aftermath of Katrina will resolve these disparities, perhaps the inequalities laid bare by the hurricane will provide a longer-term wake-up call to those who wish to actively build a more fair and meaningful democracy in the United States. In particular, we hope that new attention will be paid to the role of American political institutions in structuring and perpetuating contemporary racial, economic, regional, and gendered inequities. (Strolovitch, Warren, and Frymer 2006)

However, by the midterm elections in 2006 *none* of these issues made the short list of subjects dominating national political dialogue.[12]

More recently, the explosion of the Deepwater Horizon oil rig off the Gulf Coast on April 20, 2010, prompted both intense media coverage and high public interest. In fact, public interest in the story exceeded news coverage as measured by the difference between the percentage of Americans who claimed to be following the story closely (44 percent) and the percentage of the "news hole," or overall news coverage, that the story took up (3 percent) (PEJ 2011). The massive leakage caused by the initial explosion proved difficult to stop, and the broken oil container continued to spew oil into the ocean for more than three months. The ongoing environmental disaster prompted, as had Katrina, the rise of unusual questions about possible systemic failures regarding the regulation of large corporations that handle potentially dangerous materials, reopening a popular debate on the contours of the responsibility and potential efficacy of government in the lives of American citizens. In reviewing coverage of the disaster, the Pew Project for Excellence in Journalism found that

> press coverage matched interest initially, but the public stayed focused on three of these stories . . . long after media attention had shifted to other emerging stories . . . [L]ess than a month after the July 15 capping of the Deepwater Horizon, 44% of Americans continued to say they were following news about the spill and its aftermath more closely than any other topic. Yet just 3% of news coverage focused on the spill's aftermath, as the press focus turned toward the upcoming midterm elections. (PEJ 2011)

Conclusion

In this chapter I have explicated a model of discursive political change that I call political acceptance. I have argued that the elements that are important to consider when mapping and evaluating political change are advocates' efforts to frame their issue and the degree to which they are able to win public authority by socializing conflict. In order to articulate the relationships among challengers, media, and the public in the process of political change, I have examined two literatures that offer insight about how political communication is organized as well as what role social movements play in political change. Although both the literature on political communication and the literature on social movements have much to offer, the first focuses on a top-down approach that is inadequate for evaluating how political change from the bottom up is possible, or how it happens. The second literature focuses on how challengers are able to both take advantage of and create conditions for political change, but characterizes the relationship between movement organizations and the press as inherently antagonistic while paying little attention to the ways that challenger organizations benefit from expanding the scope of political conflict beyond the movement members and the elected officials and into the mainstream public sphere.

I propose instead that we might explain political change from the bottom up by looking through the lens of changes in mainstream political discourse, which in turn alter the *doxic* or commonplace understanding of what issues are worthy of national concern and attention. Political acceptance is not the same as political agreement. Rather, political acceptance results from challengers' ability to make a compelling case for a period of at least one year, convincing the polity, including media, official elites, and the public, that their issue is worthy to be commonly considered important and in need of address. During the period between the exposure of a new issue and when mainstream discourse begins to change regarding the matter, it is not only agreement or support that the challenger must seek, but more importantly the public incorporation of the challenger's issue into the limited lexicon of regular political subjects—those the mainstream media covers, the public acknowledges as significant, and officials are compelled to address. In the long run, it is winning this place in the discourse of American politics that makes political change from the bottom up possible.

In the following chapter, I statistically examine the political discourse and public opinion on the topics of marriage equality and the living wage over the ten-year period of each movement's emergence between 1994 and 2004. A close look at mainstream discourse on these two topics reveals that marriage equality was not only covered as a news issue nearly three times as often as the living wage, but also that the nature of the discussion on the two topics differed in

several essential ways. While public opinion throughout the period overwhelmingly favored raising the federal minimum wage and, in local polling, nearly
universally approved the idea of the living wage, the topic was rarely covered in
the news, and when it was, the arguments used in support did not present the
issue in terms that were able to overcome the pervasive "rhetoric of reaction,"
whereby suggestions that policy changes are needed are met with the notion that
attempting change will make no difference or risks losing gains that have already
been won, which can only make matters worse (Hirschman 1991). The marriage
equality debate, on the other hand, had high salience and was coherent, resonant, and articulated in a way that made the issue seem immediately important,
necessary to address, and solvable through public action. While public opinion
on the topic remained relatively stable during the decade, the public's understanding of the topic changed markedly, and political acceptance took place, laying the groundwork for the steady and dramatic change we have seen in public
opinion and policy success since 2004.

6

From Marginal to Mainstream

In this chapter I focus on the content and meaning of the mainstream discourses about the living wage and marriage equality as well as how each changed in the decade of their emergence. I have hypothesized that the difference in the way these two movement issues appeared in public discussion is a significant factor in the differential impact that each has had on American politics generally, and the differential outcomes that the two social movements have had in achieving lasting success. I lay out those differences in mainstream public discourse by submitting the text to both the qualitative textual analysis I have engaged in throughout the book, as well as the quantitative examination that is the subject of this chapter. My method of textual analysis throughout has been inductive, and the qualitative and quantitative examinations are inextricably linked.

I should say at the outset that there is no consensus on how frames may affect the way individuals process information. There are some views that conceptualize the impact of frames as additive, as with Gamson and Modigliani's concept of "interpretive packages" (Gamson and Modigliani 1989), and others like Chong and Druckman's (2007, 2010, 2013) suggesting that the impact of frames is weighted by psychological considerations or political context. I do not take a position on which of these notions is definitive because my analysis does not turn on how individuals process frames and I assume that either model could be correct and most likely, each kind of individual information processing may take place given particular conditions. Instead, I am focused on how frames shape public discourse. My model, therefore, takes account of both how many frames combine statistically and how well they cohere, because both of these possible pathways of frame impact are likely operative in actually existing politics and help me measure the probable impact of frames in shaping common public understandings of political problems.

Therefore, I undertook the investigation of the text by systematically cataloging and coding the news discourse on the living wage and marriage equality in two newspapers between 1994 and 2004. Unlike many studies that utilize content analysis as a part of their method of study, I examine the full text of the

1,190 articles that I collected from the *New York Times* and *USA Today*, rather than only the headlines and abstracts, because I am concerned with the way arguments are linked with one another and cohere together, creating the common understanding (meaning) of the public discourse on political topics. I use the textual analysis software ATLAS.ti to systematically hand code each article at the level of the paragraph, making note of frequently covered topics (such as political impact of gay marriage on a candidate or campaign), frequently used words and phrases (such as "free market" or "gay rights"), as well as recurring arguments for what is at stake in each issue ("working people deserve a decent wage" or "same-sex marriage is about equal access to the legal benefits of the institution") (table 6.1).

Along with the close reading of the discourse on these two topics, I also use a kind of statistical analysis called principal component analysis (PCA), which allows me to observe which arguments tend to occur together, creating nested packages of arguments that cohere together to form common logics regarding the political issues under discussion.[1] These argument clusters are statistically identifiable *frames*. In addition to the statistical identification of frames, principal component analysis also reveals four additional characteristics of the discourse on these topics. The first is the *salience* of each argument, or the number of arguments that appear in the *New York Times* and *USA Today* on each topic. Second, I look at the *strength* of each argument, which is measured by the magnitude of the correlation between arguments that rise and fall together in frames. The third is the level of *attention* accorded each frame. The level of attention is measured by multiplying the salience by the strength of each argument or frame. The fourth characteristic is the *resonance* of each frame. Resonance is measured by the number of distinct arguments that cluster together to create the statistically identified frames that exist in the news

Table 6.1 **Discourse Analysis Using Principal Component Analysis**

Frames	Clusters of arguments that co-occur together across texts and over time
Salience	Frequency of argument occurrence or frame co-occurrence
Strength	Magnitude of the correlation between arguments that rise and fall together in frames
Attention	Measured by multiplying the salience by the strength of each argument or frame
Resonance	Measured by the number of distinct arguments that cluster together to create the statistically identified frames that exists in the news discourse

discourse. Finally, I give an overview of public opinion on each of the two topics over the time period to show the level of public awareness on the issues as well as the way that public ideas of what is at stake change during the decade of study.

Between 1994 and 2004, gay marriage was not only routinely, but also increasingly, covered in mainstream media. Over the period, the public became more convinced of it as a political issue and elected officials were expected to take a position as a matter of course. At the same time, the living wage was certainly an emergent issue in national political discourse, but advocates were not able to enlarge the scope of conflict enough to sustain public attention. This means they were unable to generate the attendant public authority required to push against the orthodox arguments of their more powerful opponents. Instead, national reporting on the living wage was steady during the time period of interest, but of low frequency and little intensity. Publics outside the locales where living wage struggles took place were not very aware of the issue, and national elites rarely mentioned, let alone took public positions on, the topic.

Quantitative analysis of the discourse on the two topics shows that, overall, the national living wage debate was low-salience, diffuse on the advocate side but coherent on opponent side, and dissonant rather than resonant. The marriage equality debate, on the other hand was high-salience, coherent on both supporting and opposing sides, and resonant. In addition, marriage equality advocates framed their issue as urgent, necessary, and efficacious.[2] This "rhetoric of change" contradicted the "rhetoric of reaction" that says that political and social changes inevitably lead to perverse outcomes, are futile, or put what has already been gained in jeopardy (Hirshman 1991).

Frames and Media Characteristics

Before delving into the results of the analysis in detail, it is important to define some key terms. My examination of the news discourse on living wage and marriage equality focuses on identifying frames. Frames "enable individuals to locate, perceive, identify, and label occurrences within their life space and the world at large" (Snow et al. 1986, 464). Frames are the way that people organize the world conceptually, one of the linguistic tools that we use to make sense of the innumerable happenings in the world, providing a way to organize certain information into our consideration as relevant, while discarding other kinds of information. Framing is a necessary and inevitable process that takes place in both individual thought and interpersonal and mass communication. I pay special attention to the kinds of frames that emerge in mainstream discourse about the living wage and marriage equality because recurring frames reveal common understandings of political issues in our national discourse.

Obviously, print news is not the only, or even the primary source from which most Americans get their news. Television news is still the medium from which most people get most of their news. In addition, Internet sites, particularly social media like Facebook and Twitter, are rising as important sources of news consumption, especially for people aged eighteen to twenty-nine (Saad 2013). As of 2008, the Internet overtook newspapers as the second most favored site for news consumption behind television (Pew 2012a). However, the Internet was only just becoming a source for news between 1994 and 2004, the period of movement emergence for both living wage and marriage equality.

Television, on the other hand, was and is the most consumed source of news. I do not include television news in my sample, however, because procuring systematic samples of television news is prohibitively expensive. In general, though, it is important to note that television news tends to differ from print news in terms of both content and audience. In terms of content, television news contains fewer supporting facts about topical issues and more news analysis performed by anchors, expert guests, or pundits. In addition, television news tends to be more heavily weighted toward horse race or political impact coverage rather than coverage of policy content. Television news stories also tend to frame their coverage around personalities rather than topics, for example, tending to cover the personal biographies of candidates more frequently than candidate platforms (Pew 2000). In terms of audience, television news viewers during the period tended to be younger, less well educated, and less interested in news than print news consumers. Today, those demographic differences remain similar, however, television news audiences are also graying, with more and more people under the age of thirty getting their news from the Internet, particularly from articles shared on social networking cites via mobile devices (Pew 2012a).

Given what we know about the systematic differences between the information contained in newspapers and television, we might expect that TV coverage would be less nuanced than print coverage, containing fewer frames, but that those frames might be stronger, or cohere more tightly than those present in print media. If these suppositions are correct, limiting analysis to newspaper data might give an overly nuanced view of the discursive environment that most Americans engage with; however, there is no reason to believe that the most salient, strongest, attention-getting arguments in print and broadcast journalism would differ significantly from those found on TV, especially considering that TV news still looks to print (and increasingly, the Internet) to determine which are the top stories on the national political agenda. This is because, even amid the much-ballyhooed decline of print media readership and revenues in the twenty-first century, print media organizations still produce the bulk of original news reporting (Pew 2010).

Data and Methods

I examine political discourse on the living wage and marriage equality, using the *New York Times* and *USA Today* as representative of mainstream political discourse. I built a data set including all the articles mentioning gay marriage and the living wage between 1994 and 2004. I chose the *New York Times* because it is a news organ that sets the agenda for other papers with national reach and the *USA Today* because it has the highest circulation and broadest distribution in the United States. In my initial search for relevant articles in both papers using both ProQuest and LexisNexis, I used terms closely related to gay marriage and the living wage (i.e., "minimum wage," "prevailing wage," and "domestic partnership," "same-sex marriage") to make sure that I collected a data set that was as comprehensive as possible.

The data analysis has multiple steps, but I want to recount it in detail as I believe it is a useful process that other researchers can use when carrying out discourse analysis, particularly analysis of frames. Discourse analysis is inductive, from the development of the initial codes to the statistical identification of frames. At every step, the analysis I use seeks to reveal patterns that are present in the discourse rather than to test for what I think might be present. This is because my principal concern is the content and meaning that is actually present in the common public discourse on these two topics during the time period. In this way, my work is the careful and systematic catalog of content-in-context, which seeks to uncover public understandings of the two issues. As shown in table 6.2, the completed data set contains 851 articles from the *New York Times* and 339 from *USA Today*, yielding a total of 1,190 articles to analyze.

I code the entirety of the articles at the level of the paragraph, rather than focusing on their headlines and abstracts, as I am interested in the content and meaning of arguments, not only the topics and tone of coverage. This level of analysis yields 7,602 coded arguments for examination.

Once I coded all available articles, I made a quantitative matrix representing the coded data so that I could submit the discourse to statistical analysis.

Table 6.2 **Number of Articles on Living Wage and Marriage Equality in the *New York Times* and *USA Today***

	New York Times	*USA Today*	*Total*
Marriage equality	698	322	1020
Living wage	153	17	170
Total	851	339	1190

I was then able to see how arguments rose and declined in tandem over the time period. The idea behind this kind of analysis is that clusters of arguments that rise and fall together constitute "frames" that can be statistically verified. I am interested in the coverage and framing of marriage equality and the living wage during the time period, a period in which the framing of marriage equality, in contrast to that of the living wage, led to the political acceptance of the issue, an acceptance that began to pay dividends by the end of the first decade of the twenty-first century.

Baumgartner, De Boef, and Boydstun use a similar method of frame analysis in their book *The Decline of the Death Penalty and the Discovery of Innocence*, which I adapt for use with my data set (Baumgartner 2008). Because Baumgartner and coauthors are studying a well-established, rather than emerging, issue, they have six decades of news discourse available for analysis. Because my issues only emerged in the last twenty years and I am especially interested in observing political acceptance, a process that took place for one of the issues in the ten years following emergence, I focus only on data from between 1994 and 2004. While Baumgartner and his coauthors use factor analysis, developing a technique that they call evolutionary factor analysis (EFA), I use principal component analysis. I chose to use PCA for two main reasons. First, it is a statistical method that is based on identifying correlated patterns in data, just as factor analysis is; however, principal component analysis can deliver reliable estimates while requiring less data. In addition, factor analysis is particularly suited to uncover the underlying structure of data in an entire data set, while I am principally interested in how key arguments cluster together (correlate) over time. Generally speaking, PCA is a statistical method quantitative researchers use before putting data into some kind of regression analysis. It is useful for this purpose because PCA reveals how one can combine highly correlated variables in a smart way, without yielding imprecise (variables that are too highly correlated) or biased estimates (which result from excluding important data—if, say, you were to drop a variable that you thought was similar to another, but it actually statistically is not). I, too, am interested in how my variables combine, but since my variables are arguments, the payoff for me is the information that PCA reveals, rather than what further regression analysis would reveal.

PCA is also a handy tool for the analysis of discourse because discursive data have one special characteristic: they are always highly correlated. When you select discourses on the same topic, the coded elements of discourse will necessarily covary. This is a plain feature of language. When we talk to each other about particular subjects we reference similar words, phrases, and concepts because that is what conversation on a topic must consist of in order to be intelligible. PCA has the virtue of showing how correlated the entire discourse is while also giving information about specific arguments in the discourse, including whether or how they coalesce into frames and how salient, strong, attention-getting, and resonant those frames are. Given that this is so, I count arguments as making up a statistically identifiable frame only if the proportion of the variance explained by the arguments in combination yields a first component with an eigenvalue of .80 or higher.[3] Additionally, individual arguments are only considered to be a part of identified frames if the eigenvectors of their first component explains .30 or more of the entire frame.[4]

So that it is possible to read the tables that follow, let me take you through the illustrative example provided in table 6.3.

In the *New York Times* discourse on gay marriage, a frame that I dub "about equality" consists of five distinct arguments, two of which evoke the black civil rights struggle during the mid-twentieth century. The first refers to the movement in general and the second specifically evokes antimiscegenation laws that made interracial marriage illegal. A letter to the editor published in the *New York Times* on June 13, 1996, under the headline "It Boils Down to Bigotry," makes this straightforward argument clear:

> Substitute the words "black" or "Jew" for "same sex" in any argument opposing gay marriage and you will see this position for what it really is—bigotry. In time, this will seem as legally ludicrous as the miscegenation trials of the past.

The other three arguments that cohere together in this frame include one that argues that marriage rights are the next natural step in the fight against discrimination of gay people; that preventing gay people from having the right to marry prevents them from having equal access to partner benefits that straight people

Table 6.3 **Frame Analysis, the *New York Times* on Marriage Equality: "About Equality"**

Argument	Proportion of Variation Explained by Argument
Civil right invocation	.45
Equal access argument	.45
Interracial marriage analogy	.45
Gay rights	.44
Against constitutional ban	.43

Eigenvalue or total "Strength" of frame = 4.86.
Proportion of variation explained in first component = .97.

have access to; and that a constitutional ban on same-sex marriage would be writing discrimination into America's most important founding document.

The data show that these five arguments are so tightly correlated that this particular combination of arguments accounts for .97, or 97 percent, of variation observed among these terms (for a point of reference: the entire marriage equality discourse in the *New York Times* is correlated at a rate of .61). Additionally, the civil rights, equal access, and interracial marriage arguments are each correlated with all the arguments in the frame at a rate of .45. The claim that marriage rights are a natural extension of the gay rights movement is slightly less correlated with the other arguments, as they co-occur in the news discourse at a rate of .44, and the argument against a federal constitutional ban is the least correlated with the other arguments in the frame at a rate of .43.

As indicated above, the idea of looking at the way arguments correlate over time is to empirically designate which arguments cluster together into *frames*. The potency of frames can be measured in several ways. The most common way to measure frame potency is to report the number of times the argument occurs in the sample, or the frequency of the argument. In the case of news discourse, this frequency is often called *salience*. A second less commonly reported way to measure frame potency is to report the *strength* or power of the frame. This is because determining the strength of the frame requires statistical analysis. The strength of a frame is the numerical measure of how tightly the arguments in the frame are correlated. This is measured by the eigenvalue accorded the argument cluster in principal component analysis. The eigenvalue shows the magnitude (size) of the relationship between the correlated arguments. The third piece of information PCA reveals is the *attention* accorded the frame in the entirety of the sample of discourse. This is a measure of the salience multiplied by the strength of the frame. You can have a weaker and less prominent or a stronger and more prominent clustering of arguments. The fourth bit of information that PCA yields is a key term for this book: that is, PCA can reveal the *resonance* of a particular frame. In the foregoing chapters, I have developed a theory of resonance and its impact on political acceptance and the process of political change. I have posited that arguments are more likely to hold together in cohesive frames when they have certain characteristics: namely, resonant frames tend to combine some commonplace existing understandings of the way things are through common-sense logics of the way things work or relate with new arguments about what is significant or what is to be done. The alignment of these three elements can be utilized for new political purposes. In this chapter, I statistically identify the degree of resonance that can be attributed to the inductively determined frames in the discourses on marriage equality and the living wage. PCA allows me to do this by showing the number of distinct arguments that cluster together to form one single cohesive frame. I consider frames that contain four or more arguments that reveal background beliefs, linking logics, and new ideas to be resonant, while those that hold together fewer arguments are not.[5]

Describing Public Discourse on the Living Wage, 1994–2004

Public discourse on the living wage during the first ten years of the issue's emergence into the public debate was infrequent or, low salience, in national news. The *New York Times* carried 154 stories on the living wage over the ten-year period, with an average of 15.4 stories per year. There were spikes in coverage in 1996 when activists were pushing for a living wage law in New York City and an even larger spike in coverage in 2001 and 2002 when two kinds of events drew the paper's attention to the issue. The first was a spate of local legislation. Suffolk County, New York, passed a county-wide living wage law over executive veto in June 2001. And in early 2002, Albany, the state's capital city, followed suit, passing living wage legislation and prolonging coverage of the issue. The second event was a month of demonstrations by Harvard University students in support of adopting a living wage at their university and against the incoming university president, Larry Summers, who had held the reins at the Treasury department between 1999 and 2001. A story run on June 17, 2001, headlined "Harvard's Hoard," explains:

> Summers's appointment in April was barely a month old before Massachusetts Hall, which houses his new office, was taken over by dozens of students protesting Harvard's failure to provide a "living wage" of $10.25 to all its employees. Over the next 26 days, tents popped up in Harvard Yard, as students, professors and workers slept outside in sympathy. Robert Reich, the former labor secretary, dropped by to show support. Senator Edward Kennedy tried to enter the building to meet with the students, but the police wouldn't allow it. Newspapers across the country ran editorials taking Harvard to task for refusing to spend even the smallest fraction of its endowment to improve the lives of its workers. Drawings of Summers as Marie Antoinette began to go up around Harvard Yard.

The former Bush administration official provided a high-profile opponent for student activists as well as a symbolic figure of opposition for national figures supportive of labor issues. The *New York Times* seemed to relish the tableau of students at one of the nation's most respected universities taking over campus buildings and setting up encampments on the famous Harvard Yard. And, in combination with the local legislative commotions, the event provided a news peg for coverage of union organizing and low-wage work throughout New York and in the surrounding region. However, in 2003, coverage of the living wage fell from the peak coverage of thirty stories in 2002 back to the 2000 level of only ten stories during the year. In 2004, the paper ran only one story about the living wage.

As a point of comparison, marriage equality stories in the *New York Times* followed a very different pattern. There were actually more stories on the living wage than on marriage equality in 1994 and 1995. However, coverage of marriage equality increased over the period, with brief declines in coverage in 1997, 2001, and 2002 and a dramatic spike in coverage in 2003 and 2004. Even during declines in coverage, marriage equality never returned to its lowest level of coverage in 1994. Chart 6.1 compares the trends in the *New York Times'* coverage of these two issues between 1994 and 2004.

Coverage of the living wage in *USA Today* was much sparser than in the *New York Times*. In general, the frames that appear in *USA Today* are weaker than those in the *New York Times*, meaning that the eigenvalues resulting from principal component analysis are lower, indicating that the frames are less robust. The paper with the highest national circulation ran an average of 1.7 stories per year, with no coverage at all in 1994 and 2003, and peak coverage in 1998, when the paper began to run a news summary feature called "Across the USA: News from Every State," which reported all kinds of noteworthy happenings in states all over the country and sometimes provided short blurbs on the passage of new wage legislation, as in this short write-up run on December 3, 1998:

> *California* Los Angeles—Although he vetoed the original "living wage" law, Mayor Richard Riordan reportedly will let an expansion of the measure go into effect. The new ordinance would force more companies with city contracts to pay service workers about $7.50 an hour with benefits and $8.64 without them. The state minimum wage is $5.75 an hour.

These reports were provided with little to no context, and by 2000 the feature ceased to run. The paper did run traditional news articles on the living wage as well, but only very infrequently. Chart 6.2 compares the frequency of stories on the living wage in the *New York Times* and *USA Today*.

In 2004, during a presidential election year, when issues that are perceived by reporters, officials, and the public to have bearing on the national contest receive a bump in coverage and other issues experience a drop in coverage, the

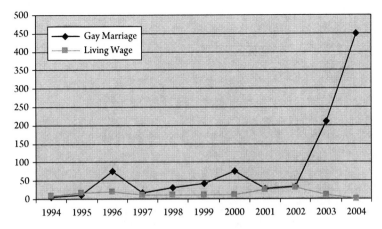

Chart 6.1 Marriage Equality and the Living Wage in the *New York Times*.

living wage had the lowest rate of coverage observed over the ten-year period, with only one story in both the *New York Times* and *USA Today*. This is especially curious as, in 2004, ACORN and affiliated living wage activists successfully organized a living wage ballot initiative in Florida, a pivotal state in every presidential contest, and especially decisive in 2004. The ballot initiative, called Amendment 5, passed with 71 percent voter approval, while at the same time, Florida voters elected to return George W. Bush to office with 52 percent of their votes going to the incumbent. Given the significance of Florida in the presidential contest and the prominence of the living wage issue in state politics during the election year, the lack of coverage of the issue in national papers is puzzling. However, it may be the case that, as has been the habit of movement activists, most of their considerable effort and skill was poured into the local campaign with the assumption that it would pay national dividends, but

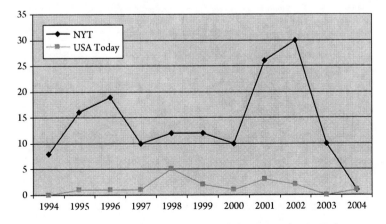

Chart 6.2 Stories on the Living Wage in the *New York Times* and *USA Today*.

without an accompanying effort to *tell the story* of the Florida living wage campaign as a part of the national election story.

New York Times

The tone of the coverage of the living wage was generally positive in the *New York Times*, as I show in chart 6.3.

Principal component analysis reveals that there are a total of seven frames in the *New York Times* coverage of the living wage (table 6.4). Six of these are positive in tone. However, the single anti-living wage frame that appears is more salient by itself than any single positive frame, with 168 arguments pointing out flaws and suspected consequences of adopting living wage legislation. Even so, as shown in chart 6.4, positive arguments appear almost twice as often as negative ones.

As table 6.5 shows, the strongest and most resonant of the six positive frames describing the living wage in the *New York Times* simply asserts that "hard-working people are entitled to make a living wage."[6]

This frame is among the most resonant on either topic, with six frames co-occurring 82 percent of the time. The arguments address the idea of the living wage from a variety of different angles, together making the case that the living wage deals with a serious moral problem that affects American workers, keeping them impoverished even when they work full time. In addition, arguments in this frame point to the need for corporations to be accountable for

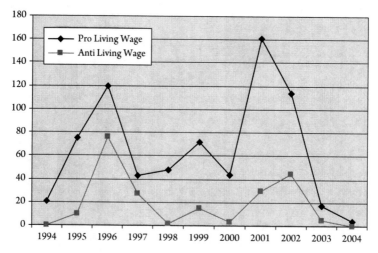

Chart 6.3 Pro- and Anti-Living Wage Arguments in the *New York Times*.

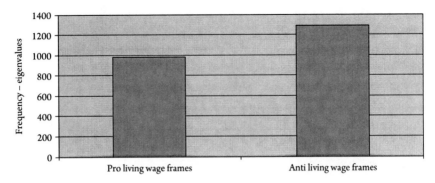

Chart 6.4 Weighted Attention to Pro- and Anti-Living Wage Frames in the *New York Times.*

Table 6.4 **Living Wage Frames Present in the *New York Times*, 1994–2004**

Pro	Anti
Full-time workers deserve living wage (132)	Anxieties about living wage (168)
Problem of poverty (57)	
Challenging economic orthodoxy (39)	
Bad conditions of low-wage work (31)	
Lifts poor from poverty (27)	
Righteous cause (22)	

Note: Number in parentheses is the frequency with which the arguments in the frame appear.

the wages that they pay workers, especially when the low wages that they pay still leave workers in need of public assistance. The other five positive frames in the *New York Times* discourse on the living wage describe the bad conditions of low-wage workers, as well as the overall problem of poverty in America. They also include claims that a living wage can lift the poor from poverty, state the difficulty of challenging economic orthodoxy, and tout the living wage as a righteous cause, but none reach the level of resonance, being made up of three or fewer arguments.

Although the tone of the coverage is positive and the most salient positive frame is both strong and resonant, it is not clear how much value the five additional positive frames add for making the case for a living wage. Indeed, it may be the case that more frames are actually harmful rather than helpful when they are not resonant—especially given that the single anti-living wage frame that exists in the *New York Times* is the strongest and most resonant of any frame in my

Table 6.5 **Frame Analysis, the *New York Times* on Living Wage: "Full-Time Workers Deserve"**

Argument	Proportion of Variation Explained by Argument
Full-time workers deserve	.43
Corporate accountability	.43
Public approval	.41
Myth of teenaged only low-wage	.41
Morally obligated	.38
Low wages equals welfare	.36

Eigenvalue or total "Strength" of frame = 4.9.
Proportion of variation explained in first component = .82.

Table 6.6 **Frame Analysis, the *New York Times* on Living Wage: "Anxieties about the Living Wage"**

Argument	Proportion of Variation Explained by Argument
So-called living wage	.26*
Business pushback	.35
Free-market principles	.33
Hurts those meant to help	.34
Limited coverage	.34
Low opinion of unions	.35
Socialists	.33
Uncertain costs	.34
Ordinance details	.32

Eigenvalue or total "strength" of frame = 7.7.
Proportion of variation explained in first component = .86.

sample on either topic. The frame, seen in table 6.6, which I call "anxieties about the living wage," consists of nine separate arguments, which co-occur together 86 percent of the time.

The overall strength of the frame is 7.7, a larger magnitude of coherence than any other frame in my data set. In addition, as shown in chart 6.4, given the strength of the frame, the weighted attention (strength × salience) to the "anxieties" frame exceeds that of all the positive living wage frames taken together.

Table 6.7 The Rhetoric of Reaction in the Living Wage Discourse

Jeopardy	Futility	Perverse Effects
Business pushback "I have serious doubt, based not on empirical evidence but on talking to business people, that we can make the leap to what is called the living wage and still remain competitive."[a]	*Limited coverage* "But the living wage movement, even if it spreads, will at most raise the pay of 75,000 workers. Only those companies with government contracts must comply, and they pay most of their workers more than the living wage already."[b]	*Hurt those meant to help* "We're in very difficult fiscal times and it's critical that the city make the most of every tax dollar that it spends. This would make the least of every tax dollar and translate into massive service reductions that hurt precisely the kinds of people the bill's proponents claim they are trying to help."[c]
Socialist "I believe employers should be aware that employees who earn under $10 cannot lead and independent life But I do not believe that government should dictate wages. We have seen this fall in Socialist and Communist countries. It will do irreparable harm."[d]	*Free-market principles* "There is no government shortcut to creating good jobs at decent wages. The best role for the city is to lower taxes and improve the overall quality of life, then let businesses create jobs and encourage their workers to acquire the skills that would earn them a better living."[e]	*Uncertain costs* "The City Council Speaker, Peter F. Vallone, who holds great sway over every piece of legislation the City Council Considers, said he supported the idea, but had reservations about the ultimate cost of the proposal and was trying to negotiate a compromise bill."[f]
		So-called living wage "To pay for a 'living wage' law, New York would face two choices: slashing services for which it uses private contractors—including low-income housing, AIDS services and foster care—or cutting back in other areas like education, libraries and transit. Either way, the poor would suffer most."[g]

[a] Louis Uchitelle, "Some Cities Flexing Fiscal Muscle to Make Employers Raise Wages," *New York Times*, April 3, 1996.
[b] Jeff Madrick, "Economic Scene: Living Wages Are Practical and Don't Let Theory Get in the Way," *New York Times*, June 24, 2001.
[c] Steve Greenhouse, "Unions Push for Higher Minimum Wage on New York City Contracts," *New York Times*, January 2, 1996.
[d] Louis Uchitelle, "Minimum Wages City by City: As More Local Laws Pass, More Businesses Complain," *New York Times*, November 19, 1999.
[e] Heather MacDonald, "'Living Wages,' Fewer Jobs," *New York Times*, January 12, 1996.
[f] Steve Greenhouse, "Unions Push for Higher Minimum Wage on New York City Contracts," *New York Times*, January 2, 1996.
[g] Heather MacDonald, "Living Wages, Fewer Jobs," *New York Times*, January 12, 1996.

In addition, the "anxieties" frame utilizes Hirschman's "rhetoric of reaction" in textbook fashion, which I break down in table 6.7. Instead of attacking the idea that workers deserve a living wage, most of the arguments in the powerfully resonant frame point to the potential jeopardy, futility, and perverse effects that might be caused by living wage legislation.

USA Today

Since the actual discursive content of each paper is different and the PCA method allows me to determine what frames are present in the debate inductively, the frames that we see in the *USA Today* are made up of similar arguments that cluster somewhat differently, yielding different frames than those that are present in the *New York Times*.

Table 6.8 shows the five frames present in the living wage debate in *USA Today*.

Table 6.8 **Living Wage Frames Present in *USA Today*, 1994–2004**

Pro	Anti
Fairness (48)	So-called living wage (25)
	Hurt those meant to help (25)
Righteous Cause (17)	Limited effects (7)

Note: Number in parentheses is the frequency with which the arguments in the frame appear

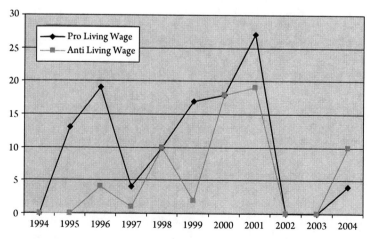

Chart 6.5 Pro- and Anti-Living Wage Arguments in *USA Today*.

The tone of the coverage of the living wage debate is more equivocal in the *USA Today* than in the *New York Times*, as we see in chart 6.5. During the ten-year period of study, positive arguments for the living wage appear more frequently than negative arguments. On the other hand, out of the five frames present in the discourse, only two are positive in tone, while three are negative. Still, as shown in chart 6.6, the weighted attention (salience x strength) to frames in the *USA Today* living wage discourse favor pro-living wage arguments.

In addition, as we see in table 6.9, the only resonant frame in the *USA Today* discourse is the positive "fairness" frame.

This frame is made up of arguments that cover worker protests and demonstrations in which quoted workers and activists point out that it is only fair to pay people who work full time enough money to live decently. In addition, the arguments in this frame emphasize the routinely high public approval for increasing minimum wages and for the living wage itself as well as highlighting religious support for living wage legislation. The frame is extremely coherent, with the

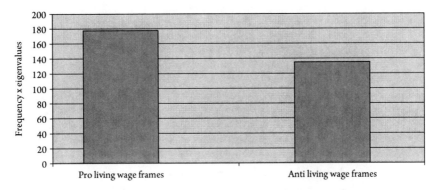

Chart 6.6 Weighted Attention to Pro- and Anti-Living Wage Frames in *USA Today*.

Table 6.9 **Frame Analysis, *USA Today* on Living Wage: "Fairness"**

Argument	Proportion of Variation Explained by Argument
Demonstrations	.52
Fairness	.52
Public approval	.52
Religious Support	.42

Eigenvalue or total "Strength" of frame = 3.4.
Proportion of variation explained in first component = .85.

four arguments covarying together 84 percent of the time and modestly strong with an eigenvalue of 3.4.

The other positive frame that appears in the *USA Today* I dub "logic of the living wage." It is made up of three arguments. The one that appears most frequently is an explanation of the term "living wage," usually painting the policy as a pragmatic, nonideological solution to an American problem. In a typical example of this argument in an article published on April 17, 1996, under the headline "States Can Take Wage Lead While Washington Waffles":

> In Washington: raising the minimum wage has been mired in partisan name-calling: Republicans accusing Democrats of carrying water for organized labor; Democrats accusing Republicans of shilling for business contributors. Meanwhile, states and cities are acting pragmatically to redeem the original premise [of the minimum wage]: assuring that honest work would generate a living wage and keep workers off the dole. If Washington is incapable of fixing the problem, states and cities have shown they can lead. Others should follow.

In the *USA Today*, this argument is often accompanied by an argument insisting that low wages cost taxpayers money in the form of workers' increased need for government disbursements.

> For four decades, the minimum wage was regularly raised, but for 10 years 1979–1989, the wage was stuck at $3.35 an hour, losing nearly half of its purchasing power to inflation. The result: increasing reliance of working families on food stamps, tax credits and other welfare to make ends meet. And that all costs tax payers money.[7]

Rounding out this frame is a collection of biographical portraits of workers who would benefit or have benefited from a living wage. Interestingly, in the *USA Today* discourse, most of these biographies are stories of immigrants who have been able to improve their lives. This is because most of the stories about the living wage were covered by West Coast reporters who routinely write stories about immigration and Latino communities. This interesting detail of the *USA Today* coverage is the result of the convergence of two factors. First, California has twenty-eight local living wage ordinances, more than any other state, and so living wage ordinances were making news more often on the West Coast from 1994 to 2004. The second is a result of the shuttering of the labor beat at most national newspapers. As political consultant Kristina Wilfore points out, "That's the problem with issues around wages: you don't have a union beat anymore. The business beat is from the perspective of business and not labor. You don't have a standing agenda to cover the issue."[8] Given that this is the case, the immigrant/immigration angle allowed the coverage of this issue in the *USA Today* more often than it otherwise might have been.

For example, an article by Abe Estimada called "'Living Wage' Is Guarantee for Only a Few," from December 28, 1999, profiles an immigrant worker:

> Adolfo Chambers struggles to say in English what Los Angeles' living wage law has meant for him and his family. With the help of his daughter, the 57-year-old from Mexico eventually makes his point by referring to the modest, two-bedroom home he rents in the Los Angeles community of South Gate. It's a castle when compared to the cramped apartment he, his wife, and their five children once shared in a dirty neighborhood near Lynwood. They were able to move thanks to the city's living wage law, which requires businesses that win public contracts or subsidies to pay a wage that keeps workers and their families above the poverty level. The federal government says that level of $16,600 for a family of four.

As we see in table 6.10, the strongest and most salient argument against the living wage in the *USA Today* was one highlighting one of the supposed perverse effects of living wage, an argument that was also quite prominent in the resonant and powerful "anxieties" frame in the *New York Times*. That is, the assertion that the living wage legislation will hurt those it is meant to help.

Being made up of only three arguments, the frame does not meet the standard for resonance, nor is it particularly strong. It is, however, quite coherent, meaning that the arguments co-occur together 89 percent of the time, which is unusual for frames in my data set that contain more than two arguments.

In order to see whether and how frames changed over time, I split the data set into two time periods, one spanning from 1994 to 1999 and the other spanning

Table 6.10 **Frame Analysis, USA Today on Living Wage: "Hurt Those Meant to Help"**

Argument	Proportion of Variation Explained by Argument
Hurt those meant to help	.58
Uncertain costs	.56
Job Better Than No Job	.57

Eigenvalue or total "Strength" of frame = 2.6.
Proportion of variation explained in first component = .89.

from 2000 to 2004. I then determined the density of each frame in each paper in both time periods. As we see in table 6.11, some of the frames were more frequent during the 1990s and less frequent in the 2000s, while others followed the opposite pattern.

In the *New York Times* the most powerful positive and negative frames, "full time workers deserve a living wage" and "anxieties about the living wage," respectively, decline in their salience in the later part of the decade of study, while three of the less overall salient frames—those arguing that the living wage lifts people from poverty, that poverty is a problem, and that it is important to challenge the economic orthodoxy on wage floors—increase in frequency of appearance. The largest change is in the decline of the salience of the argument that full-time workers deserve a living wage, which declines from a density of .80 to one of .29, a slip of .51. This is accompanied by a slight rise in the salience of the pro-living wage frame that poverty is a problem, with the density of mentions increasing from .29 to .45, a gain of .16. However, while the anti-living wage frame full of

Table 6.11 **Frame Density of Living Wage, 1994–2004**

Frame	NYT		Density	USA Today		Density
	t–1	t–2		t–1	t–2	
Pro						
full-time workers deserve	.80	.29	↓	x	x	
bad conditions	.37	.03	↓	x	x	
lifts from poverty	.14	.20	↑	x	x	
problem of poverty	.29	.45	↑	x	x	
challenging economic orthodoxy	.20	.29	↑	x	x	
righteous cause	.24	.03	↓	1.40	.28	↓
logic of living wage	x	x		1.60	4.57	↑
Anti						
anxieties living wage	1.25	.87	↓	.60	3.40	↑
hurt those meant to help	x	x		.40	3.00	↑
limited effects of living wage	x	x		.60	.14	↓

*t–1 is 1994–1999. t–2 is 2000–2004.

Note: the ratio is important because it shows us how the frame moves during the time period. Since there are more arguments than stories, the value of the ration can exceed 1. This presents no problem since the ratio is not meant to represent a meaningful mathematical value on its own.

the rhetoric of reaction stoking anxieties about the alleged jeopardy, futility, and perverse effects of living wage policies declined in salience, the drop was from a density of 1.25 to .87, yielding a level of salience that exceeded the strongest pro-living wage argument at its peak time and reflecting a decline of only .36.

Public Awareness

Overall, public discourse on the living wage as represented by these two papers presents an emergent political issue that is perceived to have broad public support and is largely portrayed in a sympathetic light. However, there are two problems with the public discourse on this issue that make it difficult for it to achieve political acceptance. First, the issue is not high salience overall, which means that the general public is not very aware of either the living wage as a political movement or the living wage policy as the solution to the problem of the working poor. This lack of salience is reflected in the available public opinion data on the topic of the living wage. Most survey questions asking people what they think of the living wage are commissioned and executed locally in municipalities where living wage campaigns are underway. As with the minimum wage, strong majorities consistently favor the living wage. Additionally, in the only survey taken in the time period that asked a national sample of adults their views on the idea of a living wage, the 2004 New American Dream Survey, surveyors asked how likely respondents would be to pay more for goods made by companies who pay overseas workers a living wage. Forty-four percent of respondents answered that they would be very or somewhat likely to do so, with 13 percent reporting that they didn't know whether they would or not and the rest saying that they would not do so (Center for a New American Dream 2004). That a question about living wages in other countries still receives relatively strong support from American respondents gives an idea of how appealing the notion of the living wage is when people are aware of it as an option and how much more so they might be if they thought the option were plausible and viable.

Since there are so few questions on national surveys about the living wage, we can extrapolate some information on the topic from what people report they feel about raising the minimum wage. Unfortunately, there is little across-time comparable data on the question of the minimum wage. The General Social Survey, the premier source for tracking opinion across time, does not include a question on the minimum wage. However, national polling outfits often ask questions about the minimum wage (especially when it pops up as a political issue in campaigns). In any case, on this topic, public opinion is decisive and clear across surveys and time: vast majorities of the public approve of raising the minimum wage and have done so consistently for decades, including the time period of the survey to the present day. Question-wording and question order effects are probably present, but in no survey that I am aware of, having been through the archives kept by Gallup, the Roper Center, and Pew Research Center, does support for increasing the minimum wage fall below 50 percent, and the rate of approval usually comfortably exceeds this threshold. For example, a 1994 NBC/ *Wall Street Journal* poll found that 75 percent of respondents favored raising the minimum wage when asked, "Do you favor or oppose increasing the minimum wage?" And, when asked a question that uses the logic of the living wage (without labeling it as such), "Some people have suggested that the living wage be increased to help people in low-paying jobs keep up with the cost of living. Other people feel that an increase in the minimum wage would increase costs to business and weaken the economy. Do you favor or oppose increasing the living wage?" 69 percent of respondents maintained support, even in the face of an argument presenting a familiar counterargument asserted by businesses opposed to paying living wages.[9] A Pew Research center poll reproduced the same question on the minimum wage in 1999 and 2004: "Please tell me if you strongly favor, favor, oppose, or strongly oppose . . . an increase in the minimum wage?" In 1999 82 percent of respondents either favored (34 percent) or strongly favored (48 percent) an increase, and in 2004 86 percent chose one of those two options, with a full 53 percent reporting that they strongly favored an increase.[10] After President Barack Obama purposed raising the minimum wage to $9 in the 2013 State of the Union address, a Gallup survey released on March 6, 2013, showed that 71 percent of respondents reported that they "would vote for raising the minimum wage to $9 per hour if given the opportunity."[11] Even more striking, a 2012 survey of likely voters conducted by Lake Research Partners asked a national sample if they would support raising the minimum wage to $10 by 2014, after presenting common opposing arguments, including the assertion that a higher minimum wage would be a "job killer," "cost taxpayers," or "hurt those it's meant to help." Support for a raise remained overwhelming at 73 percent (Lake, Gotoff, and Dunn 2012).

Second, the rhetoric of reaction that characterizes anti-living wage arguments does not seem to decrease support for the living wage in principle, but instead capitalizes on uncertainty about the plausibility of the proposal or simply shifts the living wage down on the list of national priorities. For example, a 1994 Democratic Leadership Council Poll asked respondents to rank the issue priority of raising the minimum wage as either the "single highest," "top few," "near [the] top," "mid-list," or "toward [the] bottom." The single most popular answer was "top few," which garnered a support level of 28 percent, with 21 percent putting the issue near the top and 26 percent ranking the issue mid-list. When an NBC / *Wall Street Journal* poll included raising the minimum wage in a list of multiple different issues, raising the minimum wage was ranked sixth of eight issues, behind welfare reform, healthcare reform, middle-class tax cuts, a balanced budget amendment, and a revised crime bill. In sum, people support raising the minimum wage and like the idea of a living wage, but they do not prioritize it. This may be because the living wage tends to fall into a category of ideas that members of the polity regard as ideal, but perhaps impracticable.

This puts the living wage movement in a strange position. Activists have successfully facilitated the passage of over one hundred twenty pieces of legislation all across the country on a policy that people generally approve of, and at unusually high rates. However, because living wage advocates have not been able to gain political acceptance, ushering their issue onto the short list of policies that demand regular national attention, forcing officials to take positions on their issues and holding legislatures and local governments accountable for enforcement of legislation that has been passed, the movement has had less effect than the second case that I analyze, the movement for marriage equality.

Describing Public Discourse on Marriage Equality, 1994–2004

The discourse on marriage equality showed a different pattern than that of the living wage. As chart 6.7 shows, the issue was low salience in the public discourse as represented by these two papers at the beginning of the decade but increased in salience over the ten-year period. The most dramatic increase took place between 2000 and 2004. Only about 19 percent of the total *New York Times*

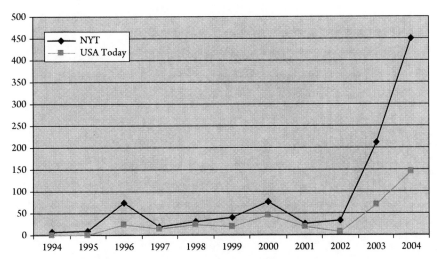

Chart 6.7 Stories on Marriage Equality in the *New York Times* and *USA Today*.

coverage takes place between 1994 and 1999 and likewise about 18 percent of the coverage of marriage equality in *USA Today* takes place during the same time. The vast majority of the coverage of marriage equality is from this period with particular increases in coverage in 2003 and 2004. This large uptick in the frequency of stories on marriage equality seems to have been amplified by the convergence of two big national stories: the *Lawrence v. Texas* Supreme Court decision declaring state sodomy laws unconstitutional on the eve of the 2004 presidential election.   .

New York Times

Like the coverage of the living wage movement, the tone of coverage of marriage equality is more positive than negative in the *New York Times*. Over the course of the decade of study, the frequency of positive arguments is greater than that of negative arguments. In presidential election year 1996, the number of positive and negative arguments reaches near parity and in the congressional election year 1998 and presidential election year 2000 anti-marriage equality arguments appeared more often than pro-marriage equality arguments. As we see in chart 6.8, unlike the living wage debate, the marriage equality discourse was characterized by not only positive and negative arguments, but also by arguments that primarily aimed to describe the impact of marriage equality on the political prospects of candidates and the contours of campaign races as well as on politics within the gay rights movement sector.

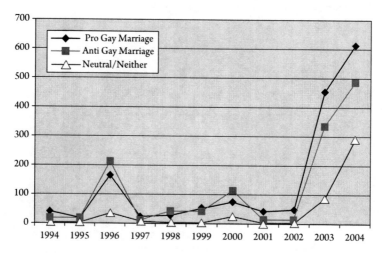

Chart 6.8 Pro-, Anti-, and Neutral Marriage Equality Arguments in the *New York Times*.

Table 6.12 shows that in the *New York Times*, the marriage equality discourse produced fifteen frames, five being positive, seven negative, and three primarily politically descriptive, or, neutral.

One of the interesting things about the marriage equality discourse is that the most frequent positive frame advocating same-sex marriage and the most resonant frame are not the same. The frame that gay people are equal citizens and so deserve the right to marry, explicated at the beginning of the chapter, is the most common in the *New York Times*; however, that frame consists of only five arguments, while the most resonant frame, shown in table 6.13, consists of seven distinct arguments making the case that families are made in all kinds of ways and should not be disrespected because adult partners are the same sex.[12]

"All kinds of families" consists of a constellation of seven pro-marriage equality arguments. These arguments include biographical portraits of gay families, often those including children, as well as accounts of how emotional the issue of marriage is for same-sex couples; claims that it is really love that constitutes a family, rather than the presence of different-sexed partners; that same-sex couples are not a threat to heterosexual families; that marriage promotes stability and monogamy, regardless of the sex of participants; that those same-sex couples who desire to marry are "regular people" with the unremarkable desire to form family units; and that marriage is an important symbol apart from its legal benefits. This frame is the most resonant in the marriage equality debate in either paper.

The last resonant frame advocating for marriage equality, shown in table 6.14, is one that consists of four arguments making the case that marriage equality is a progressive change and that progress is American.

Table 6.12 **Marriage Equality Frames Present in the *New York Times*, 1994–2004**

Pro	Anti	Neutral
About equality (690)	Social conservative (423)	Political impact (334)
All kinds of families (339)	Political conservative (351)	Legal arguments (81)
Progress is American (175)	Cultural backlash (85)	Upholding the law (32)
Economic aspects (141)	Not bigots, fair-minded (73)	
Marriage is a must (125)	Hetero marriage breakdown (61)	
	Nondiscrimination, not marriage (54)	
	Queer politics (176)	

Note: Number in parentheses is the frequency with which the arguments in the frame appear.

Table 6.13 **Frame Analysis, the *New York Times* on Marriage Equality: "All Kinds of Families"**

Argument	Proportion of Variation Explained by Argument
Biography	.40
Regular people	.40
Not a threat	.39
Stability and monogamy	.38
Love makes a family	.35
Symbolism of marriage	.35
Emotionally charged	.32

Eigenvalue or total "Strength" of frame = 5.82.
Proportion of variation explained in first component = .83.

Table 6.14 **Frame Analysis, the *New York Times* on Marriage Equality: "Progress Is American"**

Argument	Proportion of Variation Explained by Argument
Progress is American	.51
Battle for public opinion	.51
Shifting attitudes	.49.
Gay marriage is inevitable	.47

Eigenvalue or total "Strength" of frame = 3.6.
Proportion of variation explained in first component = .90.

These arguments fold together a particular vision of progress, which assert that while same-sex marriage is seemingly radical, we know from political experience that it is also inevitable. This frame dovetails nicely with the highly salient "about equality" and highly coherent "all kinds of families" frame, creating a cadre of resonant frames that make the case that this issue is like other issues that America has handled politically by granting important rights to a newly included group on the basis of fundamental similarity. If the issues in the marriage equality debate indeed concern equal rights for a group who is unjustly discriminated against, then it is hard to envision a different outcome than the ones that the American polity has produced before. It is important to remember, though, that between 1994 and 2004, the givens that make this argument so convincing were contested. Whether gay people could lay claim to a civil rights legacy was not at all obvious. A February 29, 2004, article by Lynette Clemetson headlined "Both Sides Court Black Churches in Battle over Gay Marriage," explores the matter:

> Speaking recently to a group of black evangelical ministers and lay peo-
> ple, Genevieve Wood of the conservative Family Research Council,
> made an impassioned plea. Black Christians, she said, must speak out
> against advocates of gay marriage. "They are wrapping themselves in
> the flag of civil rights," said Ms. Wood, who is white, as visitors from
> across the country shook their heads in dismay. "I can make arguments
> against that, but not nearly like you all can." As Ms. Wood has been
> brokering alliances to oppose gay marriage, Donna Payne, a board
> member of the National Black Justice Coalition, a black gay and les-
> bian organization formed to increase acceptance of gay rights among
> African-Americans, has been appealing to liberal black clergy mem-
> bers.... As debate escalates around same sex marriage, advocates on
> both sides are busily seeking support from the same source: black
> clergy members.... Each seeks the perceived moral authority and
> the sheen of civil rights that black religious leaders could lend to each
> cause. But the aggressive outreach is rife with complications. Neither
> white conservatives nor gay rights advocates have had great success
> in sustaining broad alliances with black churches in the past. The fact
> that many black Christians are both politically liberal and socially con-
> servative makes them frustratingly difficult to pigeonhole.... Many
> blacks opposed to gay marriage, for example, support equal benefits
> for gays as a matter of economic justice.

Black public opinion during the period did not embrace gay people as the heirs to the civil rights movement, and, in fact, many African Americans take umbrage at the comparison.[13] Though the discourse from the period of study does not contain black opinion on this conflation, in 2011, Ellis Cose writes eloquently about the differences he and many black people perceive between the movements. In a column for *USA Today* headlined "Don't Compare Gay Rights, Civil Rights" the journalist writes that there are two major differ-ences between the gay civil rights struggle and the black civil rights struggle. First, it is more possible for gay people to pass than it is for black people to pass, most of the time. This "ability to instantly and easily (albeit, impre-cisely) categorize was one thing that made it possible to organize an entire society around the principle of racial difference." And this racist societal orga-nization led to the second profound difference between the two groups, the reality of intergenerational economic and social disadvantage. Cose describes it this way:

> With gays, . . . [w]e are certainly looking at the workings of prejudice, which, in all its guises, ought to be condemned. But because that prejudice is not linked to a system of economic oppression that will leave gay communities permanently incapacitated, the lack of social acceptance faced by gays—and even the violence visited upon those identified as gay—will not necessarily haunt their descendants generations after attitudes begin to change. So while the gay struggle is about changing attitudes, and laws that grew out of bigoted thinking, it is not about creating a pathway to opportunity (though marriage equality does confer certain economic rights) where none now exists.

In addition, while it is true that African Americans have generally been less supportive of marriage equality than the general population, it is also the case that black people have also never been wedged into sympathy with political conservatives. No conservative politician has been able to use marriage equality to divert perceptible numbers of African American votes from Democratic candidates. In addition, it is a little-talked-about fact that African Americans have generally been *more supportive* than the general population of nondiscrimination against gay people in housing, employment, and a range of other issues.[14]

However, when marriage equality was on the ballot in states, black Americans generally voted for anti-marriage equality initiatives at higher rates than whites or Latinos. However, if we put together the fact that religious Americans tend to be more opposed to same-sex marriage, and evangelical Christians tend to be more staunchly anti-marriage equality than either mainline Protestants or Catholics, with the fact that black Americans are more religious than white Americans and most are evangelical Protestants, then the mystery of black opposition to marriage equality begins to unravel. Black American opposition to same-sex marriage, like American opposition to same-sex marriage generally, is driven by a particular interpretation of Christian doctrine.[15]

The two remaining frames supporting marriage equality in the *New York Times* are unique to the paper, and neither reaches the level of resonance. The first is a frame made up of a pair of arguments asserting that forms of partner benefits short of marriage are not enough,[16] and the second is a frame detailing the economic aspects of gay marriage, particularly speculations about the boon of gay weddings for business. The combination of these old and familiar ideas with new purposes makes a highly intelligible case, which is difficult to dismiss, even if one wishes to refute it.

As to the frames that seek to advance a position against same-sex marriage, there are two that are of nearly coequal salience and resonance as I show in tables 6.15 and 6.16: this first is a constellation of socially conservative arguments citing moral anxiety and disgust at the prospect of same-sex marriage, and the second is a group of politically conservative arguments decrying the politicization of the issue and criticizing the procedure by which it came before the American public.

The frame advancing social/religious reasons against allowing same-sex marriage is constituted by six arguments focused on the importance of marriage for traditional conceptions of society, especially as it is represented in Judeo-Christian theology. These include arguments emphasizing the need for preserving

Table 6.15 **Frame Analysis, the *New York Times* on Marriage Equality: "Social/Religious Conservative"**

Argument	Proportion of Variation Explained by Argument
Preserving traditional marriage	.44
Definitional argument	.43
Civilization at stake	.40
Clergy opinions	.40
Children best raised	.38
Natural law	.37

Eigenvalue or total "Strength" of frame = 4.85.
Proportion of variation explained in first component = .80.

Table 6.16 **Frame Analysis, the *New York Times* on Marriage Equality: "Political Conservative"**

Argument	Proportion of Variation Explained by Argument
State's rights	.43
Courts not the place	.43
Culture war	.42
Not about equal access	.39
Inappropriate recognition	.38
Divisive	.37

Eigenvalue or total "Strength" of frame = 4.81.
Proportion of variation explained in first component = .80.

traditional marriage, an argument asserting that marriage can only include one man and one woman by definition, that heterosexual marriage is the foundation of civilization and therefore cannot be altered, diverse clergy disapproving of the notion of same-sex marriage, the assertion that children are best raised by their two opposite-sex biological parents, and that only traditional marriage can be considered in accordance with procreative instincts dictated by "natural law." A November 25, 2003, letter to the editor published under the headline "Gay Marriage and Our Society" advances several of the arguments in this frame quite succinctly.

> David Brooks (column, Nov. 22) takes a bad turn when he rejects the basic principle that marriage is a covenant relationship between one man and one woman. I am a conservative to whom Mr. Brooks appeals that we must "insist on gay marriage" to keep from "drifting further into a culture of contingency." To think that homosexual marriage will reverse the existing crisis in marriage is misguided. When a country recognizes homosexual marriage it has lost its basic sense of right and wrong. There is no moral case for gay marriage and making that our stance will not protect us from the growing drift into a culture that is already awash in immorality.

The second anti-marriage equality frame also consists of six different arguments, but makes a case based on negative political consequences of marriage equality rather than negative social consequences. The two arguments that are most correlated within the frame assert that the right of states to regulate marriage in the way they see fit ought to be protected and that courts are no place to decide controversial legislation. Another dismisses the issue of marriage equality as one put forward primarily by culture warriors seeking to ignore more pressing problems. An argument in the same vein laments how needlessly divisive the issue is, and another claims that marriage recognition for same-sex couples is inappropriate, when other forms of recognition would do. Finally, this frame contains an argument that directly contests the most salient frame on the opposing side of the debate: that is, the argument asserts that the issue of same-sex marriage is not about equality. This argument forwards an understanding of marriage that avows that the institution is fundamentally for the purpose of procreation and therefore literally requires the participation of a man and a woman in order to work. A July 20, 1995, article by David Dunlap headlined "For Better or Worse a Marital Milestone" quotes a New York attorney who argues:

> Marriage is for men and women.. . . It's not about better health insurance premiums or credit ratings or access to bridal registries. We're created as

male and female for a reason. It's not to enjoy sex, it's to procreate. That's nature's mandate. And nature's mandate becomes man's law.

More interesting from a rhetorical point of view is how rare it is for arguments in either of the debates I investigate to engage in direct refutation of this kind. This is, in part, because directly refuting the claims of an opponent in public discourse, a forum for diffuse discussion rather than a dialogue conducive to direct deliberative debate, mainly serves the purpose of bringing to mind the opponent's claim, which is not necessarily advantageous.

The third resonant frame opposing marriage equality, presented in table 6.17, is one warning of the potential "cultural backlash" against gay marriage.
The frame is composed of four arguments of almost equal importance. They include assertions of the sexual perversion of "homosexuals"; derision for "the homosexual agenda"; predictions of a cultural backlash against the "immorality" of allowing state-sanctioned gay unions; and warnings that same-sex marriage is just the top edge of a slippery slope that slides inevitably toward polygamy and bestiality.

The final resonant frame against marriage equality in the *New York Times* coverage, shown in table 6.18, is unique to the paper; it was a frame cataloging the debate about the desirability of marriage within the gay community, highlighting the ambivalence and, in some cases, outright opposition to marriage equality from the left.

In the *New York Times*, the queer politics frame includes arguments questioning the wisdom of the political strategy of putting marriage at the forefront of the gay movement, arguments celebrating the benefits of families constructed outside the boundaries of nuclear-unit normality, arguments recalling the vibrancy and success of AIDS activism, arguments advocating challenging traditional gender roles that may be inscribed in marriage as an institution, and quoted

Table 6.17 **Frame Analysis, the *New York Times* on Marriage Equality: "Cultural Backlash"**

Argument	Proportion of Variation Explained by Argument
Sexual perversion	.50
Homosexual agenda	.50
Backlash	.49
Slippery slope	.49

Eigenvalue or total "Strength" of frame = 3.5.
Proportion of variation explained in first component = .88.

Table 6.18 **Frame Analysis, the *New York Times***
on Marriage Equality: "Queer Politics"

Argument	Proportion of Variation Explained by Argument
Questions of political strategy	.48
Benefits of alternative families	.47
Specter of AIDS	.44
Challenging gender	.41
Activist disputes	.40

Eigenvalue or total "Strength" of frame = 4.4.
Proportion of variation explained in first component = .88.

point-counterpoints between gay rights activists who held opposing views on the primacy of marriage in the gay movement. In an April 23, 1994, article by Jane Gross titled "After a Ruling: Hawaii Weighs Gay Marriages," a typical intra-movement point-counterpoint is presented this way:

> As Mr. Stoddard sees it, just months after his own ceremony with Walter Rieman, the issue remains "equal access to an issue of great practical and emotional importance to most Americans." For Ms. Ettelbrick, by contrast, "the true access question is whether marriage is the appropriate vehicle for determining economic rights and privileges. "I'd rather spend our resources developing a broader view of family and not replicating heterosexist institutions," she said.

As we saw in chapter 2, marriage as the lead issue of the cause of gay rights was highly controversial. Gay activists to the left of the Democratic Party and those interested in a liberatory queer politics celebrated the difference of sexual and familial practices in the gay community and generally found the notion of fighting for gay inclusion into the culturally conservative institutions of military and marriage to be morally questionable, socially backward, and, in the words of John D'Emilio, a political "unmitigated disaster" that had "created a vast body of new anti-gay law" (D'Emilio 2010). Amid the harrowing of the sea change in public opinion on marriage equality, which became apparent late in the first decade of the twenty-first century, it is tough to remember that marriage equality lost almost every legislative battle and most court battles brought on behalf of the issue from its inception until the mid-2000s. Far from being a sure political winner, marriage equality seemed a fool's errand to many political activists during the time, and they had a mass of indicators of political failure from across the

United States to point to in declaring the seemingly empirically proved folly of marriage politics. However, the mistake that many political observers made was in believing that policy success is the primary indicator of movement success. As we see in the two cases that I review, this is not always the case. Policy success may not herald movement success, and policy failure may obscure more fundamental changes in the political meanings of new and contested issues.

Along with these resonant frames, the marriage equality discourse in the *New York Times* includes three additional frames. One laments a general "marriage crisis" that includes postponing marriage, declining marriage rates, cohabitation, and divorce in the perceived worrisome trends in heterosexual relationships. Another acknowledges that discrimination against gay people in various areas of American public life and policy is problematic, but marriage is no way to answer these concerns. And the final frame is another direct refutation of a major charge that proponents of marriage equality level, which claims that since the majority of Americans were against marriage equality during the period, they cannot all be bigots, but are rather "fair-minded Americans" attempting to protect the arrangement of society that we have allegedly always known.

In addition to frames making the case for or against marriage equality, there are three frames, only one of which is resonant (shown in table 6.19), that reserve judgment on the social and political good or ill of same-sex marriage and rather attempt to describe the legal ramifications and political impact of gay marriage.

The only resonant neutral frame is about the political impact of marriage equality during the period. This frame consisted of arguments discussing the content and politics of both a proposed ban on same-sex marriage in the federal Constitution and the legislative and constitutional bans that were passed in the

Table 6.19 **Frame Analysis, the *New York Times* on Marriage Equality: "Political Impact"**

Argument	Proportion of Variation Explained by Argument
Constitutional ban	.47
State bans	.47
National debate	.46
Protests and demonstrations	.46
Campaign issue	.34

Eigenvalue or total "Strength" of frame = 4.4.
Proportion of variation explained in first component = .88.

majority of states. Also included were arguments involving the veracity of the national debate on the topic as well as coverage of the issue in campaigns across the country and protests and other extraelectoral actions taken by proponents or opponents of marriage equality.

Generally speaking, in the *New York Times* coverage, marriage equality was seen as a boon for Republican candidates for two reasons. First, the prospect of same-sex marriage seemed to mobilize conservative activist like no issue other than abortion. Second, majority public opinion was against same-sex marriage during the entire decade of study. National polling on the same-sex marriage did not become common until 1996, the first presidential election year after the marriage equality movement's emergence. In that year, Gallup, Pew Research Center for the People and the Press, the *Washington Post*, and *Newsweek* began asking same-sex marriage questions that they have continued to ask annually. In 1996, Gallup found that 27 percent of respondents supported same-sex marriage while 68 percent opposed. By 2004, the same poll reported that support had risen to 42 percent and opposition was 55 percent.[17] While the movement suggested is significant, opposition to same-sex marriage was still the majority position, and there was quite a bit of variation in support for legalizing marriage equality depending on how the questions were worded and in what order they were presented. For example, support for marriage equality increased when the marriage question was asked after questions about other aspects of gay rights such as discrimination in employment and housing. And support for marriage decreased significantly when surveys allowed a tripartite preference between marriage, civil unions, and no legal recognition, rather than forcing a choice between marriage and nonrecognition (Brewer and Wilcox 2005).

The other two descriptive or neutral frames present in the *New York Times* marriage equality discourse were neither particularly salient nor resonant. One deals with the myriad real and hypothetical legal implications of marriage legislation. And the other contains two arguments noting the awkward position that civil servants are put in while attempting to uphold the law as it fluctuated between favorable court rulings and ballot initiative bans (or vice versa).

As seen in chart 6.9, although there were more frames opposing marriage equality than supporting it in the *New York Times*, the proponents' frames were both more salient and more resonant than the opponents' frames.

This feature of the marriage equality discourse suggests that, when it comes to changing the public understanding of the political meaning of a new issue, the repetition and consistency of resonant arguments is of prime importance. Public discourse is able to contain complex ideas, but they may be more memorable and intelligible when they come in a resonant package rather than in a number of distinct frames from differing perspectives.

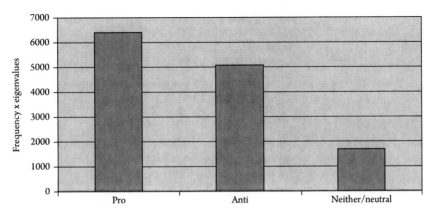

Chart 6.9 Weighted Attention to Pro-, Anti-, and Neutral Marriage Equality Frames in the *New York Times*.

USA Today

As we see in table 6.20, the discourse on marriage equality in *USA Today* contains fifteen frames. Six of the frames make arguments for marriage equality, six of the frames make arguments against, and three are descriptive or neutral.

As is the case with the living wage, the discourse on marriage equality in *USA Today* is less salient than that in the *New York Times*. This means that there is less coverage of the issue overall and fewer stories and arguments on the topic of same-sex marriage. Indeed, there are no stories about same-sex marriage in the *USA Today* in 1994 and 1995. The paper did not cover the emergent issue until 1996, a presidential election year.

As we see in chart 6.10, coverage in the *USA Today* is more mixed in tone than that of the *New York Times*. From 1996 to 1999, the more salient frames in the paper make arguments for marriage equality. However, in 2000, 2003, and 2004, the more salient frames in the paper make arguments against marriage equality. As chart 6.11 shows, taking into account the weighted attention accorded each frame, the discourse on marriage equality contained in the *USA Today* is more negative than positive, overall.

The frames in *USA Today* are similar to those in the *New York Times*, but the positive arguments cohere less well, producing multiple, similar, non-resonant frames, instead of fewer frames that consist of more arguments co-occurring together in a coherent way. There are also fewer resonant frames overall in *USA Today* than in the *New York Times*. As we see in table 6.21, in total, there are only four resonant frames: one positive, two negative, and one neutral.

Table 6.20 **Marriage Equality Frames Present in *USA Today*, 1994–2004**

Pro	Anti	Neutral
About equality (210)	Social conservative (289)	Political impact (357)
Shifting attitudes (113)	Political conservative (115)	Legal arguments (78)
All kinds of families (91)	Cultural backlash (62)	Overreaction (24)
Biography (56)	Civil unions (96)	
	Tolerance, not approval (57)	
Benefits of alternative families (53)	Values breakdown (47)	
Hypocrisy/Bigotry (43)		

Note: Number in parentheses is the frequency with which the arguments in the frame appear.

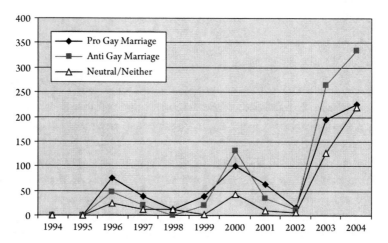

Chart 6.10 Pro-, Anti-, and Neutral Marriage Equality Arguments in *USA Today*.

The "about equality" frame in *USA Today* is almost identical to the one that appears in the *New York Times*, except that the latter supports an additional argument about the movement for gay rights, in particular. The frame is not as strong as its similar in the *New York Times*, nor does it cohere as well. However, the frames in *USA Today* are generally weaker and less coherent, so the more relevant comparison is to the two resonant frames that make arguments against marriage equality in the same paper. The most resonant anti-gay marriage frame in *USA Today*, as demonstrated in table 6.22, is the "social conservative" frame, which is the most resonant argument in the paper (on either issue), containing six arguments.

The argument is nearly identical to the frame of the same name in the *New York Times*. The arguments contained in the frame are consistent, and the

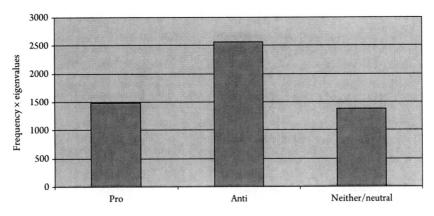

Chart 6.11 Weighted Attention to Pro-, Anti-, and Neutral Marriage Equality Frames in *USA Today*.

Table 6.21 **Frame Analysis, *USA Today* on Marriage Equality: "About Equality"**

Argument	Proportion of Variation Explained by Argument
Interracial marriage analogy	.51
Equal access	.50
Against Constitutional ban	.50
Civil rights	.47

Eigenvalue or total "Strength" of frame = 3.56.
Proportion of variation explained in first component = .89.

strength of the frame differs by only a tenth of a point. This means that social conservatives made remarkably similar arguments against marriage equality over the ten-year period. Underscoring the consistency of the anti-marriage equality frames across the two papers is the fact that the second resonant frame making arguments against same-sex marriage is the "political conservative" frame, one we also encountered in the *New York Times* discourse. As we see in table 6.23, the frame is constituted slightly differently in *USA Today* than in the *New York Times*.

Notably, the politically conservative case against marriage equality contains only four arguments in *USA Today*, while its similar in the *Times* contains six. The arguments that the debate is divisive and that marriage is an inappropriate recognition for gay couples do appear in *USA Today*, but they are low salience

Table 6.22 **Frame Analysis, *USA Today* on Marriage Equality:**
"Social Conservative"

Argument	Proportion of Variation Explained by Argument
Children best raised	.44
Natural law	.43
Preserving traditional marriage	.40
Civilization at stake	.39
Definitional argument	.39
Clergy opinions	.36

Eigenvalue or total "Strength" of frame = 4.94.
Proportion of variation explained in first component = .82.

Table 6.23 **Frame Analysis, *USA Today* on Marriage**
Equality: "Political Conservative"

Argument	Proportion of Variation Explained by Argument
Culture war	.51
State's rights	.50
Courts not the place to decide	.50
Not about equal access	.46

Eigenvalue or total "Strength" of frame = 3.58.
Proportion of variation explained in first component = .89.

and do not co-occur with the other four arguments consistently enough to be included in the frame. Finally, as shown in table 6.24, the *USA Today*, like the *Times*, contains a resonant argument describing the political impact of marriage equality on campaigns and elections during the period.

The frame contains four arguments that are also found in the *New York Times* discourse, though with slightly different emphases as well as the notable absence of any argument describing protests and demonstrations focused on the issue of marriage equality.

This frame profile means that *USA Today*'s discourse emphasized social arguments against marriage equality over politically conservative arguments, while the only resonant positive frame emphasized a rights-based political argument, rather than the arguments built around the fundamental similarities of families or the primacy of love and commitment therein. This is an

Table 6.24 **Frame Analysis, the *New York Times***
on Marriage Equality: "Political Impact"

Argument	Proportion of Variation Explained by Argument
Constitutional ban	.53
Campaign issue	.53
State bans	.49
National debate	.46

Eigenvalue or total "Strength" of frame = 3.28.
Proportion of variation explained in first component = .82.

interesting lack of congruence, which suggests that the idea of public discourse as a debate, rather than a diffuse discussion in which people are seeking to understand what the political meaning and stakes at issue are, may be flawed in a way that prevents analysts from grasping the way that public discourse impacts political behaviors.

In terms of the way that the marriage equality discourse changed over time, the chief thing to note, as demonstrated in figure 6.1, is how the most resonant arguments are deployed in the 1990s versus the 2000s.

In the *New York Times*, the "about equality" frame, which is less salient from 1994 to 1999 than it is from 2000 to 2004, remains constant as a proportion of the discourse across both periods, while the "all kinds of families" frame, emphasizing fundamental or essential qualities of care among same and different sex-headed households, decreases in density from .50 to .33. In *USA Today* both of these arguments decrease as a proportion of the total discourse on gay marriage. On the other hand, the social and politically conservative frames containing arguments against marriage equality increase, and, in the case of the socially conservative frame, increase dramatically from a density of .24 to 1.01, in *USA Today*, while decreasing as a ratio of the discourse in the *New York Times*. In both papers, though, the socially conservative frames more densely populate the discourse on marriage equality throughout the entire decade of study.

The resonant coterie of arguments that do increase in density in the *New York Times* is the "progress is American" frame, which goes from a density of .10 to .20. And the "cultural backlash" frame comes to make up a greater proportion of the discourse in both papers, though the movement is greater in *USA Today*, in which the frame increases in density from .02 to .20. It is also interesting to note that the frame unique to the *New York Times* that opposes marriage equality from left of the marriage equality movement, the "queer dissent" frame, is much less prevalent in the 2000s than in the 1990s, going from a density of .43 to .12.

Frames	NYT		Density	USA Today		Density
	t–1	t–2		t–1	t–2	
Pro						
all kinds of families	.50	.33	↓	.33	.22	↓
about equality	.44	.44	=	.65	.54	↓
progress is American	.10	.20	↑	x	x	
rights, not marriage	.21	.10	↓	x	x	
economic aspects	.25	.12	↓	x	x	
hypocrisy/bigotry	x	x		.08	.11	↑
benefits of alternative	x	x		.16	.27	↑
shifting attitudes	x	x		.25	.35	↑
love makes a family	x	x		.13	.16	↑
Anti						
social/religious conservative	.63	.43	↓	.24	1.01	↑
political conservative	.38	.36	↓	.20	.34	↑
cultural backlash	.06	.09	↑	.02	.20	↑
hetero marriage breakdown	.02	.07	↑	x	x	
values breakdown	x	x		.01	.16	↑
civil unions	x	x		.19	.29	↑
tolerance, not approval	x	x		.03	.19	↑
non-discrimination, not marriage	.01	.06	↑	x	x	
queer dissent	.43	.12	↓	x	x	
not bigots, fair minded	.25	.03	↓	x	x	
Neutral/ Neither						
political impact	.00	.42	↑	.46	1.18	↑
Overreaction	x	x		.01	.08	↑
legal arguments	.27	.03	↓	.19	.21	↑
upholding the law	.00	.03	↑	x	x	

Figure 6.1 Frame Density of Marriage Equality Debate, 1994–2004.
*t–1 is 1994–1999. t–2 is 2000–2004.
**Density = Frequency of frame / # of articles in time period.

The "political impact" frame, resonant in both papers, becomes a much greater proportion of the discourse in both papers in the 2000s, with the frame going from nonexistent in the *New York Times* to a density of .42 and increasing from .46 to 1.18 in *USA Today*.

Overall, then, the discourse on marriage equality becomes more constituted by the political impact frame over the time period. Since my analysis is at the level of arguments and frames, this does not mean that there are more stories that lead with the political impact frame, but only that the perceived political impact of the issue becomes more and more constitutive of the discourse as a whole. It is also interesting to note that the positive frames that assert the fundamental similarity of family, love, and relation in both same- and opposite-sex relationships become less constitutive of the discourse, while the equality frame maintains a relatively stable place. The rise of the socially conservative frame as a constitutive part of the debate and the concomitant decline of the politically conservative frame is also worth observing. I believe this fluctuation in the density of frames across the time period, showing us the ways that the discourse becomes differently constituted at different times, points to common understandings of the stakes of the issue and the way that those stakes can be understood differently at different times. In the public discourse on marriage equality as represented in these two papers, the stakes of the marriage equality debate seem to center around social similarity, political equality, and socially conservative values across the decade, but the emphasis shifts from social similarity to political equality in the 2000s, while the socially conservative frames remain the dominant opposition and the political impact of the issue becomes much more central to the discourse. This is the discursive profile of political acceptance. The political argument and its political implications become the dominant way of understanding the issue. However, it is also likely the case that without the frames asserting some kind of fundamental similarity, the equality argument might not have been intelligible or remained resonant.

Public Awareness

According to a 2003 report by Pew Research Center, "Numerous survey organizations have tracked public attitudes toward 'homosexuality' in a variety of ways, and virtually all measures show the same pattern. While many Americans harbor concerns about legalizing gay marriage, the public is a much more tolerant toward homosexuals than it was twenty years ago" (Pew 2003b) Unlike the minimum wage, the General Social Survey has been tracking whether or not people feel sexual relationships between people of the same sex are wrong or not since 1973 and began specifically asking about same-sex marriage in 1988. Gallup has been asking whether "homosexuality" ought to be considered an "acceptable alternative lifestyle" and whether "homosexuals should have equal rights" since 1982. The earliest question about marriage equality in particular was asked in 1985, but questions about support or opposition to marriage equality did not start appearing regularly until 1992.[18] Also in 1985, the Pew Research Center asked, "Do you strongly favor, favor, oppose, or strongly oppose allowing gays and lesbians to marry legally?" In 1989 a Yankelovich, CNN, *Time* magazine poll asked, "Do you think marriages between homosexual men or homosexual women should be recognized as legal by the law or not?" Throughout the early 1990s, questions about whether respondents supported or opposed marriage equality began to appear across issue polls more frequently, and by 1996 questions about marriage equality were ubiquitous on public opinion polls from most major polling organizations including Pew, Gallup, ABC/*Washington Post*, Harris, *Newsweek*, and various university polling centers. During the late 1990s the issue was also becoming a topic that was more and more frequently covered in mainstream public discourse, with national parties beginning to stake out positions in their public platforms in 1996. As we have seem in election years 2000 and 2004, marriage equality also became a major issue in the presidential campaign, and coverage spiked in national papers.

Over that time, the general familiarity and comfort of the American public with gay people, images, culture, and rights increased markedly. According to a National Opinion Research (NORC) poll conducted yearly since 1977, those reporting that "homosexual" relationships are "always wrong" has been steadily decreasing, with the most notable drops in those reporting an intolerant sentiment in the young, those with college or more education, those making more than $75,000, and those living in the West and Northeast. Still, in 2004, even in the most permissive demographics, a large plurality, never less than one-third (33 percent), reported the view that sexual relations between people of the same sex is always wrong (Bowman and O'Keefe 2004). On the other hand, support for marriage equality in particular remained low even as news coverage increased and the most salient arguments and frames presented in public discourse changed. Between 1992 and 2004 a version of the question "Do you think marriages between homosexual men or homosexual women should be recognized as legal by the law or not?" was asked every year by most polling organizations, and while support for legal recognition for same-sex marriage increased, it never rose above 33 percent. Indeed, opposition to such recognition was quite consistent, with the proportion of respondents indicating their opposition never dropping below 60 percent (Bowman and O'Keefe 2004).

Interestingly, while a majority of respondents regularly reply that sexual relations between adults of the same sex is "morally wrong," Americans have tended to reject outlawing such relationship, with nearly two-thirds affirming that sexual relations between two adults of the same sex "should be legal." As with all other indicators evaluating aspects of sexual relationships between people of the same sex, the number of those tolerant of same-sex relations steadily increased throughout the time period of interest. Interestingly, there was a particular increase in support in the spring of 2003, before both the *Lawrence* decision and the bulk of the 2004 presidential campaign. In addition, large majorities of

Americans say that gay men and lesbians should be accorded equal employment access and equal treatment on the job.

Also of interest is that during the period more Americans perceived their fellows to be intolerant of "homosexual behavior" than disapproved of same-sex pairings themselves. In 2001 NORC asked respondents, "What is your impression of how most Americans feel about homosexual behavior—do most Americans think it is acceptable or not acceptable?" Seventy-four percent believed that most Americans viewed "homosexual behavior" as unacceptable, a figure that outdoes the actual rate of public disapproval by at least ten percentage points (Bowman and O'Keefe 2004). This difference adds credence to the notion that a part of what matters in public opinion is how people believe others perceive the issue. In addition, although gay rights generally and marriage equality in particular have been issues on which much official grandstanding and the outcome of several local and at least one national election may have turned, when Pew asked in 2003 whether "more acceptance of gays and lesbians would be a good thing or a bad thing for the country—or that it would not make much difference either way?" a large plurality, 42 percent, indicated that they thought it would not make much difference either way. These results are intriguing and lend credence to the notion that people are able to separate their personal feelings from what they believe to be politically important. While 51 percent of respondents personally rejected gay marriage, most of them also believed, by the end of the decade of study, that the country would suffer no adverse effects should their personal beliefs not be reflected in policy.

Moreover, throughout the 1990s majorities of Americans reported that their personal level of comfort rose in engaging with gay people in a variety of activities in daily life, from buying something from a gay salesperson, to voting for a political candidate who is gay, or allowing one's child to play in the home of a child with a gay or lesbian parent. In fact, of the six "personal comfort level" indicators that the Yankelovich/CNN/*Time* annual poll asks about, every single one showed an increase in personal comfort level between 1994 and 1998 of no less than four and as many as fourteen percentage points (Bowman and O'Keefe 2004). There are also some interesting generational differences in public opinion that have only become more profound since 2004. Those eighteen to twenty-nine are least likely to report that gay sexual relations are "always wrong," and nearly 60 percent of college freshman reported in 2004 that same-sex couples "should have the right to legal marital status," compared with only 50 percent of the general population (Bowman and O'Keefe 2004).

The general increase in comfort and tolerance did not begin to dramatically affect opinion on marriage until about 2004. That year, 48 percent of respondents in a February 2004 Harris/CNN/*Time* poll reported that they would be less likely to vote for a candidate for political office who was in favor of legalizing gay marriage. Since that time, the general public's approval of marriage equality has been increasing, on average, by about two percentage points per year.[19] Until, in 2010, surveys began to find more support than opposition to marriage equality and, in 2012, most pollsters began to find consistent support from just over 50 percent of respondents. In addition, most people now report that a candidate's position on marriage equality "would not make much difference" in their candidate choice.[20]

It is critical to recognize that though marriage equality did not receive public approval during the period of study, civil unions, a policy accommodation developed in response to the Vermont State Supreme Court's ruling in *Baker v. Vermont*, became overwhelmingly approved by the public. When the question of same-sex partnership was parsed in polls between 2000 and 2004, allowing for the intermediate civil union status, about two-thirds of the public supported either marriage equality or civil unions, with less than a third (27 percent) reporting that they believed that same-sex relationships deserved no legal recognition (Bowman and O'Keefe 2004). This policy accommodation quickly became a popular position for Democratic politicians to endorse, giving them a plausible middle ground between embracing marriage equality outright and completely alienating core constituents. Interestingly, a Pew Research Center study found that the number of people who supported civil unions increased substantially when respondents were asked about gay marriage first. "When respondents have already had the opportunity to express their opposition to marriage equality on the survey, more feel comfortable with allowing some legal rights as an alternative. But when respondents are asked about legal rights without this context, they draw a firmer line" (Pew 2003b).

In addition, there is another element of public opinion that is hard to capture with the kinds of survey questions that had generally been asked in the 1990s and early 2000s. It is the aspect of position-taking and persuasion, which is public, less about the reporting of survey respondents' fundamental principles than about what different issue positions are seen to signify in the polity.

In a 2003 article written for the *National Review* in July 2003, Ramesh Ponnuru elucidates the issue nicely. He writes:

> Another shift in public sentiment is less easily captured in poll numbers: the rise of what one might call an "anti-anti-gay" bloc. People in this group may have qualms about homosexuality and may not support gay marriage. But they are at least as uncomfortable with anything that strikes them as hostile to gay people, with rhetoric that singles them out for criticism, with political figures who seem to spend too much time worrying about them. It is this group—more than gays themselves or

even unequivocal supporters of gay rights—that has caused the Bush
White House to take a moderate line on gay issues. (Ponnuru 2003)

This sentiment created a complex situation for elites taking positions. On the
one hand, the Republican Party had incentive to capitalize on the negative popularity of gay marriage; on the other, when they were seen to be too mean-spirited
they risked losing votes. But, not only did national politicians risk alienating
potential voters, they also added credence to the resonant argument that those
opposed to same-sex marriage might be bigots akin to those who opposed interracial pairings. This is how public persuasion works. If what is at stake in the
politics of marriage equality is one's fundamental moral beliefs about "homosexuality," then people make their decision based on that signification. On the
contrary, if what is at stake is the equal access of people who are judged fundamentally similar to a legal institution that provides hundreds of practical rights
and privileges, then the policy preferences of citizens might be different, even if
they maintain negative moral assessments of "homosexual behavior."

In a 2004 *New York Times* article headlined "Bush's Push for Marriage Falls
Short for Conservatives," Republican pollster Ed Goeas explains, "I think there
are a lot of people that don't want to endorse a lifestyle contrary to their personal
values, but they want to be tolerant . . . and quite frankly they don't like to be
put into a situation where they look to be intolerant."[21] When George W. Bush
endorsed a constitutional amendment to ban gay marriage during the 2004 presidential campaign, pleasing conservative activists, he also broke with majority
opinion, perhaps crossing the discursively constructed line between "upholding personal values" and "intolerance." Though most people opposed same-sex
marriage, most also opposed tinkering with the nation's founding document
for what they perceived as a low-priority political issue. This line crossing did
not prevent George W. Bush from being re-elected, given that most voters felt
that marriage equality was the least important issue discussed in the presidential
campaign, but it played a part in the changing meaning of what taking sides in
the marriage equality debate signified in public discourse.

The politics of marriage equality were not simple for the Democratic Party
during the period, either. Bill Clinton handed his fellow Democrats a stinging
defeat in the form of "Don't Ask, Don't Tell," a bill adopted in 1993 that said that
gay people could not serve openly in the military. Three years later Clinton again
bargained away gay rights, signing the Defense of Marriage Act into law in order
to forestall marriage equality as a potential campaign issue in his re-election bid
against Bob Dole. Though the politics of same-sex marriage in the Democratic
Party of today is quite clearly pro-equality, the case was not nearly so clear cut
twenty years ago. While Democrats in the polity were generally more supportive of marriage equality than the general public between 1994 and 2004, that

support was hardly overwhelming, with only half of Democrats identifying themselves as in favor of gay marriage. As a result, candidates running under the Democratic banner tended to affirm the "definition of marriage" as between a man and a woman, while stating support for policy accommodations such as civil unions or robust domestic partner benefits, and deriding the Republican push for a constitutional amendment banning same-sex marriage. This nuanced positioning did not please Democratic Party activists any more than the initial attempt of the Bush re-election campaign to avoid a push for amending the Constitution pleased the Republican Party base. Pulitzer Prize–winning playwright and gay rights activist Tony Kushner put it simply in a 2003 *New York Times* article headlined "The Democrats Have Done an Appallingly Bad Job of Running Around in Circles on This."[22] However, progressive Democratic Party activists held less sway over their party's positioning than did conservative activists in the Republican Party during the period of observation.

The steady swing of public opinion toward a majority marriage equality position accelerated around 2004 (Silver 2013), after the uptick in coverage of the issue precipitated by the *Lawrence v. Texas* decision, Massachusetts' legalization of gay marriage, and the presidential campaigns of 2004. Though most Americans regarded marriage equality as a low-priority issue during the period, given the news coverage, the general public could not help but be aware of the issue, and candidates running for office and officeholders regularly pronounced positions regarding the issue and policy accommodations, beginning with Vermont's civil union laws in 2000. The issue of marriage equality attained political acceptance on the short list of issues that are regularly debated in national politics, even though it had yet to win political agreement from either elected officials or the general public.

Conclusion

Political acceptance is measured by media salience, public awareness, and the prevalence of position-taking and policy accommodation of elected officials and other political decision-makers. By these measures, we see that while the living wage movement has valiantly persisted since its emergence, it has not achieved political acceptance, while the movement for marriage equality has. This political acceptance was not synonymous with political agreement in 2004 and still does not reflect an overwhelming consensus. While public opinion in support of marriage equality has and continues to increase, Congress invalidated the "Don't Ask, Don't Tell," statue preventing gay people from serving openly in the military, and the Supreme Court has since ruled that the Defense of Marriage Act is invalid, the issue "remains . . . very divisive."[23] A poll conducted by Pew Research in May 2013 found 51 percent of respondents avowing that same-sex marriage ought to be legal, but 42 percent maintain that it ought to be illegal. Interestingly, both groups reported believing, at a rate of 85 percent among proponents and 59 percent among opponents, that the legalization of same-sex unions is "inevitable" (Pew 2013a). This constellation of opinions is indicative of what political acceptance can create over time—a sense that the political issue will be revisited again and again until it is resolved, likely according to the terms that are the most resonant in mainstream public discourse.

On the other hand, President Obama proposed raising the national minimum wage in his 2013 State of the Union address using a living wage argument:

> We know our economy is stronger when we reward an honest day's work with honest wages. But today, a full-time worker making the minimum wage earns $14,500 a year. Even with the tax relief we've put in place, a family with two kids that earns the minimum wage still lives below the poverty line. That's wrong. Tonight, let's declare that in the wealthiest nation on Earth, no one who works full-time should have to live in poverty, and raise the federal minimum wage to $9.00 an hour. This single step would raise the incomes of millions of working families.

Though this elite position-taking has increased the salience of the minimum wage (using the logic of the living wage) the issue remains marginal in terms of media coverage and public awareness, as well as official position-taking and policy accommodation.

The most important lesson that we learn from the examination of the discourse on these two topics is that there is more to being a successful social movement than winning immediate favorable policy attributable to direct pressure by advocates. The *salience, strength, attention,* and *resonance* of the frames that appear in the mainstream political debate on these issues reveal that while the living wage was racking up policy wins and marriage equality was taking a policy drubbing, the terms of the marriage equality debate were shifting in a way that favored the public understanding that gay rights advocates put forward and which ultimately prefigured the policy success that marriage equality has begun to enjoy. This is because social movements seem to have their most lasting and permanent effect not through particular policy victories, but instead by *changing politics itself,* rewriting the common understandings present in the discursive field upon which political possibilities are considered and wherein binding decisions are made.

Conclusion

After Acceptance: The Tea Party, Occupy, and Prospects
for Political Transformation

Everything can be explained to the people, on the single condition that
you want them to understand.

—Franz Fanon, *The Wretched of the Earth*

This book is a pragmatist's genealogy. It is a history of the present, or more precisely, how the normalized present came to be under contingent discursive circumstances. But, unlike most genealogists, I am not interested in how discourses and orders of knowledge constitute subjectivities. I am interested, instead, in how they constitute polities.

Many have railed against the presupposition of methodological individualism in empirical political science, and I, too, think the bias for this notion limits the conceptual apparatus of the field in significant ways. My objection is not rooted in the belief that behaviorist approaches are too prevalent or that statistical methods are too dominant (though I think each claim carries some truth), but instead in the way that the assumptions of methodological individualism cause us to conceive of the public. Both statistically oriented political science and communicatively oriented political theory take the public to be an aggregate of individuals who make choices, evaluations, and judgments based on their (more or less) reasonable, (relatively) unconstrained preferences. I think this is rather misguided. Publics are made up of individuals with their own minds, certainly, but the interests, values, evaluations, and judgments processed therein are always enabled and constrained by large-scale, multifaceted interactions that produce publically intelligible meanings. It is in those meanings, not only in the decisions and choices based upon them, that much of politics is located.

I have argued that political meanings are created, shaped, and changed primarily in public discourse and that the arguments that frame these discourses, as well as the ways that they change over time, can and do alter what people understand public problems and their solutions to be. The interplay between these levels of individual understanding, choice, innovation, and public constraint is what politics consists of: providing a field of action that is, at once, practically bounded and potentially infinite. For political challengers, especially those who lack access to traditional political resources, this field of discourse and action is an indispensible site of power. While political challengers do not have the influence to directly rework the systems, institutions, and social practices that result in outcomes that they deem unjust, they can impact the public meanings that govern common interpretations of the way things are and, most importantly, the way they might be changed for the better.

Although I have knitted together the insights of a diverse array of thinkers from the subfields of American politics, political theory, and political communications, as well as the neighboring field of sociology, the basic premise of this book is simple: *what we say and what we mean matters for how we understand, experience, and act politically.* I have argued that for political challengers, it is more important to change the public understandings of contested issues than to win particular policy victories. This is because in changing common public understandings, movements *change the politics* surrounding their issue, creating political possibilities that are more favorable to their civic vision, and which may serve to usher in political victories on a range of related policy issues over the long term.

The way that political challengers can accomplish this feat is by winning political acceptance through the use of resonant arguments, which, over time, coalesce into coherent frames. This political acceptance is not synonymous with political approval or agreement and does not ensure that their favored set of policies will be adopted immediately, or in full. Instead, political acceptance allows those who wish to challenge status quo distributions of power and privilege to win an effective hearing in public, enabling them to make their case in terms that ordinary citizens, going about the regular process of their lives, can readily understand and apply to their political decision-making.

The Political Acceptance of the Tea Party

In this book, I have used the examples of the living wage and marriage equality movements to illuminate the importance of political acceptance to movement success. However, the theory of political acceptance is broadly applicable. For example, take the most vibrant American movements of the early twenty-first century: the Tea Party movement and Occupy Wall Street. Although I have not conducted statistical analysis of the news discourse surrounding these movements over the past half-decade, the logic of the theory of political acceptance is still instructive as it provides a plausible explanation for what has enabled the Tea Party's influence, while also suggesting a major reason for Occupy's abeyance.

The Tea Party movement was born in mainstream, public discourse. Conceptually, the mother of the movement was Keli Carender, a young libertarian and improv comedian who wrote the blog *Redistributing Knowledge*, under the name Liberty Belle. In 2009, she organized a "Porkulus Protest" against the $787 billion dollar American Recovery and Reinvestment Act, sponsored by then newly elected President Barack Obama. On February 16 of that year, about one hundred people attended the demonstration in Seattle, Washington (Malkin 2010). The next day, a similar protest, spearheaded by the Colorado chapter of Americans for Prosperity, featured a live pig and drew about two hundred activists who shouted "No more pork" outside the Denver Museum of Nature and Science, where Obama signed the Recovery Act into law. The protestors, who were hailed as heroes in the right-wing blogosphere but largely ignored by national media, decried the "generational theft" that they believed the bill portended, warning that each American would be saddled with $30,000 worth of debt as a result of the stimulus bill.[1] On February 18, for the third day in a row, this time in Mesa, Arizona, five hundred protestors showed up for an anti–Recovery Act protest promoted by local conservative talk radio channel KFYI (Malkin 2009).

Then, on February 19, 2009, Rick Santelli, a CNBC pundit, launched into a five-minute on-air rant in which he railed against the idea that the newly elected president would dare to put money into helping homeowners who had been devastated by the housing market crash that caused the Great Recession. Santelli shouted to the commodities traders on the floor of the Chicago Mercantile Exchange:

> [Do] we really want to subsidize the losers' mortgages? . . . This is America! How many people want to pay for your neighbor's mortgage, that has an extra bathroom and can't pay their bills? Raise your hand! President Obama, are you listening? You know Cuba used to have mansions and a relatively decent economy. They moved from the individual to the collective. Now they're driving '54 Chevys. *It's time for another tea party.* What we are doing in this country will make Thomas Jefferson and Benjamin Franklin roll over in their graves. (Ethridge 2009; emphasis added)

Santelli's declaration drew immediate response in the blogosphere, cheeringly hailed on the right and loudly mocked on the left (Ethridge 2009). What is important for our purposes, however, is that his new terminology, the doxic invocation of the "Tea Party"—the American defiance of British authority in 1773, an event depicted in every elementary school American history textbook—stuck immediately, replacing the clumsy and silly-sounding "porkulus" among protest organizers. The newly minted Tea Partiers sloughed off the porky imagery for eighteenth-century costumes and patriotic slogans emphasizing the importance of "freedom" and "liberty" as epitomized by "small government" and unregulated markets. Throughout the rest of 2009, groups who identified themselves as affiliated with the Tea Party movement, some sponsored by long-standing Washington, DC–based organizations like Freedomworks and Americans for Prosperity and some organized by bloggers and local activists, organized actions, including the highly effective infiltration of the town hall meetings of Congress members during the August recess that year. These Town Hall actions captivated the national media, and through them, Tea Partiers gained a platform to condemn Obama administration initiatives from the Recovery Act to the Affordable Care Act (colloquially, "Obamacare") for engaging in irresponsible spending, increasing the size of government, illegitimately "redistributing" taxpayer money, and courting socialism.

In the early stages of the Tea Party movement there was quite a bit of speculation that the movement was not at all grass-roots, but was instead "Astroturf," or an elite, professional campaign falsely claiming to be a mass movement (Good 2009). This speculation has proved untrue as Tea Party groups self-organized and proliferated, many having no connection to large national groups and others feuding with, defying, or cutting ties to established political players in order to support their favored candidates and causes, even when it has cost the national Republican Party political gains, as it did during the 2012 election cycle. Despite the various affiliations of the Tea Party groups around the country, the movement has maintained a simple, clear, consistent message containing the elements of resonance. Tea Party discourse is anchored by a doxic depiction of patriotic defiance in the face of coercion and in defense of liberty. It utilizes a common-sense logic that disparages spending more than one takes in, by employing a (largely inaccurate) "national budget is like a family budget" analogy.[2] And it offers the natal idea that in the face of government overspending, general incompetence, and even maleficent tendencies, the only solution is to "starve the beast," which shrinks the size of government and curbs the bad behavior of economic "losers."

Thus the Tea Party has achieved political acceptance through the use of consistent and coherent discourse, which has penetrated public awareness and prompted elite position-taking and policy accommodation. As with the case of marriage equality, political acceptance does not necessarily indicate political approval. The Tea Party has often earned itself electoral rebuke, running candidates like Sharon Angle and Christine O'Donnell in 2010, each of whom repeatedly made bizarre statements during her campaign, the former suggesting "Second Amendment remedies" as the best way to deal with her opponent,

Senate Majority Leader Harry Reid, and the latter releasing a campaign ad assuring voters that she was "not a witch."[3] Likewise in 2012, the Tea Party put forward Todd Akin in Missouri, who set off a national firestorm when he asserted that victims of "legitimate rape" rarely get pregnant because "the female body has ways to try to shut that whole thing down" (D. Cohen 2012). That race cost national Republicans a winnable Senate seat, returning Democratic incumbent Claire McCaskill to Washington, DC, after a re-election campaign that had been tough and uncertain up until Akin's comments rendered him a national lightning rod. That same pattern was repeated in Indiana with Tea Party favorite Richard Mourdock claiming that pregnancies resulting from rape were circumstances "God intended to happen," and therefore should not be undone (McAuliff 2012). Note that these campaign implosions took place for Tea Partiers deviating from the movement's original message advocating freedom from the financial coercion of "big government."

Underscoring the point that acceptance is not synonymous with approval, public opinion regarding the Tea Party movement has also been tepid since its emergence. At the peak of the movement's popularity in November 2010, 32 percent of respondents polled by Gallup described themselves as supporters. By May 2014, that number was down to 22 percent, with 30 percent of respondents describing themselves as opposed to the Tear Party and an additional 48 percent claiming to have no opinion.[4] In addition, the movement has an increasingly fraught relationship with the Republican Party "establishment," often working at cross-purposes with national party leaders.

Despite this evidence of tepid approval in the general public and ambivalence among party elites, the Tea Party and the views it espouses enjoy quite a bit of currency in national discourse. A Google search for news stories about the Tea Party in 2014 returns 172 million results, and national politicians, both Republican and Democrat, routinely take positions for and against Tea Party causes and attempt to make policy accommodations as gestures toward movement concerns.[5]

Occupy in Abeyance

The Occupy movement is a contrasting case. Occupy Wall Street was a part of a wave of uprisings that took place all over the world, beginning with the Arab Spring in late 2010 and early 2011, continuing with uprisings against austerity measures in Greece and antieviction occupations in Spain, among other rebellions across Europe. The American instantiation of this swell of resistance began as an encampment in New York City's Zucotti Park on September 17, 2011, and spread to cities and towns throughout the country. The movement immediately

captured the attention of the nation using two novel tactics. The first was a viral
online campaign. The #occupy hashtag tagged images of people holding placards
or sheets of paper that told the stories of their struggles in the Great Recession.
These testimonials were not deployed for sympathy, but were instead intended
to highlight the consequences of public policies that disadvantage the labor-
ing "99%" while benefitting the wealthy "1%." Here is an example of a typical
testimonial:

> I am 62 years old. I have worked honestly and hard my whole life (since
> I was 14) because that is how you realize the "American Dream." I was
> a home builder and designer. In 1980, the savings and loan crisis forced
> me out of work and out of business. (The government helped the
> banks survive. . .). I slowly rebuilt my life and business. In 2007, the
> "sub-prime mortgage crisis" crushed me again. I lost my home, my wife,
> and my belief in that "American Dream." (The government saved the
> banks again. . .). We are the 99%.[6]

Often these testimonials focused on the stories of people who had "played by
the rules," but were nevertheless let down, ignored, or crushed by laws and institutional rules that seemed designed to ensure their failure. These visual testimonials, or memes, dominated social media, including Facebook, Twitter, and
Tumblr, through much of the autumn of 2011. The "99%" argument combined
with the #occupy meme was an amazing communicative tactic and enabled anyone with access to social media to identify with the mobilizations that were taking place all over the country. The movement meme, coupled with the novel
protest tactic of encampment—the practice of literally occupying public space
for weeks or months—drew broad attention to the movement from the general
public and mainstream media alike, and focused attention on the systemic corruption, inequality, and injustice that activists believed was powerfully symbolized by New York City's financial district.

The argument that 99 percent of people are disadvantaged by current economic and political arrangements is a powerful one that many people agreed
with, as is evidenced by the robust public approval of the movement in the first
few months after its emergence. In October 2011, a *Time* magazine poll found
that 54 percent of respondents held a favorable view of Occupy[7] and an ABC /
Washington Post poll conducted between October 31 and November 3 of 2011
found that 44 percent of respondents described themselves as either strongly
supportive or somewhat supportive of the Occupy Wall Street movement.[8]

However, the Occupy movement's discourse never took on all the elements
of resonance. While the idea of the 99 percent was consistently repeated, and
was anchored in the doxic notion of what the "American dream" is supposed to

deliver if one is "hardworking" and "plays by the rules," the argument of the movement seemed to end there, never coalescing into a coherent and resonant frame.
Resonant frames must also include a commonplace logic and a natal solution, and
Occupy, with all its visceral appeal and tactical innovation, never moved beyond
calling attention to the systematic nature and broad impact of the problem.

Occupy did not omit these elements by chance or out of ineptness. Instead,
Occupy organizers and participants had serious philosophical reservations about
definitively characterizing the systematic problems that their testimonials called
attention to and an even stronger aversion to committing as a group to an official
set of solutions, particularly if those solutions would point back to partisan politics, electoral politics, or public policy prescriptions that would fail to challenge
what they saw as basic flaws in the current economic and political order.

Bernard Harcourt has argued that this aversion to the usual group-based politics that characterized twentieth-century activism was among Occupy's positive
innovations. Instead of practicing the "civil disobedience" of the iconic but, in
their view, limited movements that had preceded them, Occupy practiced "political disobedience." Harcourt explains the difference thusly:

> Civil disobedience accepted the legitimacy of political institutions, but
> resisted the moral authority of resulting laws. Political disobedience,
> by contrast, resists the very way in which we are governed: it resists
> the structure of partisan politics, the demand for policy reforms, the
> call for party identification, and the very ideologies that dominated the
> post-War period. (Harcourt 2011)

For Occupy participants, there were principled reasons for getting together in
the streets in order to draw attention to a pervasive problem, while simultaneously resisting the pressure to speak with one, assured voice. Activists used
#occupy memes and the encampments to build solidarity, while simultaneously
avoiding hierarchy, blunting the impact of any one ideology, and limiting the
exercise of dominative power by any one demographic group, which would seek
to speak for the whole, the kind of situation that results in "respectability politics" (Higginbotham 1993) and "secondary marginalization" (Cohen 1999).

Harcourt goes on to argue that "political disobedience" can be seen as the
active, political embodiment of a Foucauldian style of "critique," which rejects
what has come before and demands

> constant vigilance of all the micro and macro rules that permeate our
> markets, our contracts, our tax codes, our banking regulations, our
> property laws—in sum, all the ordinary, often mundane, but frequently
> invisible forms of laws and regulations that are required to organize and

maintain a colossal economy in the 21st-century and that constantly distribute wealth and resources.[9]

By these lights, there is no solution to the urgent and well-articulated problem of the 99 percent; instead, there is only "constant vigilance." This disbelief in solutions is the flip side of the Foucaultian assessment of power. If power is an ever-present effect of relation, then there is no way to nullify its impact. Power simply is because it is produced by human relation and it will remain with us as long as we remain. The best we can do, then, is to be aware of this fact and to be vigilant about what power does and how power does it, hence the importance of the genealogical method. However, what those who take this perspective often downplay or ignore is that not all of power's effects are equally destructive and, through public discourse, we are perfectly capable of deciding between the effects of power that are broadly acceptable and those that are not. The fact that what we accept as a public may not be just, in a philosophical sense, is not a sign of futility or defeat, but a call to persuade.

While Occupy demonstrated the power to mobilize and built solidarity among participants and observers, it did not seek to persuade. Like the attitude that has often afflicted labor advocates on the left, those who participated in Occupy believed the impetus for their cause was self-evident. Occupiers also seemed to believe that necessary remedies would emerge from the process and that the ethical dangers of falling into old political traps and ideological troupes were greater than those of seeming incoherent and directionless.

Reasonable people can disagree about the merits of the trade-off that Occupy chose. If the movement is in abeyance, rather than disbanded, it may re-emerge in a decade with a sense of itself that is more finely honed, practically focused, and articulate, while maintaining its disobedient ethic. However, what we know of the immediate political outcome of the Occupy Wall Street uprising is that while public support for Occupy started strong, by November 2011, a Quinnipiac poll showed that only 30 percent of respondents still held a favorable view of the movement, while 39 percent had come to oppose it.[10] Noting the swift swing in public support, a Public Policy Polling analyst opined on November 16, 2011, the day after New York mayor Michael Bloomberg ordered the forcible removal of the Zucotti Park encampment:

> I don't think the bad poll numbers for Occupy Wall Street reflect Americans being unconcerned with wealth inequality. Polling we did in some key swing states earlier this year found overwhelming support for raising taxes on people who make over $150,000 a year. In late September we found that 73% of voters supported the "Buffett rule" [which would establish a minimum tax rate for high-income taxpayers]

with only 16% opposed. And in October we found that Senators resistant to raising taxes on those who make more than a million dollars a year could pay a price at the polls. I don't think any of that has
changed—what the downturn in Occupy Wall Street's image suggests
is that voters are seeing the movement as more about the "Occupy"
than the "Wall Street." The controversy over the protests is starting to
drown out the actual message.[11]

A message that never coalesced beyond the compelling cry that "shit is fucked up
and bullshit," as one oft-shared Zucotti Park sign declared.[12]

In 2014, four years from the emergence of Occupy, polling agencies no longer ask respondents what they think of the movement. As I mentioned above, a
Google search for news stories about the Tea Party returns 172 million results; a
parallel search for news stories about Occupy, a movement that initially enjoyed
more public support, now returns only 18 million results. And though the affecting language of the 1 percent still lingers in our public discourse, it is not linked
to any consistent analysis or set of remedies.

To "dream a world," as Langston Hughes wrote, can be not only inspiring
and fulfilling, but also a necessary and useful act, but then that dream must be
translated into something that can be made manifest in political reality. The fact
that there is always something lost in translation is both simply the reality of the
political and a call to further action down the line. Such action is only possible
if political challengers have a clear idea of what they want the world to look like
and are willing to sustain a politics that relentlessly articulates itself in resonant
terms, making it practicable, if not perfect.

Political Acceptance or Political Transformation?

One final question that is worth addressing is whether this pragmatist genealogy
leaves room for anything beyond political acceptance. One of the goals of those
who spend their time thinking about and organizing for social justice is precisely
challenging popular understandings and pushing the boundaries of what counts
as commonplace. I have encountered many scholars and activists who argue that
the gulf between *is* and *ought* is so vast that to traverse the space incrementally,
while largely adhering to the conventions that have spawned the gap, is counter-
productive. What is needed instead is a radical politics that seeks transformation
rather than acceptance.

Michael Warner, for example, writes about a desire for a kind of politics that
seeks to challenge common understandings, transforming, or "queering," common linkages between background understandings, common-sense logics, and

personal, social, and political purposes. In the case of marriage equality, queer activists ask whether this movement's progress should be considered success at all. Marriage, after all, is an institution that reinscribes traditional forms of sexual and property relation that can be oppressive. In addition, as an institution, marriage is becoming more and more the purview of the economically and educationally privileged (Greenstone and Looney 2012). Yasmin Nair and Ryan Conrad, cofounders of the organization Against Equality, argue that marriage is "neoliberalism's handiest little tool," asserting:

> The entire framework that we use to understand our "resources," like health care or housing or knowledge, etc. is of the economic model of capitalism and scarcity. Here in the States, through marriage we see the privatization of what we believe are collective benefits, like access to health care, to specifically classed family units. Instead of fighting for everyone's right to live, like queer folks did so loudly and proudly here and elsewhere in the 80s, we see LGBTs now demanding that only married people have the right to these things.[13]

The political project of marriage equality is one of inclusion, not disruption, and as such is not only inadequate, by these lights, but can actually be damaging. Making marriage the premier issue of the gay rights movement not only erases the experience of those whose gender identities, notions of the good life, or material access to needed resources is not addressed by marriage, but draws away resources from movements for universal healthcare, antipoverty programs, and the like that might help a broader swath of people: gay, straight, queer, married or not.

This critique brings up a number of valid issues. It is true that legalizing same-sex marriage in no way helps unmarried people—gay, straight, or otherwise—to gain access to basic services like healthcare and housing, for example. More troubling than the problems marriage does not address is the fact that the gay politics of respectability that has been practiced in the marriage equality movement makes relatively wealthy, mostly white, usually male, and generally gender-conforming individuals the public face of gay politics. This creates a skewed perception of the LGBTQ community, which includes many more poor and moderate-income individuals and people of color than popular representations suggest. This misrepresentation matters not only in terms of inadequate descriptive representation, but much more importantly because those who lend the movement their faces also tend to dominate the movement's agenda, prioritizing the concerns that impact their demographic group(s) and downplaying or ignoring those of the more marginal and less "respectable."

Given these concerns, what can a theory of political acceptance offer those who want to get beyond a politics of inclusion and move toward a politics that prioritizes social justice? My answer is that this theory does not proscribe the scope of change, but instead underscores the importance of persuasion if the change activists seek is to be widespread and enduring. The theory of political acceptance points out that public meaning is an indispensible site of movement power and clarifies the necessary contours of a positive and practicable project for political change, whether the goal is inclusion or transformation.

Often radical politics begins in critique—an effort to uncover the inconsistencies and limits of a doctrine, ideology, or orthodoxy. Intellectually, critique is undertaken for its own sake; politically, people undertake critique in order to evoke radical consciousness. It is thought that such consciousness, if it is shared broadly enough, may stimulate the kind of revelation that is required for revolution. Radical politics is anchored by skepticism and geared toward questioning. Politics that seeks transformation in relations of power asks that members of the polity view the normalizing institutional, cultural, and practical edifices of personal, social, and political life as both monumental and devious. As such, the task of those who seek justice, as defined from this point of view, must be to relentlessly take institutions to task: demystifying, deconstructing, and denouncing their failings.

However, in the process of this "de"-ing, the converse and politically necessary "re"-ing—reinterpreting, rearticulating, and reconstructing—often remains obscured, permanently deferred. It can often seem that radical politics is *only* a politics of undoing and subverting. These activities are necessary, but they are not sufficient to the task of challenging status quo arrangements of power and privilege. This is because highlighting problems of political understanding and policy is not enough, particularly if it is carried out in language that is careless about whether it is intelligible to the ordinarily competent person.

Some might argue that this kind of political pragmatism is the antithesis of radicalism. But I see no reason why that should be the case. If we take the meaning of the word "radical" seriously, as derived from the Latin *radix*, or root, it means to think, speak, or act in a way that affects the fundamental nature of a thing, specifically, of political and social arrangements. Radicalism requires no particular methodology, but instead a particular orientation toward recognizing problems and conceiving solutions. I should be clear that a well-articulated, practical politics does not have to be conducted with allegiance to traditional ideologies (although it will build from them, mixing and matching, as is the wont of activists) or via electoral politics or any other particular form. Instead, a politics that takes into account the lessons of political acceptance must seek to persuade, and in doing so must be focused, well articulated, and consistent, attempting to answer the inevitable rhetoric of reaction with a rhetoric of change. It is unreasonable and, more importantly, politically impracticable to ask members of the polity to change direction—to revise beliefs, common logics, practices, policies, or, certainly, political structure, without articulating a clear and intelligible vision, conveying that vision in a way that links to some beliefs and values that are already deeply held.

Tapping into the natal capacity inherent in political action requires a constructive and declarative way forward. A politics that understands the necessity of political acceptance for lasting change should acknowledge the importance and usefulness of critique as a tool of analysis, but does not presume that such analyses will give rise to radical consciousness or imagine that such consciousness provides self-evident steps in the desired direction. Neither does this philosophically pragmatic politics assume that spontaneous revolt, should it occur, would automatically satisfy most conceptions of justice. Instead, lasting political change requires a positive project: one that seeks to articulate, not only interrogate, one that seeks to translate, not only raise consciousness, and one that seeks to persuade, not only provoke political revelation and the revolution that might accompany it. This is because revelation and revolution are singular, illusive heights of insight and action that, should they be reached, still beg the question: what does revelation mean to the we who are the polity, and how should revolution shape what comes next?

Appendix A

PRINCIPAL COMPONENT ANALYSIS FOR THE EXAMINATION OF ARGUMENTS AND FRAMES: STEP BY STEP

Step 1: Construct a matrix of all coded variables. Run principal component analysis (PCA) on the entire data set in order to shed light on two things. The first is how many components are relevant for your data set. The second is how correlated the entire data set is. In my data set, the first component accounted for .61, or 61%, of the variance, and the next two components accounted for 18% and 12%, respectively. Seven additional components accounted for 3% or less of the variance. I focused my attention on the first three components, as they accounted for the vast majority of the variance in the data set.

Step 2: Take a look at the eigenvectors for each coded variable. These eigenvectors capture the weights given to each variable when calculating the components. Here, see whether any of the variables have particularly large or small loadings. Mine did not. They varied, but not shockingly so, between .05 at the smallest and .168 at the largest. What interested me more at this early stage were the signs of the loadings. This gives a clue as to how the arguments might relate to one another when pulled out and grouped together as potential frames. However, these loadings are only clues and do not yet determine which arguments are most closely related or how they are related (only the researcher can posit that).

Step 3: Begin to classify arguments together in order to test them to see if they statistically resolve into frames.

Step 4: Run PCA on hypothesized frames to see how well they cohere. Start narrowing down which variables (arguments) make up distinct frames based upon both frame coherence (percentage of total variance explained by the first component) and the robustness of arguments in the frame (percentage of variance accounted for by a single argument within a frame). In my data set, I chose to consider those clusters of arguments that together accounted for at least .80, or 80%, of variance. This high standard is necessary because the entire data set is highly correlated. In terms of how tightly correlated the individual arguments were with others in the frame, I chose to set the eigenvector value at greater than .30 because by the conventions of statistical analysis in political science, variables that are more than 30% correlated, can no longer be considered independent of one another.

Step 5: The hypothesized frames are likely not exactly right. In my data set, in some cases, I wasn't even close. But each additional component analysis gives you a lot of information. Every time you run a comparison, you get to see which eigenvector loadings are higher and which are lower. In each case, I took the ones with lower loadings (below .30) out of the PCA and then ran them with each other in order to see whether there were relationships that I simply hadn't considered.

Step 6: With orphaned arguments—those that do not fit into any frame—think about the possible connections between them, given your familiarity with the entire discourse. Put together other arguments that seem logically related. Look at their loadings and coherence measure. Sometimes the orphaned arguments belong in a frame that has already been created. Sometimes they combine with each other in unexpected ways (the way the code "rights for gay couples" paired with "economic aspects of gay marriage," rather than the "equality" frame or the "all kinds of families" frame is an example of this kind of unexpected result).

Step 7: Name and define the substantive frames that emerge.

Step 8: Once the frames have been determined, you can then use PCA to assess salience (frequency) and strength (eigenvalue/vector). These two values multiplied give a score for attention (or "weighted attention" if using the terminology of Baumgartner, De Boef, and Boydstun 2008); as well as resonance (number of arguments that hang together).

Appendix B

New York Times: Gay Marriage

abortion and gay marriage
adoption and GM
"all-but-married"
"America is not ready"
apolitical
article
backlash
battle for public opinion
benefits of alternative families
biography
Bush not antigay
campaign issue
challenging gender
children best raised by two heterosexual parents
church and state
civil-state-marriage-church
civil rights invocation
civil war analogy
civilization at stake
clergy opinions
Clinton burned by supporting gay rights before
"comity"
constitutional ban on GM
courts not the place to decide GM
culture war
debate focused
definitional argument

love makes a family
making history
marriage is a social good
"marriage lite"
"marriage movement"
marriage versus civil unions
national debate
natural law
nondiscrimination
normalization of civil unions
"normal people"
not a threat to the family
not about equal access
novelty
overreaction on GM
personal relationships
politics of state GM bans
preserving traditional marriage
problems with heterosexual marriage
progress is American
public/religious/spiritual recognition
questions of political strategy
redefinition of marriage/family
right to marry
rights for gay couples
rights, not marriage
sanctity of marriage
"sex-partner subsidies"
sexual perversion
sexuality is chosen
shifting attitudes
"the sky does not fall"
slavery analogy
slippery slope argument
"sneak attack"
special rights
specter of AIDS
stability and monogamy
state's rights
symbolism of marriage
take the state out of marriage

"this is something that people get"
tolerance
traditional understanding
"trendy moral relativism"
upholding the law
"wedge politics"
"the world as we know it"
World Trade Center spouses
writing discrimination into Constitution
"wrong side of history"

New York Times: Living Wage

1960s invocation
"accountability and responsibility"
alternative growth
"appeal to average Americans"
article
bad condition of workers
biography-negative outcome
biography-positive outcome
business pushback
business threat
challenging eco orthodoxy
companies can afford
"corporate welfare"
demonstrations
development not produced good jobs
downsizing-privatization
empirical LW
even in the face of evidence
fairness
free-market principles
"full-time workers deserve"
"giving America a raise"
gulf between rich and poor
high public approval for wage floor
hurt those meant to help
immigrant labor dimension
laying the groundwork
lifts poor from poverty

limited coverage of LW ordinances
living wage
low public opinion of unions
low wage = social decay
LW definition
LW drives business away
LW helps business
LW hurts small business
LW in quotes
LW is union stalking horse
LW leads to job loss
LW local strategy
LW movement success
LW not shown gains to working poor
LW oversight
LW prices workers out of market
LW saves public money
minimum wage
moral obligation to pay
myth of the teenager
no LW, more government programs
ordinance details
original idea
paid less than legal minimum
"paper ordinances"
poverty
poverty-level income amount
prevailing wage
religious support
"reward work"
"self-sufficiency wage"
"social contract"
"socialist"
social justice
state reversal
uncertain LW costs
underemployment, not unemployment
unfair to business
Wal-Mart
Washington, DC, not acting
welfare (and wages)

"working families"
"working harder for less"
"working poor"

USA *Today*: Gay Marriage

abortion and gay marriage
adoption and gay marriage
"all-but-married"
all kinds of families
"America is not ready"
apolitical
article
backlash
battle for public opinion
benefits of alternative families
biography
Bush not antigay
campaign issue
challenging gender
children best raised with two heterosexual parents
church and state
civil rights invocation
civilization at stake
clergy opinions
Clinton burned by supporting gays
constitutional ban on gay marriage
courts not the place to decide
culture war
definitional argument
demonstrations
discrimination
divided/divisive
do the right thing
DOMA
economic aspects of gay marriage
emotionally charged
equal access argument
fair-minded Americans
freedom to marry
full faith and credit

"fundamentally ugly"
"gay baiting"
gay biology
gay lobby
gay parents
gay rights
gay wedding announcements
gay marriage's inevitability
gay marriage for the children
homosexual agenda
human rights
"hypocrisy, bigotry!"
inappropriate recognition
insider/outsider
interracial marriage analogy
"it's not right"
just a couple of regular people
legal opinion versus public opinion
"linguistic rights" to the word "marriage"
litmus test
love makes a family
making history
"marriage lite"
"marriage movement"
marriage versus civil unions
national debate
natural law
nondiscrimination
normalization of civil unions
not a threat to the family
not about equal access
not like black civil rights
novelty
overreaction on gay marriage
personal relationships
politics of state gay marriage ban
polls
postmarriage era?
preserving traditional marriage
problems with cohabitation
problems with heterosexual marriage

progress is American
questions of political strategy
redefinition of marriage/family
religious/legal/public recognition
right to marry
rights, not marriage
"sanctified but separate"
"sanctity of marriage"
"sex-partner subsidies"
sexual perversion
sexuality is chosen
shifting attitudes
"the sky does not fall"
slavery analogy
slippery slope
special rights
specter of AIDS
stability and monogamy
state's rights
symbolism of marriage
take the state out of marriage
"this is something that people get"
tolerance
"trendy moral relativism"
upholding the law
wage referendum
World Trade Center spouses
writing discrimination into the Constitution
"wedge politics"
"wrong side of history"

USA Today: Living Wage

alternative growth
"appeal to average Americans"
article
biography-positive outcomes
biography-negative outcomes
business pushback
business threats
companies can afford

demonstrations
empirical LW
fairness
"full-time workers deserve LW"
gulf between rich and poor
high public approval for LW
hurt those meant to help
immigrant labor dimension
laying the groundwork
lifts poor from poverty
limited coverage of LW ordinances
living wage
low public opinion of unions
LW definition
LW drives business away
LW helps business
LW in quotes
LW is union stalking horse
LW leads to job loss
LW local strategy
LW movement success
LW not shown gains to WP
LW oversight
LW prices workers out of market
minimum wage
moral disapproval for low wages
no LW, more government programs for poor
ordinance details
original idea
"paper ordinances"
poverty-level income
religious support
"reward work"
uncertain of LW costs
unfair to business
Wal-Mart
Washington, DC, not acting
welfare (and wages)
"working families"
"working poor"

NOTES

Introduction

1. The discursive disarray that characterizes the movement during the primary decade of study has had periods of abatement, but only when subjected to the message discipline of national elites allied with the movement—a movement that then becomes invisible in the familiar and temporary (that is, election-cycle-specific) glare of traditional party competition. This has happened twice in the period since 2004: first, during the congressional debate preceding the amendment of the Fair Labor Standards Act in 2007, which raised the federal minimum wage from $5.15 to $7.25, and more recently, following President Obama's proposal, in the 2014 State of the Union, to increase the current federal minimum wage from $7.25 to $10.10.

2. New media forms have altered this equation somewhat, enabling clever cultural critics to have the kind of voice that can interrupt dominant discourses, sometimes bypassing official gatekeepers in traditional media, but the vast majority of information that most people have access to still flows through those credentialed to speak by their profession or position.

3. Lukes takes on the problems of attributing a consistent "nature" and "judgment" that can dictate "real interests" in the second edition of *Power: A Radical View* (2005) and concludes that nature and judgment are clearer categories than any of their alternatives, especially "identity" and "preference." He goes on to defend the notion of "real interests" by claiming that "there is no reason to believe that there exists a canonical set of such interests that will constitute 'the last word on the matter,'" but that should not preclude observers from employing the concept of real interests as a useful category of analysis that "simply takes what count as 'real interests' to be a function of one's explanatory purpose, framework, and methods, which in turn have to be justified" (148). I find this to be an elision of the question. In my view, what is needed is a method of analysis that allows us to hold these concepts in dynamic tension, as people actually experience them, rather than creating a hierarchy of importance or dismissing one in favor of the other.

4. In his essay "What Is Critique?" Foucault wrote: "the question is being raised: 'what, therefore, am I,' who belong to this humanity, perhaps to this piece of it, at this point in time, at this instant of humanity which is subjected to the power of truth in general and truths in particular? The first characteristic of this philosophical-historical practice, if you will, is to de-subjectify the philosophical question by way of historical contents by examining the effects of power whose truth affects them and from which they supposedly derive" (2002, 199).

5. While sociological study has shown that contemporary lovers are skeptical of this Jane Austen-esque idea of love, often describing their own relationships in "prosaic-reali[st]" terms, which emphasize the gradualness, ambiguity, open-endedness, and contingency of love as people experience it in their everyday lives, the mythic notion of love persists in

popular culture and pops up unexpectedly amid the prosaic accounts that people offer of their own love lives. There are some who would attribute this persistence to the hegemonic power of the love myth, the false consciousness of lovers who despite their lived experience reject the "truth" of love's prosaic nature. Swidler counters, "Mythic love persists because, while the prosaic view is more realistic as a description of experience, description is not the only or most important use to which cultural meanings can be put. Culture does not describe external reality so much as it organizes people's own lines of action. [And] criticism of the dominant ideal will not eliminate it as long as it provides a useful guide to action.. . . The basic structure of the love myth corresponds to, and helps organize, the lines of action individuals construct whether to enter or leave a marriage" (Swidler 2001, 129).

6. Of course, this means that marriage equality advocates also reinforce and reinscribe notions of bourgeois love that queer critics define as one of the major problems preventing the just distribution of rights and resources in the American context. For example, the idea that marriage is a choice, but one has to marry one's partner in order to obtain health insurance, does not ring true to many queer activists. Cf. Conrad 2010. See also the tremendous archive of related articles at http://www.againstequality.org/.

7. For more evidence and in-depth analysis of this phenomenon see Jennifer Hochschild's *What's Fair* (1986).

Chapter 1

1. A way to underscore this distinction is to reference the difference between memory-based and online information-processing models that have been developed in the public opinion literature. Memory-based models posit that people make decisions based on the information that is the most accessible, and that is usually information that is highly salient (Zaller 1992). Online processing, or running-tally, models are based on the theory that people spontaneously cull affectively relevant details from political information that they encounter the moment that they encounter it (Lodge et al. 1995). What individuals find affecting is usually attributed to psychological and sociological processes (Goffman 1974, Pan and Kosicki 1993, Scheufele and Tewksbury 2007).

2. See *Oxford English Dictionary* under the entry "persuade," retrieved from http://dictionary. oed.com.proxy.uchicago.edu/cgi/entry/50176313?query_type=word&queryword=persua ded&first=1&max_to_show=10&single=1&sort_type=alpha on December 12, 2007.

3. It is important to acknowledge that the idea that marriage increases well-being is hotly disputed, especially within gay communities, but the internal debate, which raged pretty seriously among advocates throughout the 1990s, rarely emerged into mainstream discourse. Instead, the common idea that marriage is the ideal result of mature sexual relations and personal commitment was repeatedly referenced in articles regardless of the author's stand on the political issue.

Chapter 2

1. Appearances can be deceiving. There were and continue to be heated and divisive battles in the LGBTQ community about every aspect of advocacy for gay rights. In addition, there is a whole sector of organizations on the queer left dedicated to critiquing and delegitimizing marriage as an appropriate goal for gay rights organizations. Cf. Against Equality: http:// www.againstequality.org/

2. Interview conducted with Jen Kern April 11, 2008.

3. Interview with Jen Kern, April 11, 2008.

4. Living Wage Resource Center homepage retrieved on July 12, 2008, from http://www.livingwagecampaign.org/index.php?id=1961.

5. Living Wage Resource Center homepage retrieved on July 12, 2008. from http://www.livingwagecampaign.org/index.php?id=1961.

6. Interview with Jen Kern, April 11, 2008.

7. Interview with Jen Kern, April 11, 2008.

8. Interview with Kristina Wilfore. April 22, 2008.
9. National Employment Law Project, "Living Wage Laws," http://www.nelp.org/content/content_issues/category/living_wage_laws/ (March 10, 2013).
10. Interview with Jen Kern, April 11, 2008.
11. Interview with Stephanie Luce, April 21, 2008.

Chapter 3

1. Troy Perry, founder of the Metropolitan Community Church, performed a public marriage between two people of the same sex in 1969. In 1970, the Metropolitan Community Church filed the first lawsuit petitioning for the right for same-sex partnerships to be legally recognized as marriages (Chauncey 2004).
2. It is important to note that the history of striving to gain legal recognition of partnerships in the gay rights movement precedes the marriage movement. Beginning in 1979 and through the 1980s, gay rights advocates designed and pushed for the legal recognition of "domestic partnerships" in cities around the country. Like living wage policies, the eligibility, rights, and benefits of domestic partners are highly localized, recognized by cities, counties, states, or employers, but with no federal recognition. Some gay rights activists prefer domestic partnerships to civil unions or marriages because they can be regarded as recognizing a larger variety of relationships—for example, cohabitating, nonconjugal relationships—thereby seeking to "reflect and honor the diverse ways in which people find and practice love, form relationships, create communities and networks of caring and support, establish households, bring families into being, and build innovative structures to support and sustain community." Retrieved on June 16, 2014, from http://www.beyondmarriage.org/full_statement.html It is also worth noting that domestic partnerships (and the larger degree of flexibility in household construction that they might provide) have been increasingly invalidated or eliminated in locales where equal marriage is available, resulting in what independent scholar Yasmin Nair has called "compulsory marriage." See Joshua Pavan's interview with the cofounders of Against Equality, "Capitalism's Handiest Little Tool," *No More Potlucks*, retrieved on June 16, 2014, from http://nomorepotlucks.org/site/%E2%80%9Cneoliberalism%E2%80%99s-handiest-little-tool%E2%80%9D-against-equality-on-marriage/.
3. Carey Goldberg, "Couple Who Stirred Issue of Same-Sex Marriage Still Hopeful," *New York Times*. July 27, 1996.
4. Goldberg, "Couple Who Stirred Issue."
5. Defense of Marriage Act (DOMA), Pub. L. No. 104-199, 110 Stat. 2419 (Sept. 21, 1996) and codified at 1 U.S.C. § 7 and 28 U.S.C. § 1738C.
6. Interview with Evan Wolfson, April 29, 2008.
7. It should be noted that during the 1980s a handful of cities had recognized "domestic partnerships," a status that could be entered into by same or opposite sex couples for certain limited benefits. Interestingly, like living wage ordinances, laws recognizing domestic partnerships were often enacted at the municipal level and, in several cases, only applied to city employees or to firms contracting with the municipality.
8. "The World According to Cheney, Lieberman," *USA Today*, October 6, 2000.
9. "Legislating Who Can Say I Do," *New York Times*, July 7, 1996.
10. While she argues that AIDS made this path seem like the best at the time, she is ultimately critical of the "degaying, desexualizing, decoupling of AIDS-specific reform from systemic reform" that, in her view, amounted to "short-term, quick-fix strategies that yielded dramatic, but short-lived gains" (Vaid 1995, 74). As recently as 2013, men who have sex with men account for the majority of new HIV infections, and gay men are the only segment of the population whose HIV infection rate is currently rising, while public discourse on the domestic AIDS crisis has plummeted. Her claim should be taken seriously.
11. Each of the organizations has focused a lot of attention on marriage. Between 1995 and 2005, 35 percent of the Human Right's Campaign's press releases were on the topic of gay marriage; no other issue received as much attention from the organization. Marriage rights were the National Gay and Lesbian Task Force's third most predominant issue, with 24 percent of

their press releases devoted to the topic, behind employment issues and hate crimes legislation (Mucciaroni 2008, 5).

12. Although this speculation was widely questioned by scholars and public opinion researchers, the myth of the gay marriage wedge issue took hold (Taylor 2006).

13. Michael Paulson, "Conference Cuts Funding for ACORN," *Boston Globe*, November 12, 2008.

14. Paulson, "Conference Cuts Funding for ACORN."

15. Human Rights Campaign Annual Reports Archive, retrieved on May 20, 2013, from http://www.hrc.org/the-hrc-story/annual-reports.

16. Lambda Legal Defense and Education Fund 2011 Annual Report, retrieved on May 20, 2013, from http://www.lambdalegal.org/publications/ar_2011_making-the-case-for-equality. Lambda Legal's budget was about the same between 2009 and 2011 according to publically available tax forms retrieved on May 20, 2013, from http://www.guidestar.org/organizations/23-7395681/lambda-legal-defense-education-fund.aspx.

17. See the discussion and linked economics articles in Konczal 2013.

18. Specifically the politics of African American Christian women at the turn of the twentieth century and its practice can be traced to the beginning of black American social movements and followed like a thread through black American political thought from David Walker to W. E. B. Dubois and E. Franklin Frazier, right up to contemporary thinkers like William Julius Wilson.

19. Bayard Rustin, the openly gay chief organizer of the 1963 March on Washington, was barred from giving a public speech at the lectern lest the fact that he was gay be used to impugn the moral uprightness of the larger movement.

Chapter 4

1. It is important to note here that, following Slavoj Žižek, I do not mean to argue that cynical reception is synonymous with or antecedent to rejection; on the contrary, as Žižek argues in *The Sublime Object of Ideology*, the cynical subject "knows the falsehood very well" and is "well aware of a particular interest hidden behind an ideological universality, but still . . . does not renounce it" (1989, 29).

2. Although Habermas owes the teleological form of his "communicative reason" approach to Aristotle, he chooses not to use the ancient philosopher's insight on the subject of rhetoric to make his theory more applicable to democratic communication as it is actually practiced. I believe the realities of mediation in practical democratic experience, especially in the current era, might require a revision of the usual theoretical tools. For this reason, it is important to supplement the dominant Habermasian analysis of communication with the old insights of Aristotle so that we can better understand the function of communication as it is generally practiced. The most comprehensive explanation of Habermas's discourse ethics is in *Between Facts and Norms* (1996).

3. Pew Research Center for the People and the Press, "Abortion, the Court, and the Public," October 3, 2005, retrieved from http://people-press.netcampaign.com/commentary/display.php3?AnalysisID=119 on May 12, 2008.

4. Frank Browning, "Why Marry?" *New York Times*, April 17, 1996.

5. Aristotle does make this point when he explains that rhetorical argument best proceeds through the use of enthymeme (a syllogism in which part of the argument is assumed because it "goes without saying") as opposed to the dialectic's syllogism (in which a proof must be constructed). For in rhetoric it is most important that the argument persuade the judges, not necessarily that that the argument is shown to be logically consistent (Aristotle 1991, 42).

6. The unconscious, here, is meant in the simplest way possible. That is: things that we know that we do not (and perhaps cannot) explicitly explain because our knowledge of them has not been codified.

Chapter 5

1. Ideology is meant here in Marx's sense as the dominant or hegemonic ideas, not in its common American politics usage denoting a unidimensional liberal-to-conservative scale. Also, hegemony theorists mean to apply the famously compelling, but underspecified, notion of hegemony authored by Antonio Gramsci in his *Prison Notebooks* (1992).
2. This flow of information is not merely directive, "as with real world cascading waterfalls, each level in the metaphorical cascade also makes its own contribution to the mix and flow of ideas." Entman also notes that "as we go down . . . the flow of information . . . [is] increasingly limited to the selected highlights, processed through schemas, and then passed on in ever-cruder form." In addition, Entman does allow for the flow of information from bottom to top (public to administration); however, he seems unconvinced that this upward flow makes very much difference in regular political communication (2004, 12, 21).
3. Doug McAdam's idea that successful movements require members to undergo "cognitive liberation" as a prerequisite to mobilization is a widely acknowledged precursor to Snow and Benford's influential work.
4. Sidney Tarrow, David Snow, Robert Benford, and other scholars of cultural framing acknowledge that the general public will require different kinds of frames than the membership, but these authors do not then examine how member frames and public frames are or ought to be different.
5. Survey results published on the IGM forum website published by the University of Chicago Booth School of Business, retrieved from http://www.igmchicago.org/igm-economic-experts-panel/poll-results?SurveyID=SV_br0IEq5a9E77NMV on December 4, 2014.
6. There are exceptions to this rule. Ruud Koopmans and Susan Olzak (2004) did a study in which they analyze the connection between public discourse and radical Right violence in Germany. In it, they argue that public discourse is a mediating factor between political opportunity and internal framing processes. Also, Shane Gunderson's short article "Social Movement, Spectacle and Momentum" (2008b) explores the notion that "popular intellectuals" can be the authors of arguments that they seek to insert in mass-mediated discourse via spectacles that dramatize issues and cause public outcry. See also Gunderson 2008a.
7. Pew Forum on Religion and Public Life, November 18, 2003, "Religious Beliefs Underpin Opposition to Homosexuality," retrieved from http://pewforum.org/docs/?DocID=37 on November 16, 2007.
8. The key phrases in this definition, "the people" and "common interest," are both somewhat ambiguous terms, which have inspired volumes of philosophical examination and scrutiny, but I have a thin conception of each term. I take John Dewey's definition of "the people" from *The Public and Its Problems* (1927) as a group that emerges in response to a shared situation or set of problems. Likewise, common interest, in this conception, is merely the problems that a public acknowledges need to be addressed or solved.
9. It could certainly also be represented in "everyday talk" as elaborated by Jane Mansbridge (1999).
10. "Religion and Politics: Contention and Consensus" (Pew 2003a). Pew has not repeated this survey since 2003. There is some evidence, that since the financial crash of 2008, this calculus may have changed. An NBC/*Wall Street Journal* poll conducted April 5–8, 2013, found that 50 percent of Americans now say that the "most serious problems in our society stem mainly from economic and financial pressures on the family," while only 43 percent point to a "decline in moral values" (Harwood 2013).
11. Originally, I had hoped to include television news in this analysis, but obtaining a representative sample of television coverage was prohibitively expensive.
12. According to the Pew Research Center for the People and the Press, the issues getting intense media coverage as campaign issues during the summer of 2006 were government surveillance, global warming, abortion, gay marriage, and the inheritance tax. Incidentally, these were not the issues that voters listed as their top priority; those included education, Iraq, terrorism, healthcare, and the economy. Corruption, racism, and income disparity did not make the list of issues voters indicated as very important (Pew 2006).

Chapter 6

1. My analysis of frames and resonance is adapted from the evolutionary frame analysis technique developed by Frank Baumgartner, Suzanne De Boef, and Amber Boydstun in their book *The Decline of the Death Penalty and the Discovery of Innocence* (2008). I chose to use principal component analysis rather than factor analysis because principal component analysis allows you to extract the same kind of information about discourse with a smaller data set.

2. These three terms constitute the "rhetoric of change" that William Gamson and David Meyer offer, which states that arguments that counter what Albert Hirschman dubbed "rhetoric of reaction" must include frames that convey "urgency," "necessity," and "possibility." See Gamson and Meyer 1996. However, I think that what they are detailing is not a rhetoric of political change, but instead a rhetoric that encourages political activism. These are not necessarily synonymous, given that much of the success of political change rests on the perceptions of people who are not activists, but interested observers who are members of the polity.

3. The customary level of correlation that is considered too highly correlated to use as independent variables in a regression analysis is .30.

4. The one exception to this rule is the "so-called living wage" argument in the "anxieties about the living wage" frame. I included this argument because it seemed that .26 level of correlation was an artifact of the unusually high number of arguments contained in the frame.

5. For a more detailed account of this methodology see appendix A.

6. Quote from Senator Alfonse D'Amato (D-NY) as reported in the *New York Times* article "Senate Votes Down Higher Minimum Wage, Citing Squeeze," by Katharine Q. Seelye, published on September 22, 1998.

7. "States Can Take Wage Lead While Washington Waffles," *USA Today*, April 17, 1996.

8. Interview with Kristina Wilfore, April 22, 2008.

9. *NBC News / Wall Street Journal* Poll conducted December 10–13, 1994, by Hart and Teeter Research Companies.

10. Pew Research Center for the People and the Press Poll conducted December 1–16, 2004 by Princeton Survey Research Associates International.

11. Gallup Poll conducted March 2–3, 2013, Gallup Daily Tracking Survey.

12. "Sex" here maintains both its meanings, as a designation of biological difference, and a reference to the romantic act. This is significant in the marriage equality discourse, as the first meaning comes to overshadow the second during the course of the debate for strategic political reasons.

13. "Nationwide Poll of African American Adults," conducted February 14–20, 2013, by Zogby Analytics Polling Market Research, retrieved on July 8, 2013, from http://www.rljcompanies.com/phpages/wp-content/uploads/2013/03/Results-of-a-National-Opinion-Poll-Conducted-by-Zogby-Analytics-Black-Opinions-in-the-Age-of-Obama_2013.pdf.

14. "Americans Overwhelmingly Support Executive Action to Ban Anti-LGBT Work Discrimination," conducted November 9–13, 2011, for the Human Rights Campaign by Greenberg Quinlan Rosner Research, retrieved on July 8, 2013, from http://www.hrc.org/resources/entry/americans-overwhelmingly-support-executive-action-to-ban-anti-lgbt-workplac.

15. See Pew 2009, as well as the commentary of the CEO of the Public Policy Institute of California, Mark Baldassare (2008).

16. It should be noted that many queer advocates preferred domestic partnership or civil union rights to same-sex marriage on the grounds that marriage is a conservative and exclusive institution, marred by a patriarchal history and practice that cements regressive and essentialist gender roles that political progressives should not seek to reinscribe in a new form. A March 23, 1996, letter to the editor in the *New York Times* argues: "Many homosexuals, myself included, also oppose this grab for a bogus 'right.' This issue stems from a desire by assimilationist homosexuals to abandon sexual liberation in favor of middle class respectability."

17. That percentage remained basically unchanged between 2004 and 2011, when Gallup found a majority of respondents in favor of marriage equality for the first time. "For First Time, Majority of Americans Favor Legal Gay Marriage," Gallup, retrieved on May 12, 2013, from http://www.gallup.com/poll/147662/First-Time-Majority-Americans-Favor-Legal-Gay-Marriage.aspx.

18. From data compiled Charles Franklin (2008).
19. Nate Silver, "How Opinion on Same Sex Marriage Is Changing and What It Means," *New York Times,* March 26, 2013.
20. NBC News / *Wall Street Journal* poll conducted on February 29–March 3, 2012, by Peter Hart and Bill McIntruff polling organizations.
21. David Kirkpatrick, "Bush's Push for Marriage Falls Short for Conservatives," *New York Times,* January 14, 2004.
22. Elisabeth Bumiller, "What Partisans Embrace Politicians Fear," *New York Times,* November 23, 2003.
23. According to an interview with Pew Research Center's Mike Dimock conducted by BBC News, retrieved on June 27, 2013, from http://www.bbc.co.uk/news/world-us-canada-23070752.

Conclusion

1. "President Signs Massive Stimulus in Denver," February 19, 2009, *ABC 7 News Denver,* retrieved on July 6, 2014, from http://www.thedenverchannel.com/news/politics/president-signs-massive-stimulus-in-denver.
2. Jake Tapper, "If Obama's Budget Were Yours," *ABC News,* February 13, 2012, retrieved on July 11, 2014, at http://abcnews.go.com/WNT/video/obamas-budget-familys-15577806.
3. Robert Costa, "Where Is Christine O'Donnell still famous? CPAC," *Washington Post,* March 7, 2014, retrieved on July 11, 2014, at http://www.washingtonpost.com/blogs/the-fix/wp/2014/03/07/christine-odonnell-is-still-famous-at-cpac/.
4. "Support for Tea Party Continues to Decline," Gallup, May 9, 2014 retrieved on July 11, 2014, at http://www.gallup.com/video/168950/support-tea-party-continues-decline.aspx.
5. Paul Steinhauser, "Fewer Wins This Time, but Tea Party Has Changed the GOP," *CNN,* July 1, 2014 retrieved on July 11, 2014, from http://www.cnn.com/2014/07/01/politics/midterm-elections-halftime/.
6. Retrieved on July 11, 2014, from http://weknowmemes.com/wp-content/uploads/2011/10/we-are-the-99-percent.jpg.
7. Alex Altman, "Obama Leads Head to Head Match-ups with Republican Rivals," *Time,* October 13, 2011, retrieved on July 11, 2014, from http://swampland.time.com/2011/10/13/time-poll-obama-leads-head-to-head-match-ups-with-republican-rivals/.
8. From pollingreport.com, retrieved on July 11, 2014, from http://www.pollingreport.com/politics.htm.
9. From pollingreport.com, retrieved on July 11, 2014, from http://www.pollingreport.com/politics.htm.
10. Josh Kraushaar, "Poll: Voters Viewing Occupy Wall Street Unfavorably," *National Journal,* November 3, 2011 retrieved on July 11, 2014, from http://www.nationaljournal.com/blogs/decoded/2011/11/poll-voters-viewing-occupy-wall-st-unfavorably-03.
11. "Occupy Wall Street Favor Fading," Public Policy Polling, November 16, 2011, retrieved on July 11, 2014, from http://www.publicpolicypolling.com/main/2011/11/occupy-wall-street-favor-fading.html.
12. Sign retrieved on July 11, 2014, from https://www.flickr.com/photos/jimkiernan/6224561169/. See also Norton 2012.
13. Joshua Pavan, "Neoliberalism's Handiest Little Tool: Against Equality on Marriage," *No More Potlucks,* retrieved on June 20, 2014, from http://nomorepotlucks.org/site/%E2%80%9Cneoliberalism%E2%80%99s-handiest-little-tool%E2%80%9D-against-equality-on-marriage/.

BIBLIOGRAPHY

ACORN. Living Wage Resource Center. 2007. http://livingwagecampaign.org/index. php?id=2071 (accessed April 6, 2007).

Alinsky, Saul. (1971) 1989. *Rules for Radicals: A Pragmatic Primer for Realistic Radicals*. New York: Vintage.

Allegretto, Sylvia, Arindrajit Dube, and Michael Reich. 2011. "Do Minimum Wages Really Reduce Teen Employment? Accounting for Heterogeneity and Selectivity in State Panel Data." *Industrial Relations* 50(2): 205–240.

Alvarez, Michael, and John Brehm. 1995. "American Ambivalence toward Abortion Policy: Development of a Heteroskedastic Probit Model of Competing Values." *American Journal of Political Science*: 1055–1082.

———. 1997. "Are Americans Ambivalent toward Racial Policies." *American Journal of Political Science*: 345–374.

Andersen, Margaret, and Patricia Hill Collins. 2006. *Race, Class, and Gender: An Anthology*. New York: Wadsworth.

Ansoblehere, Steven, Roy Behr, and Shanto Iyengar. 1993. *The Media Game: American in the Television Age*. New York: Macmillan.

Anthias, Floya, and Nira Yuval-Davis. 1983. "Contextualizing Feminism: Gender, Ethnic and Class Divisions." *Feminist Review*: 62–75.

Arendt, Hannah. 1965. *On Revolution*. New York: Viking Press.

———. 1993. "What Is Authority?" In *In Between Past and Future*. New York: Penguin.

———. 1994. "Understanding and Politics." In *Essays in Understanding, 1930–1954: Formation, Exile and Totalitarianism*, ed. Jerome Kohn, 307–327. New York: Schocken Books.

———. (1958) 1998. *The Human Condition*. 2nd ed. Chicago: University of Chicago Press.

Aristotle. 1991. *On Rhetoric: A Theory of Civic Discourse*. New York: Oxford University Press.

Atlas, John. 2010. *Seeds of Change: The Story of ACORN, Americas Most Controversial Antipoverty Community Organizing Group*. Nashville: Vanderbilt University Press.

Badgett, M. 1995. V. Lee. "The Wage Effects of Sexual Orientation Discrimination." *Industrial and Labor Relations Review*: 726–739.

Bagdikian, Ben H. 2004. *The New Media Monopoly*. New York: Beacon Press.

Bailey, Robert W. 1999. *Gay Politics, Urban Politics: Identity and Economics in the Urban Settting*. New York: Columbia University Press.

Baldassare, Mark. 2008. "Why the Same-Sex Marriage Ban Passed." Public Policy Institute of California. http://www.ppic.org/main/commentary.asp?i=897 (accessed July 8, 2013).

Ball, Terence, James Farr, and Russell L. Hanson. 1989. *Political Innovation and Conceptual Change*. Cambridge, UK: Cambridge University Press.

Banaszak, Lee Ann. 1996. *Why Movements Succeed or Fail*. Princeton, NJ: Princeton University Press.

Baumgartner, Frank, Jeffrey Berry, Marie Hojnacki, David Kimbal, and Beth Leech. 2009. *Lobbying and Policy Change: Who Wins, Who Loses and Why*. Chicago: University o Chicago Press.

Baumgartner, Frank, Suzanna L. De Boef, and Amber Boydstun. 2008. *The Decline of the Death Penalty and the Discovery of Innocence*. Cambridge: Cambridge University Press.

Bennett, W. Lance. (1983) 2011. *News: The Politics of Illusion*. 9th ed. New York: Pearson.

Bennett, W. Lance, and Robert Entman. 2000. *Mediated Politics: Communications and the Future of Democracy*. Cambridge: Cambridge University Press.

Bernstein, Mary. 1997. "Celebration and Suppression: The Strategic Uses of Identity by the Lesbian and Gay Movement." *American Journal of Sociology* 103: 531–565.

Bernstein, Mary. 2002. "Identities and Politics: Toward a Historical Understanding of the Lesbian and Gay Movement." *Social Science History*: 531–581.

Bourdieu, Pierre. 1977. *Outline of a Theory of Practice*. Trans. Richard Nice. Cambridge: Cambridge University Press.

Bowman, Karlyn, and Bryan O'Keefe. 2004. "Attitudes about Homosexuality and Gay Marriage." American Enterprise Institute. http://www.aei.org/publication/attitudes-about-homosexuality-and-gay-marriage/ (accessed December 19, 2014).

Boykin, Keith. 1997. *One More River to Cross: Black and Gay in America*. New York: Anchor.

Brenner, Mark. 2004. "The Economic Impact of Living Wage Ordinances." Political Economy Research Institute: Working Paper No. 80.

———. 2005. "The Economic Impact of the Boston Living Wage." *Industrial Relations*: 59–83.

Brenner, Mark, Jeannette Wicks-Lim, and Robert Pollin. 2002. "Measuring the Impact of Living Wage Laws: A Critical Appraisal of David Neumark's *How Living Wage Laws Affect Low-Wage Workers and Low-Income Families*." Political Economy Research Institure: Working Paper No. 43.

Brewer, Paul, and Clyde Wilcox. 2005. "Same-Sex Marriage and Civil Unions." *Public Opinion Quarterly* 69(4): 599–616.

Brewer, Marilynn B., and Michael D. Silver. 2000. "Group Distinctiveness, Self-Identification and Collective Mobilization." In *Self, Identity and Social Movements*, ed. Timothy J. Owen, Robert W. White, and Sheldon Stryker, 153–171. Mineapolis: University of Minnesota.

Brooks, David. 2005. "The Storm after the Storm." *New York Times*. September 1. http://www.nytimes.com/2005/09/01/opinion/01brooks.html (accessed May 3, 2013).

Brown, Wendy. 2003. "Neoliberalism and the End of Liberal Democracy." *Theory and Event* 7(1). http://brisbin.polisci.wvu.edu/r/download/114178 (accessed December 19, 2014).

Bucheler, Steven. 1995. "New Social Movement Theories." *Sociological Quarterly*: 441–464.

Cain, Patricia. 1993. "Litigating for Lesbian and Gay Rights: A Legal History." *Virginia Law Review*: 1551–1641.

Campbell, Angus, Phillip Converse, Warren Miller, and Donald Stokes. (1960) 1980. *The American Voter*. Chicago: University of Chicago Press.

Card, David. 1992. "Do Minimum Wages Reduce Employment? A Case Study of California, 1987–89." *Industrial and Labor Relations Review*: 38–54.

Card, David, and Alan Krueger. 1994. "Minimum Wages and Employment: A Case Study of the Fast Food Industry in New Jersey and Pennsylvania." *American Economic Review*: 772–793.

———. 1995. "Time-Series Minimum Wage Studies: A Meta-analysis." *American Economic Review*: 238–243.

Carpenter, Dale. 2012. *Flagrant Conduct: The Story of Lawrence v. Texas*. New York: W.W. Norton.

Center for a New American Dream. 2004. "New American Dream Survey Report." September. http://www.newdream.org/resources/publications/new-american-dream-survey-report-2004 (June 4, 2014).

Chapman, Jeff, and Jeff Thompson. 2006. "The Economic Impact of Local Living Wages." February 15. http://www.epi.org/publication/bp170/ (accessed June 15, 2006).

Chauncey, George. 2004. *Why Marriage? The History Shaping Today's Debate over Gay Equality*. New York: Basic Books.

Chauncey, George. 2005. *Why Marriage: The History Shaping Today's Debate Over Gay Equality*. New York: Basic Books.

Chong, Dennis, and James Druckman. 2007. "A Theory of Framing and Opinion Formation in Competitive Elite Environments." *Journal of Communication*: 99–118.

———. 2010. "Dynamic Public Opinon: Frame Effects over Time." *American Political Science Review*: 663–680.

———. 2013. "Counterframing Effects." *Journal of Politics*: 1–16.

CNN. 2012. December 19. http://politicalticker.blogs.cnn.com/2012/12/19/cnn-poll-majori ty-dissatisfied-but-dont-think-administration-misled-on-benghazi-attack/ (accessed May 3, 2013).

Cohen, Bernard. 1973. *The Public's Impact on Froeign Policy.* Boston: Little, Brown.

Cohen, Cathy. 1999. *The Boundaries of Blackness: AIDS and the Breakdown of Black Politics.* Chicago: University of Chicago Press.

Cohen, David. 2012. "Todd Akin: 'Legitimate Rape' Victims Rarely Get Pregnant." *Politico.* August 19. http://www.politico.com/news/stories/0812/79864.html (June 20, 2014).

Conrad, Ryan. 2010. *Against Equality: Queer Critiques of Gay Marriage.* Lewiston, ME: Against Equality Publishing Collective.

Crenshaw, Kimberle. 1991. "Mapping the Margins: Intersectionality, Identity Politics and Violence against Women of Color." *Stanford Law Review*: 1241–1299.

Cunningham, Brent. 2003. Re-thinking Objectivity. *Columbia Journalism Review.* July 11. http://www.cjr.org/feature/rethinking_objectivity.php?page=all (accessed July 5, 2013).

Dahl, Robert. 1956. *A Preface to Democratic Theory.* Chicago: University of Chicago Press.

———. 1957. "The Concept of Power." *Behavioral Sciences*: 201–215.

———. 1961. *Who Governs? Democracy and Power in an American City.* New Haven: Yale University Press.

Dawson, Michael. 2001. *Black Visions: The Roots of Contemporary African American Political Ideologies.* Chicago: University of Chicago Press.

De Boef, Suzanne L., and John Nagler. 2005. "Do Voters Really Care Who Gets What? Economic Growth, Economic Distribution and Presidential Popularity." Midwest Political Science Association Annual Conference. Chicago.

Delgado, Gary. 1986. *Organizing the Movement: The Roots and Growth of ACORN.* Philadelphia: Temple University Press.

———. 2009. "Does ACORN's Work Contribute to Movement Building." In *The People Shall Rule: ACORN, Community Organizing and the Struggle for Economic Justice,* ed. Robert Fisher, 251–274. Nashville: Vanderbilt University Press.

D'Emilio, John. 2010. "The Marriage Fight Is Setting Us Back." In *Against Equality: Queer Critiques of Gay Marriage,* ed. Ryan Conrad, 37–42. Lewiston, ME: Against Equality Publishing Collective.

Dewey, John. 1954. *The Public and Its Problems.* New York: H. Holt.

Diamond, Sara. 1995. *Roads to Dominion: Right Wing Movement and Political Power in the United States.* New York: Guilford Press.

Doucouliagos, Hristos, and T. D. Stanley. 2009. "Publication Selection Bias in Minimum Wage Research? A Meta-Regression Analysis." *British Journal of Industrial Relations*: 406–428.

Dreier, Peter. 2009. "Community Organizing, ACORN, and Progressive Politics in America." In *The People Shall Rule: ACORN, Community Organizing and the Struggle for Economic Justice,* ed. Robert Fisher, 3–39. Nashville: Vanderbilt University Press.

Drezner, Daniel, and Henry Farell. 2007. "Introduction: Blogs, Politics and Power a Special Issue of Public Choice." *Public Choice*: 1–13.

Druckman, James. 2001. "The Implications of Framing Effects for Citizen Competence." *Political Behavior*: 225–256.

———. 2010. "Competing Frames in a Political Campaign." In *Winning with Words: The Origins and Impact of Framing,* ed. Brian F. Schaffner and Patrick J. Sellers, 101–120. New York: Routledge.

Druckman, James, and R. Kjersten Nelson. 2003. "Framing and Deliberation: How Citizens' Conversations Limit Elite Inluence." *American Journal of Political Science*: 729–745.

Dube, Andrajit, William Lester, and Michael Reich. 2011. "Minimum Wage Effects across State Boarders: Estimates Using Contiguous Counties." *Review of Economics and Statistics*: 945–964.

Dugan, Kimberly. 2008. "Just Like You: The Dimensions of Identity Presentations in an Antigay Contested Context." In *Identity Work in Social Movements,* ed. Jo Reger, Daniel Myers, and Rachel Einwohner, 21–46. Minneapolis: University of Minnesota.

Duke, Brendan V., and Ike Lee. 2014. "Retailer Revelations: Why America's Struggling Middle Class Has Businesses Scared." Center for American Progress. http://cdn.american-progress.org/wp-content/uploads/2014/10/CorporateMiddleOut_report3.pdf (accessed December 4, 2014).

Eliasoph, Nina. 1998. *Avoiding Politics: How Americans Produce Apathy in Everyday Life.* Cambridge: Cambridge University Press.

Entman, Robert. 1989. "How the Media Affect What People Think: An Information Processing Approach." *Journal of Politics:* 347–370.

———. 2004. *Projections of Power: Framing News, Public Opinion, and U.S. Foreign Policy.* Chicago: University of Chicago Press.

Ethridge, Eric. 2009. "Rick Santelli: It's Tea Party Time." *Opinionator.* February 20. http://opin-ionator.blogs.nytimes.com/2009/02/20/rick-santelli-tea-party-time/ (July 6, 2014).

Farrow, Kenyon. 2012. "Afterword: A Future beyond Equality." *Scholar and Feminist Online.* Fall–Spring. http://sfonline.barnard.edu/a-new-queer-agenda/afterword-a-future-beyond-equality/ (accessed March 10, 2013).

Fisher, Robert, ed. 2009. *The People Shall Rule: ACORN, Community Organizing and the Struggle for Economic Justice.* Nashville: Vanderbilt University Press.

Foucault, Michel. 2002. "What Is Critique?" In *The Political,* ed. David Ingram. Oxford: Blackwell.

Franklin, Charles. 2008. "Gay Marriage Support and Opposition." *Pollster.com.* May 21. http://www.pollster.com/blogs/gay_marriage_support_and_oppos.php (July 20, 2008)

Fraser, Nancy. 1990. "Rethinking the Public Sphere: A Contribution to the Critique of Actually Existing Democracy." *Social Text* 25/26: 56–80.

Gamson, Joshua. 1995. "Must Identity Movements Self-Destruct? A Queer Dilemma." *Social Problems:* 390–407.

———. 1996. "The Organizational Shaping of Collective Identity: The Case of Lesbian and Gay Film Festivals in New York." *Sociological Forum:* 231–261.

———. 1997. "Messages of Exclusion: Gender, Movements, and Symbolic Boundaries." *Gender and Society:* 178–199.

Gamson, William. 2006. "Movement Impact on Cultural Change." In *Culture, Power and History: Critical Studies in Sociology,* ed. Stephen Pfohl, Aimee Van Wagenen, Patricia Arend, Abigail Brooks, and Denise Leckenby, 103–125. Boston: Brill Academic Publishers.

———. 1992. *Talking Politics.* Cambridge: Cambridge University Press.

Gamson, William, and David Meyer. 1996. "Framing Political Opportunity." In *Comparative Perspectives on Social Movements,* ed. Doug McAdam, John D. McCarthy, and Mayer Zald, 275–290. Cambridge: Cambridge University Press.

Gamson, William, and Andre Modigliani. 1989. "Media Discourse and Public Opinion on Nuclear Power: A Constructionist Approach." *American Journal of Sociology:* 1–37.

Gans, Herbert. 2005. *Deciding What's News: A Study of CBS Evening News, NBC Nightly News, Newsweek, and Time.* 2nd ed. Evanston, IL: Northwestern University Press.

Gecan, Michael. 2002. *Going Public.* New York: Anchor Books.

Geertz, Clifford. 1983. "Common Sense as a Cultural System." In *Local Knowledge,* 73–93. New York: Basic Books.

Gilens, Martin. 2011. "Two-Thirds Full? Citizen Competence and Democratic Governance." In *New Directions in Public Opinion,* ed. Adam J. Berinsky, 52–76. New York: Routledge.

Ginsburg, Helen. 1983. *Full Employment and Public Policy: United States and Sweeden.* New York: Lexington Books.

Gitlin, Todd. 1996. *Twilight of Common Dreams: Why America Is Wracked by Culture Wars.* New York: Holt Paperbacks.

———. (1980) 2003. *The Whole World Is Watching: The Mass Media and the Making and Unmaking of the New Left.* 2nd ed. Berkeley: University of California Press.

Goffman, Irving. 1974. *Frame Analysis: An Essay on the Organization of Experience.* Cambridge, MA: Harvard University Press.

Goldberg-Hiller, Jonathan. 2002. *The Limits to Union: Same Sex Marriage and the Politics of Civil Rights.* Ann Arbor: University of Michigan Press.

Good, Chris. 2009. "The Tea Party Movement: Who's in Charge?" *Atlantic*. April 13. http://www.theatlantic.com/politics/archive/2009/04/the-tea-party-movement-whos-in-charge/13041/ (July 10, 2014).

Goodwin, Jeff, and James Jasper. 2004. *Rethinking Social Movements: Structure, Meaning and Emotions*. New York: Rowman and Littlefield.

Gramsci, Antonio. 1992. *Prison Notebooks*. Ed. Joseph A. Buttigieg. Trans. Joseph A. Buttigieg and Antonio Callari. New York: Columbia University Press.

Grant, Jaime M., Lisa A. Mottet, Justin Tanis, Jack Harrison, Jody L. Herman, and Mara Keisling. 2011. *Injustice at Every Turn: A Report of the the National Transgender Discrimination Survey.* Survey Report, Washington: National Center for Transgender Equality and National Gay and Lesbian Task Force.

Greenstone, Michael, and Adam Looney. 2012. "The Marriage Gap: The Impact of Economic and Technological Change on Marriage Rates." *Brookings*. http://www.brookings.edu/blogs/jobs/posts/2012/02/03-jobs-greenstone-looney (June 20, 2014).

Groffman, Bernard, Alex Trechsel, and Mark Franklin. 2013. *The Internet and Democracy: Voters, Candidates, Parties and Social Movements*. New York: Springer.

Gunderson, Shane. 2008a. "Protest Actions, Image Events and the Civil Rights Movement in Birmingham." *American Communication Journal* 10(4). http://ac-journal.org/journal/pubs/2008/Winter%2008%20-%20Talking%20a%20Good%20Game/Article_4.pdf (accessed December 19, 2013).

Gunderson, Shane. 2008b. "Social Movement, Spectacle and Momentum." *Resistance Studies Magazine*: 23–34.

Habermas, Jürgen. 1996. *Between Facts and Norms: Contributions to a Discourse Theory of Law and Democracy*. Trans. William Rehg. Cambridge, MA: MIT Press

———. (1996) 2000. *The Inclusion of the Other: Studies in Political Theory*. Ed. Ciaran Cronin and Pablo De Greif. Cambridge, MA: MIT Press.

Haider-Markel, Donald P. 2002. *GLBTQ Social Sciences: An Encyclopedia of Gay, Lesbian, Bisexual, Transgender and Queer Culture*. http://www.glbtq.com/social-sciences/nat_gay_lesbian_tf.html (accessed May 20, 2013).

Haider-Markel, Donald, and Kenneth J. 1996. Meier. "The Politics of Gay and Lesbian Rights: Expanding the Scope of Conflict." *Journal of Politics*: 332–349.

Harcourt, Bernard. 2011. "Occupy's New Grammar of Political Disobedience." *Guardian*. November 30. http://www.guardian.co.uk/commentisfree/cifamerica/2011/nov/30/occupy-new-grammar-political-disobedience (accessed July 5, 2013).

Harris-Perry, Melissa. 2004. *Barbershops Bibles and BET: Everyday Talk and Black Political Thought*. Princeton, NJ: Princeton University Press.

Hartz, Louis. 1955. *The Liberal Tradition in America: An Interpretation of American Political Thought since the Revolution*. New York: Harcourt Brace.

Harwood, John. 2013. "US Problems about More Than 'Moral Values': WSJ/NBC Poll." *CNBC*. April 12. http://www.cnbc.com/id/100635460 (June 15, 2013).

Higginbotham, Evelyn Brooks. 1993. *Righteous Discontent: The Women's Movement in the Black Baptist Church: 1880–1920*. Cambridge: Harvard University Press.

Hirschman, Albert O. 1970. *Exit, Voice and Loyalty: Responses to Decline in Firms, Organizations, and States*. Cambridge, MA: Harvard University Press.

———. 1991. *Rhetoric of Reaction: Perversity, Futility, Jeopardy*. Cambridge, MA: Belknap Press of Harvard University Press.

Hochschild, Jennifer L. 1986. *What's Fair*. Cambridge, MA: Harvard University Press.

Honneth, Axel. 1995. *The Struggle for Recognition: The Moral Grammar of Social Conflicts*. Cambridge, MA: MIT Press.

Howes, Candace. 2005. "Living Wage and Retention of Homecare Workers in San Fransisco." *Industrial Relations*: 139–163.

Ingram, Gordon Brent, Anne-Marie Bouthillette, and Yolanda Retter. 1997. *Queers in Space: Communities, Public Places, Sites of Resistance*. Seattle: Bay Press.

Iyengar, Shanto. 1987. "Television News and Citizens Explanations of National Affairs." *American Journal of Political Science*: 815–831.

———. 1991. *Is Anyone Responsible? How Television Frames Political Issues.* Chicago: University of Chicago Press.

Iyengar, Shanto, and Stephen Ansolabehere. 1995. *Going Negative: How Political Advertisements Shrink and Polarize the Electorate.* New York: Free Press.

Iyengar, Shanto, and Donald Kinder. 2010. *News That Matters.* Updated ed. Chicago: University of Chicago Press.

Izadi, Elahe. 2013. "Gay Marriage Is a 2016 Litmus Test for Democrats." *National Journal.* March 18. http://www.nationaljournal.com/politics/gay-marriage-is-a-2016-litmus-test-for-democrats-20130318 (May 18, 2013).

Jahoda, Marie. 1980. "Work, Employment and Unemployment: An Overview of Ideas and Research Results in the Social Science Literature." SPRU Occasional Paper Series. Sussex: Sussex University Press.

Jamieson, Kathleen Hall, and Paul Waldman. 2003. *The Press Effect: Politicians, Journalists and the Stories That Shape the Political World.* New York: Oxord University Press.

Johnson-Cartee, Karen S. 2005. *News Frames: Constructing Political Reality.* New York: Rowman and Littlefield.

Katznelson, Ira. 1981. *City Trenches: Urban Politics and the Patterning of Class in the United States.* Chicago: University of Chicago Press.

Kelber, Harry. 2005. "AFL-CIO's 50 Year Organizing Record under Meany, Kirkland and Sweeny." *Truthout.* March 30. http://www.truth-out.org/archive/item/53349:aflcios-50year-organizing-record-under-meany-kirkland-and-sweeney (November 13, 2013).

Keynes, John Maynard. 2009. *The General Theory of Employment, Interest, and Money.* New York: Signalman.

Kinder, Donald R., and D. Roderick Kiewiet. 1981. "Sociotropic Politics: The American Case." *British Journal of Political Science*: 129–161.

Kitschelt, Herbert P. 1986. "Political Opportunity Structures and Political Protest: Anti-nuclear Movements in Four Democracies." *British Journal of Political Science*: 57–85.

Klar, Samara, Joshua Robison, and James Druckman. 2013. "Political Dynamics of Framing." In *New Directions in Media and Politics*, ed. Travis N. Ridout, 171–192. New York: Routledge.

Konczal, Mike. 2013. "Minimum Wage 101." *The American Prospect.* February 14. http://prospect.org/article/minimum-wage-101 (accessed May 6, 2013).

Koopmans, Ruud, and Susan Olzak. 2004. "Discursive Opportunities and the Evolution of Right-Wing Violence in Germany." *American Journal of Sociology*: 198–230.

Lake, Celinda, Daniel Gotoff, and Alex Dunn. 2012. "Public Support for Raising the Minimum Wage." Lake Research Partners. http://nelp.3cdn.net/0be1c6315f2430afa6_arm6bq9wu.pdf (July 8, 2013).

Lippmann, Walter. 1922. *Public Opinion.* New York: Harcourt Brace.

Lipset, Seymour Martin, and Stein Rokkan. 1967. *Party Systems and Voter Alignments: Cross-National Perspectives.* Toronto: Free Press.

Lodge, Milton, Marco R. Steenbergen, and Shawn Brau. 1995. "The Responsive Voter: Campaign Information and the Dynamics of Candidate Evaluation." *The American Political Science Review* 89(2): 309–326.

Luce, Stephanie. 2004. *Fighting for a Living Wage.* Ithaca, NY: Cornell University Press.

———. 2009. "ACORN and the Living Wage Movement." In *The People Shall Rule: ACORN, Community Organizing and the Struggle for Economic Justice*, ed. Robert Fisher, 131–152. Nashville: Vanderbilt University Press.

———. 2012. "Living Wage Laws: Worth the Effort?" *Labor Notes.* February 27. http://labornotes.org/2012/02/living-wage-laws-worth-effort (accessed February 28, 2013).

Lukes, Steven. (1974) 2005. *Power: A Radical View.* 2nd ed. New York: Palgrave.

Malkin, Michelle. 2009. "Mesa, Arizona: Anti-Porkulous Protestors Raise Their Voices." *Michelle Malkin.* February 18. http://michellemalkin.com/2009/02/18/mesa-arizona-anti-porkulus-protesters-raise-their-voices/ (July 10, 2014).

———. 2010. "Anniversary of a Porkulous Protest: The Roots of the Tea Party Movement." *Michelle Malkin.* February 15. http://michellemalkin.com/2010/02/15/anniversary-of-a-porkulus-protest-the-roots-of-the-tea-party-movement/ (July 11, 2014).

Mansbridge, Jane. 1999. "Everyday Talk in the Deliberative System." In *Deliberative Politics: Essays in Democracy and Disagreement*, ed. Steven Macedo. New York: Oxford University Press.

Mansbridge, Jane, and Katherine Flaster. 2007. "The Cultural Politics of Everyday Discourse: The Case of 'Male Chauvinist.'" *Critical Sociology*: 627–660.

Marx, Karl. 2008. *Capital: An Abridged Edition*. Ed. David McLellan. Oxford: Oxford University Press.

Mayhew, David. (1974) 2004. *Congress: The Electoral Connection*. 2nd ed. New Haven: Yale University Press.

McAdam, Doug, and David A. Snow. 2000. "Identity Work Processes in the Context of Social Movements: Clarifying the Identity/Movement Nexus." In *Self, Identity and Social Movements*, ed. Timothy J. Owen, Robert W. White, and Sheldon Stryker, 41–67. Minneapolis: University of Minnesota Press.

McAdam, Doug. (1982) 1999. *Political Process and the Deveopment of Black Insurgency 1930–1970*. 2nd ed. Chicago: University of Chicago Press.

McAdam, Doug, David McCarthy, and Mayer Zald. 1996. *Comparative Perspectives on Social Movements: Political Opportunities, Mobilizing Structures, and Cultural Framings*. Cambridge: Cambridge University Press.

McAdam, Doug, and David A. Snow. 2009. *Readings on Social Movements*. 2nd ed. New York: Oxford University Press.

McAdam, Doug, Sidney Tarrow, and Charles Tilly. 2001. *Dynamics of Contention*. Cambridge: Cambridge University Press.

McAuliff, Michael. 2012. "Richard Mourdock: Pregnancy from Rape Is 'Something God Intended.'" *Huffington Post*, October 23, 2012. http://www.huffingtonpost.com/2012/10/23/richard-mourdock-abortion_n_2007482.html (June 25, 2014).

McCarthy, John, and Mayer Zald. 1977. "Resource Mobilization and Social Movements: A Partial Theory." *American Journal of Sociology*: 1212–1241.

McCombs, Maxwell, Lance Holbert, Spiro Kiousis, and Wayne Wanta. 2011. *The News and Public Opinon: Media Effects on Civic Life*. New York: Polity.

McCombs, Maxwell, and D. Shaw. 1972. "The Agenda-Setting Function of Mass Media." *Public Opinion Quarterly*: 176–187.

McQuail, Denis. 2005. *McQuail's Mass Communication Theory*. 5th ed. New York: Sage.

Mermin, Jonathan. 1999. *Debating War and Peace: Media Coverage of U.S. Intervention in the Post–Vietnam War Era*. Princeton, NJ: Princeton University Press.

Meyer, David. 2004. "Protest and Political Opportunities." *Annual Review of Sociology*: 125–145.

Meyer, David, and Debra Minkoff. 2004. "Conceptualizing Political Opportunity." *Social Forces*: 1457–1492.

Miller, Joanne, and Jon Krosnick. 1998. "The Impact of Candidate Name Order on Election Outcomes." *Public Opinion Quarterly*: 291–330.

Mucciaroni, Gary. 2008. *Same Sex, Different Politics: Success and Failure in the Struggles over Gay Rights*. Chicago: University of Chicago Press.

Mutz, Diana. 1994. "Contextualizing Personal Experience." *Journal of Politics*: 689–714.

Mutz, Diana, and Joe Soss. 1997. "Reading Public Opinion: The Influence of News Coverage on Perceptions of Public Sentiment." *Public Opinion Quarterly*: 431–451.

Myers, Daniel. 2008. "Ally Identity: The Politically Gay." In *Identity Work in Social Movements*, ed. Jo Reger, Daniel Myers, and Rachel Einwohner, 167–188. Minneapolis: University of Minnesota Press.

Myrdal, Gunnar. 1944. *An American Dilemma: The Negro Problem and Modern Democracy*. New York: Harper and Row.

Nelson, Thomas E., Rosalee A. Clawson, and Zoe M. Oxley. 1997. "Media Framing of a Civil Liberties Conflict and Its Effect on Tolerance." *American Political Science Review*: 567–583.

Nelson, Thomas E., and Donald Kinder. 1996. "Issue Frames and Group-Centrism in American Public Opinion." *Journal of Politics*: 1055–1078.

Nelson, Thomas E., and Zoe M. Oxley. 1999. "Issue Framing Effects on Belief Importance and Opinion." *Journal of Politics* 61(4): 1040–1067.

Neumark, David, and William Wascher. 2000. "The Effect of New Jersey's Minimum Wage Increase on Fast Food Employment: A Re-evaluation Using Payroll Records." *American Economic Review*: 1362–1396.

Norton, Quinn. 2012. "A Eulogy for #Occupy." *Wired*. December 12. http://www.wired.com/201 2/12/a-eulogy-for-occupy/ (July 11, 2014).

Okin, Susan Moller. 1999. "Is Multiculturalism Bad for Women?" In *Is Multiculturalism Bad for Women?* ed. Joshua Cohen and Matthew Howard, 8–24. Princeton, NJ: Princeton University Press.

Ortner, Sherry. 1997. *Making Gender: The Politics and Erotics of Culture*. Boston: Beacon Press.

Paige, Benjamin, and Robert Shapiro. 1992. *The Rational Public: Fifty Years of Trends in Americans Policy Preferences*. Chicago: University of Chicago Press.

Pan, Zhongdang, and Gerald M. Kosicki. 1993. "Framing Analysis: An Approach to News Discourse." *Political Communication* 10(1): 55–75.

Parenti, Michael. 1993. *Inventing Reality The Politics of the Mass Media*. 2nd ed. New York: St. Martin's Press.

Patterson, Thomas, and Robert McClure. 1976. *The Unseeing Eye: The Myth of Television Power in National Politics*. New York: Putnam's Sons.

Peffley, Mark, and Jon Hurwitz. 2007. "Persuasion and Resistance: Race and the Death Penalty in America." *American Journal of Political Science*: 996–1012.

PEJ. 2011. *Pew Research Center Project for Excellence in Journalism Annual Report*. http://stateofthe-media.org/2011/mobile-survey/a-year-in-news-narrative/ (accessed May 6, 2013).

Petro, Anthony. 2013. "Koop's Crusade." *Slate*. February 27. http://www.slate.com/articles/health_and_science/medical_examiner/2013/02/c_everett_koop_and_aids_he_defied_and_collaborated_with_the_religious_right.html (accessed March 4, 2013).

Pew. 2000. "Television vs. Print." Pew Research Journalism Project. February 3. http://www.jour-nalism.org/node/409 (accessed April 23, 2013).

———. 2003a. "Religion and Politics: Contention and Consensus." Pew Research Center for the People and the Press. July 23. http://people-press.org/reports/display.php3?ReportID=189 (October 29, 2007).

———. 2003b. "Religious Beliefs Underpin Opposition to Homosexuality." Pew Research Center for the People and the Press. November 18. http://people-press.org/report/?pageid=765 (July 26, 2008)

———. 2006. "Democrats More Eager to Vote, but Unhappy with Party." Pew Research Center for the People and the Press. June 27. www.people-press.org/2006/06/27/democrats-more-eager-to-vote-but-unhappy-with-party/ (October 31, 2014).

———. 2009. "African-Americans and Religion." Pew Research Religion and Public Life Project. January 30. http://www.pewforum.org/African-Americans-and-Religion.aspx (July 8, 2013).

———. 2010. "How News Happens: A Study of the News Ecosystem of One American City." Pew Research Journalism Project. January 11. http://www.journalism.org/analysis_report/how_news_happens (accessed April 23, 2013).

———. 2012a. "In Changing News Landscape, Even Television Is Vulnerable." Pew Research Center for the People and the Press. September 27. http://www.people-press.org/2012/09/27/in-changing-news-landscape-even-television-is-vulnerable/ (accessed April 23, 2013).

———. 2012b. "Election, Tragedies Dominate Top Stories of 2012." Pew Research Center for the People and the Press. December 20. http://www.people-press.org/2012/12/20/election-tragedies-dominate-top-stories-of-2012/ (accessed May 3, 2013).

———. 2013a. "In Gay Marriage Debate, Both Supporters and Opponents See Legal Recognition as Inevitable." Pew Research Center for the People and the Press. June 6. http://www.people-press.org/2013/06/06/in-gay-marriage-debate-both-supporters-and-oppon ents-see-legal-recognition-as-inevitable/ (June 27, 2013).

———. 2013b. "Republicans Followed Benghazi Probe News More Closely Than Democrats." Pew Research Center for the People and the Press. January 23. http://www.pewresearch.org/daily-number/republicans-followed-benghazi-probe-news-more-closely-than-democrats/ (accessed May 3, 2013).

Phelan, Jo C., and Bruce G. Link. "Conceptualizing Stigma." 2001. *Annual Review of Sociology*: 363–385.

Phelan, Shane. 1989. *Identiy Politics: Lesbian-Feminism and the Limits of Community.* Philadelphia: Temple University Press.

Phillips, Anne. 1987. *Divided Loyalties: Dilemmas of Sex and Class.* London: Virago.

Pichardo, Nelson A. 1997. "New Social Movements: A Critical Review." *Annual Review of Sociology*: 411–430.

Plotke, David. 1990. "What's So New about New Social Movements?" *Socialist Review*: 81–102.

Polleta, Francesca, James Jasper, and Jeff Goodwin. 2001. *Passionate Politics.* Chicago: University of Chicago Press.

Pollin, Robert. 1998. "Living Wage, Live Action." *Nation.* November 23.

Pollin, Robert, Mark Brenner, and Stephanie Luce. 2008. *A Measure of Fairness: The Economics of Living Wages and Minimum Wages in the United States.* Ithaca, NY: Cornell University Press.

Pollin, Robert, and Stephanie Luce. 1998. *The Living Wage: Building a Fair Economy.* New York: New Press.

Ponnuru, Ramesh. 2003. "Coming Out Ahead: Why Gay Marriage Is on the Way," *National Review.* July 28.

Popkin, Samuel. 1994. *The Reasoning Voter: Communication and Persuasion in Presidential Campaigns.* Chicago: University of Chicago Press.

Queers for Economic Justice. 2007. "Tidal Wave: LGBT Poverty and Hardship in a Time of Economic Crisis." http://www.q4ej.org/Documents/qejtidalwave.pdf (accessed May 18, 2013).

Rampell, Catherine. 2013. "Part-Time Work Becomes Full-Time Wait for Better Job." *New York Times.* April 19. http://www.nytimes.com/2013/04/20/business/part-time-work-becomes-full-time-wait-for-better-job.html?pagewanted=1&_r=1&hp& (accessed July 14, 2013).

Rathke, Wade. 2009. "Understanding ACORN: Sweat and Social Change." In *The People Shall Rule: ACORN, Community Organizing and the Struggle for Economic Justice,* ed. Robert Fisher, 40–62. Nashville: Vanderbilt University Press.

Reger, Jo, Daniel J. Myers, and Rachel L. Einwohner. 2008. *Identity Work in Social Movements.* Minneapolis: University of Minnesota Press.

Rimmerman, Craig, Kenneth Wald, and Clyde Wilcox. 2000. *The Politics of Gay Rights.* Chicago: University of Chicago Press.

Rimmerman, Craig, and Clyde Wilcox. 2007. *The Politics of Same-Sex Marriage.* Chicago: University of Chicago Press.

Rochon, Thomas. 1998. *Culture Moves: Ideas, Action, and Changing Values.* Princeton: Princeton University Press.

Rochon, Thomas R. 2000. *Culture Moves: Ideas, Activism, and Changing Values.* Princeton, NJ: Princeton University Press.

Roosevelt, Franklin D. 1937. "Second Inaugural Address." *Inaugural Addresses of the Presidents.* January 20. http://www.bartleby.com/124/pres50.html (accessed June 7, 2013).

Ropponen, Olli. 2011. "Reconciling the Evidence of Card and Krueger (1994) and Neumark and Wascher (2000)." *Journal of Applied Econometrics* 26(6): 1051–1057.

Rosenberg, Gerald. 1991. *The Hollow Hope: Can Courts Bring About Social Change?* Chicago: University of Chicago Press.

Saad, Lydia. 2013. "TV Is Americans' Main Source of News." Gallup. July 8. http://www.gallup.com/poll/163412/americans-main-source-news.aspx?version=print (accessed July 8, 2013).

Schattschneider, E. 1975. E. *The Semisovereign People: A Realist's View of Democracy in America.* New York: Wadsworth.

Scheufele, Dietram, and David Tewksbury. 2007. "Framing, Agenda Setting and Priming: The Evolution of Three Media Effects Models." *Journal of Communication*: 9–20.

Schlozman, Kay L. 1984. "What Accent the Heavenly Chorus? Political Equality and the American Pressure System." *Journal of Politics*: 1006–1032.

Schlozman, Kay L., Sidney Verba, and Henry Brady. 2012. *The Unheavenly Chorus: Unequal Political Voice and the Broken Promise of American Democracy.* Princeton, NJ: Princeton University Press.

Bibliography

Schmitt, John. 2013. "Why Does the Minimum Wage Have No Discernible Effect on Employment." Center for Economic and Policy Research. http://www.cepr.net/documents/publications/min-wage-2013-02.pdf (accessed December 4, 2014).

Schroedel, Jean Reith, and Pamela Fiber. 2000. "Lesbian and Gay Policy Priorities: Commonality and Difference." In *The Politics of Gay Rights*, ed. Craig Rimmerman, Kenneth Wald, and Clyde Wilcox, 97–120. Chicago: University of Chicago Press.

Schudson, Michael. 1995. *The Power of News*. Cambridge, MA: Harvard Unversity Press.

Shoemaker, Pamela, and Stephen Reese. 1996. *Mediating the Message: Theories of Influence on Mass Media Content*. 2nd ed. New York: Longman.

Shoenberger, Erica. 2000. "Living Wage in Baltimore: Impacts and Reflections." *Review of Radical Political Economics*: 428–436.

Shudson, Michael. 2001. "The Objectivity Norm in American Journalism." *Journalism*: 149–170.

Silver, Nate. 2013. "How Opinion on Same Sex Marriage is Changing and What It Means." *Five Thirty Eight*. March 26. http://fivethirtyeight.blogs.nytimes.com/2013/03/26/how-opinion-on-same-sex-marriage-is-changing-and-what-it-means/?_r=0 (accessed March 26, 2013).

Skowronek, Stephen. 2006. "The Reassociation of Ideas and Purposes: Racism, Liberalism and the American Political Tradition." *American Political Science Review*: 385–401.

Smith, Rogers. 1997. *Civic Ideals: Conflicting Visions of Citizenship in U.S. History*. New Haven: Yale University Press.

———. 2003. *Stories of Peoplehood: The Politics and Morals of Political Membership*. Cambridge: Cambridge University Press.

Sniderman, Paul, and Sean Theriault. 2004. "The Structure of Political Argument and the Logic of Issue Framing." In *Studies in Public Opinion*, ed. Willem E. Saris and Paul Sniderman, 133–165. Princeton, NJ: Princeton University Press.

Snow, David A., and Doug McAdam. 2000. "Identity Work Processes in the Context of Social Movements: Clarifying the Identity/Movement Nexus." In *Self, Identity and Social Movements*, ed, Sheldon Stryker, Timothy Owens, and Robert White, 41–67. Minneapolis: University of Minnesota.

Snow, David A., and Robert Benford. 1988. "Ideology, Frame Resonance and Participant Mobilization." *International Social Movement Research*: 197–217.

———. 1992. "Master Frames and Cycles of Protest." In *Frontiers in Social Movement Theory*, ed. Aldon Morris and Carol Mueller, 133–155. New Haven: Yale University Press.

———. 2000. "Framing Processes and Social Movements: An Overview and Assesment." *Annual Review of Sociology*: 611–639.

Snow, David, Rochford, R. Burke, Worden, Steven K., and Benford, Robert D. 1986. "Frame Alignment Processes, Micromobilization, and Movement Participation." *American Sociological Review* 51: 464–481.

Sowell, Thomas. 2010. *Basic Economics: A Commonsense Guide to the Economy*. 4th ed. New York: Basic Books.

Stein, Marc. 2012. *Rethinking the Gay and Lesbian Movement*. New York: Routledge.

Strolovitch, Dara, Dorian Warren, and Paul Frymer. 2006. "Katrina's Political Roots and Divisions: Race, Class, and Federalism in American Politics." *Understanding Katrina: Perspectives from the Social Sciences.*. June 11. http://understandingkatrina.ssrc.org/FrymerStrolovitchWarren/ (accessed May 3, 2013).

Stryker, Sheldon, Timothy J. Owen, and Robert W. White, eds. 2000. *Self, Identity and Social Movements*. Minneapolis: University of Minnesota.

Sullivan, Andrew. 1996. *Virtually Normal: An Argument about Homosexuality*. New York: Vintage Books.

Sullivan, Andrew. 1989. "Here Comes the Groom: A (Conservative) Case for Gay Marriage." *The New Republic*. http://www.newrepublic.com/article/79054/here-comes-the-groom (accessed December 3, 2014).

Swarts, Heidi. 2008. *Organizing Urban America: Secular and Faith-Based Progressive Movements*. Minneapolis: University of Minnesota Press.

Swartz, David. 1997. *Culture and Power: The Sociology of Pierre Bourdieu*. Chicago: University of Chicago.

Swidler, Ann. 1986. "Culture in Action: Symbols and Strategies." *American Sociological Review*: 273–286.

———. 1995. "Cultural Power and Social Movements." In *Social Movements and Culture*, ed. Hank Johnston and Bert Klandermans, 25–40. Minneapolis: University of Minnesota Press.

———. 2001. *Talk of Love: How Culture Matters*. Chicago: University of Chicago Press.

Tarrow, Sidney. 1992. "Mentalities, Political Cultures, and Collective Action Frames: Constructing Meanings through Action." In *Frontiers in Social Movement Theory*, ed. Aldon Moriss and Carol Mueller, 174–202. New Haven: Yale University Press.

———. 1994. *Power in Movement: Social Movements, Collective Action and Politics*. New York: Cambridge University Press.

———. 1998. *The Social Movement Society: Contentious Politics for a New Century*. New York: Rowman and Littlefield.

Taylor, Paul. 2006. "Wedge Issues on the Ballot: Can State Initiatives on Gay Marriage, Minimum Wage Affect Candidate Races?" Pew Research Center. July 26. http://www.pewresearch.org/2006/07/26/wedge-issues-on-the-ballot/ (May 13, 2013).

Taylor, Verta, and Nancy Whittier. 1992. "Collective Identity in Social Movement Communities: Lesbian Feminist Mobilization." In *Frontiers in Social Movement Theory*, ed. Aldon Morris and Carol McClurg Mueller, 104–129. New Haven: Yale University Press.

Theimer, Sharon, and Pete Yost. 2009. "Did ACORN Get Too Big for Its Own Good?" *NBC News*. September 20. http://www.nbcnews.com/id/32925682/ns/politics-more_politics/t/did-acorn-get-too-big-its-own-good/#.UZpse1HYB8E (May 18, 2013).

Tilly, Charles. 1978. *From Mobilization to Revolution*. New York: McGraw Hill.

Vaccari, Cristian. 2013. "From Echo Chamber to Persuasive Device? Rethinking the Role of the Internet in Camapaigns." *New Media and Society*: 109–127

Vaid, Urvarshi. 1995. *Virtual Equality: The Mainstreaming of Gay and Lesbian Liberation*. New York: Doubleday.

Vedder, Richard K., and Lowell E. Galloway. 1997. *Out of Work: Unemployment and Government in Twentieth-Century America*. New York: NYU Press.

Verba, Sidney, Kay Schlozman, and Henry Brady. 1995. *Voice and Equality: Civic Voluntarism in American Politics*. Cambridge, MA: Harvard University Press.

Wald, Kenneth. 2000. "The Context of Gay Politics." In *The Politics of Gay Rights*, ed. Craig Rimmerman, Kenneth Wald, and Clyde Wilcox, 1–30. Chicago: University of Chicago Press.

Warner, Michael. 1991. "Introduction: Fear of a Queer Planet." *Social Text*: 3–17.

———. 1999. *The Trouble with Normal: Sex, Politics, and the Ethics of Queer Life*. Cambridge, MA: Harvard University Press.

———. 2002. "Publics and Counterpublics." *Public Culture*: 49–90.

Wedeen, Lisa. 2002. "The Influence of News Coverage on Perceptions of Public Sentiment." *American Political Science Review*: 713–728.

Wittgenstein, Ludwig. 2001. *Philosophical Investigations: The German Text, with a Revised English Translation*. Trans. G. E. M. Anscombe. 3rd ed. Malden, MA: Blackwell.

Woirol, Gregory R. 1996. *The Technological Unemployment and Structural Unemployment Debates*. Westport, CT: Greenwood Press.

Woodly, Deva. 2008. "New Competencies in Democratic Communication? Blogs, Agenda-Setting, and Political Participation." *Public Choice*: 109–123.

———. 2014. "Seeing Collectivity: Structural Relation through the Lens of Youngian Seriality." *Contemporary Political Theory*. September 23, doi:10.1057/cpt.2014.34.

———. *Changing Politics: Political Acceptance and the Process of Political Change*. Oxford University Press, forthcoming.

Wright, Erik Olin. 1996. "The Continuing Relevance of Class Analysis—Comments." *Theory and Society*: 693–716.

Young, Iris Marion. 1990. *Justice and the Politics of Difference*. Princeton, NJ: Princeton University Press.

Young, Iris Marion. 1994. "Gender as Seriality." *Signs*: 713–738.

Zald, Mayer, and John McCarthy. 1979. *The Dynamics of Social Movements: Resource Mobilization, Social Controls and Tactics*. Cambridge, MA: Winthrop.

Zaller, John. 1992. *The Nature and Origin of Mass Opinion*. Cambridge: Cambridge University Press.

Zaller, John, and Stanley Feldman. 1992. "A Simple Theory of Survey Response." *American Journal of Political Science*: 579–616.

Žižek, Slavoj. 1989. *The Sublime Object of Ideology*. New York: Verso.

INDEX

Figures, notes, and tables are indicated by f, n, and t following the page number.